Book design by Steven Tarnay
www.freedomlovegold.com

Chief Editor
Catherine J. Hedge
www.catherinehedge.com

Artistic Illustration
Eszter Rékassy
rekassy66@gmail.com

Interior design
Michael Campbell, MC Writing

A Carpathian Folk Song

Freedom, Love, Gold

*The Tarnay Family and
the Struggle to Save the
Hungarian National Treasury*

FREDERICK ELMER TARNAY
and
KATHERINE TARNAY

To the New Hungarian Generation

Figure 1: Frederick E. (Frici), Katherine (Kati), Fred B. (Little Frici), Steven (István), and Matt (Hapsi, Géza)

Composers
Steven A. Tarnay – Design, Editing, and Translation
Matt G. Tarnay – Editing and Publishing
Fred B. Tarnay – Editing, Archives, and Memoirs

Chief Editor
Catherine J. Hedge

Artistic Illustration
Eszter Rékassy

CONTENTS

THE DANUBE STURGEON: A SYMBOL FOR HUNGARY

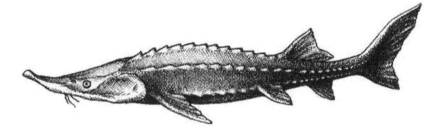

Figure 2: The sturgeon is a symbol for Hungary. A beautiful, majestic fish, it is an ancient giant. The sturgeon has fed the poor and toasted kings with its caviar for centuries. It is a perfect design that has barely changed through time. It is coming back from the verge of extinction.

REVIEWS

"The Tarnay story is a story that begs to be told. It is many stories: a love story, a historically important story, a dramatic story, a tragic story and given its significance to an entire nation, it is a poignant story."

— WILLIAM LOWER, *BUDAPEST TIMES* COLUMNIST

Figure 3: Our father's Ex Libris book mark, "Knowledge, Strength, and Country"

PREFACE

By Steven Tarnay

During the 20th century, Hungary endured the most drastic changes in its thousand-year history. It lost the environmental stewardship of Europe's beautiful natural boundary, the Carpathian Basin. A hundred percent of this boundary and over 70 percent of the integrity of this ecosystem was destroyed after World War I with the Treaty of Trianon on June 4, 1920. Soon after, World War II and Nazi occupation devastated much of the country, especially Budapest. This was followed by the Soviet Communist "liberation" and the tragic outcome of the 1956 Revolution that sealed the fate of Hungarians.

Forty-five years of Soviet Communist rule stripped the people of their identities, languages, and cultures. Europe suffered a great environmental and cultural loss.

War-time mayhem, plunder, retaliation, and treason were experienced by people driven by survival instinct, fear, patriotism, greed, and so much more. It brought out the best and the worst in human actions. It was through this maze that our parents lived their incredible story.

The base of the Hungarian economy, thirty-two tons of gold and the most precious Hungarian national treasure, the crown of St. Stephen, was at stake. With the help of a German Commissioner and our father, Fred Tarnay as a secret courier, the personnel of the Magyar Nemzeti Bank saved the National Treasury. They hid it from retreating Nazis and advancing Russian forces and turned it over to the Americans in the last days of World War II. Labeled gold robbers, the families had little choice but to flee. Returning to Hungary would have meant facing the Gulags or death.

Katherine (Katalin/Kati) and Frederick (Frigyes/Frici) Tarnay were an integral part of this adventure. They met as bank employees and advanced to high positions. The events of war separated them. They were only together five years as a family of the 19 years they were married. Ironically, this separation furnished the source material for this story *Freedom, Love, Gold.* Through their intimate letters, documents, pictures, and diaries, our parents shared their human struggles and love of family that helped them survive the war and to find a home in a new land.

This document is written with every attempt to be authentic, credible, and a reflection of the Hungarian culture and its beautiful language embedded in the thousand years of Christianity founded by St. Stephen.

Much of the documentation was assembled by the family. A great part comes from my research and experience during the last 8 years as I live part-time in Hungary.

Figure 4: Hungary after the WWI Trianon Peace Treaty. The center area was the new Hungary, only 28% of the prewar Kingdom of Hungary. (Graphic alteration approved and use granted by the artist) Lerner, Janos. N. pag. Magyar Tájak Kárpát – Medence útikőnyv. Web. June & July 2013. <http://www.karpat-medence.hu/>.

NOTE TO OUR READERS

Unless otherwise noted, the writing is that of our parents, Kati and Frici Tarnay. The italicized introductions and captions are the explanatory pieces written by myself and my brothers. In addition, letters and documents have been put into paragraphs matching current use.

In this document, The Magyar Nemzeti Bank is referred to as "the Bank", MNB, and "the Hungarian National Bank."

Figure 5: ID card pictures for our father in 1932 and our mother in 1934, when they started to work for the Hungarian National Bank, the MNB.

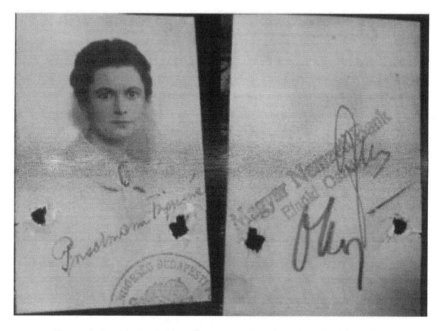

Figure 6: Our Mother's Identification card at the MNB. This shows her
signature as Mrs. Puschmann after she married our father (Puschmann)
in 1938. In 1942 the family changed to our mother's Hungarian Tarnay
name for security reasons under the German occupation

INTRODUCTION:
FROM THE WRITINGS OF
FREDERICK E. TARNAY

"THE GOLD RUSH FROM HUNGARY" (1956)

[Complete document in Appendix]

Attached please find the manuscript of a true story titled "The Gold Rush from Hungary," written by myself. The story was inspired by the article "The Secret Voyage of Britain's Treasure" [by Leland Stowe] published in the November 1955 issue of *The Reader's Digest,* and presents in a way a counterpart to that story relating how a similar gamble was undertaken on the side of the Axis powers during World War II. It is, however, rather a personal account of the whole transaction in which I played an active part.

...When I finished reading this story [*Stowe, "Secret Voyage"*] a crowd of memories started swarming in my mind, memories of a similar venture of a small nation in South East Europe which tried to save its treasures from being captured by Russians and "secured" by the Germans under the most turbulent and adventurous circumstances in the very middle of the fighting between the German and the Red Army. This country was Hungary. The valuables involved were of course smaller than those of Britain's treasures, but for a small nation they meant just as much as the gigantic amounts for a world power....

I was born in Hungary in 1906. As a graduate of the College for World Trade in Vienna, I entered the services of the National Bank of Hungary in 1932 and was working in the Foreign Exchange and Foreign Trade Department of the Bank. When World War II entered its last phase in 1944, I was head of the Foreign Trade Section. In October 1944 when the constitutional government was overthrown by the Germans and replaced by a Nazi puppet government, I offered my resignation to the new Board of Directors. This, however, was not accepted and I was warned by the new general manager if I did not stay at my post and follow the new regime's policy, I'd be put to death.

The story of my family's flight before the Russian invasion is told in my article.

THE MNB UNDERGROUND RESISTANCE FORCE AGAINST GERMANY

Hungary's alliance with the Axis was an act of self-preservation to maintain some political independence and to keep Germany from completely taking over the country. Hungary managed to stave off this event until October 15, 1944. Up until that time the MNB, with our father's direction, worked effectively in reducing and delaying "war important supplies" to Germany. The MNB implemented foreign exchange and clearing policies that impeded Germany and at the same time made it easier for Allied countries to do business in Hungary.

Our father was head of the Foreign Exchange and Clearing Section of the MNB. His main focus was with Germany because of the difficult conditions Hungary had under Hitler's Reich. Father stayed in touch with all the countries with which Hungary was officially doing business. He was instrumental in creating and carrying out the policies of the Bank, including this resistance. His stance against the Reich helped to keep war supplies from going to Germany.

In the summer of 1945, the Americans in Frankfurt interviewed the MNB bank representatives who accompanied the gold. They inquired about bank transactions with foreign countries during the war. Father was asked to write this report to the Americans in English.

This "Underground Financial Resistance" by the MNB against Germany showed Hungary's support for the Western Allies and significantly helped the Allies in their war efforts against Germany. Unfortunately, this was never recognized.

—〰—

Figure 7: The board room at the MNB in 1936. Our father is the third to the left of the speaker. It appears to be a press conference.

REPORT TO THE AMERICANS IN FRANKFURT, 1945

German-Hungarian Economic Negotiations 1934-1945
With Special Regard to the Settlement of Payments
By
Frederick E. Tarnay

In the course of the German-Hungarian economic negotiations the National Bank of Hungary (hereinafter referred to as Bank) constantly performed an opposing attitude against the German aspirations. The Bank recognized that the German aspirations in the economic field were by political aims and were not in accordance with the economic principles and laws followed by the traditional policy of the Bank. The Bank thanked its foundation to the Western Anglo-Saxon Powers and was conscious of the fact that after the World War I Hungary could consolidate her economic life only with the effective aid of these Powers. These relations with the Western Powers determined the spirit of the Bank's financial policy and thus it was evident that sooner or later it must come to clash with the Nazi economic policy.

In the following text we give evidence of the manifold controversies between the German aspirations and the Bank's counteraction during the economic negotiations between Nazi Germany and Hungary:

I. The Settlement of payments arising from the merchandise traffic.

When Nazi Germany on the basis of the New Plan set on to intensify the economic relations to the Southeastern European countries and so to revive the merchandise traffic with these countries, the Bank endeavor was to replace the stiff clearing system by a more free payment machinery by which export and import may hold the balance and by which the German aspirations would be restricted to the limits determined by the laws of economy.

This point brought about the first conflict.

When the efforts of the Bank to decrease the premium of the reichsmark (RM) i.e. the devaluation of the reichsmark failed, the Bank continued its counteracting policy by refusing the purchase of RM surpassing the limit of 15 million. The effect of this measure was that the Hungarian exporter did not receive immediately the sales price of his shipment and if he wanted cash money, he was obliged to ask an advance from his bank upon his claim.

The time element in such transaction caused a loss of interests to him and also a certain degree of devaluation was also realized.

On the top of her power and victory Germany could not tolerate the devaluation of her currency and strived to make disappear the devaluation of the RM everywhere. At the end of 1940 the Germans wanted Hungary to raise the premium of the RM to the level of that of the free exchanges. The Bank opposed this want in the sharpest manner because it considered this proposition as an economic absurdity, which would entail the upset of the equilibrium in the merchandise traffic and to enable Germany to buy much cheaper at the cost of Hungary. Although Germany promised to paralyze the disadvantages of this policy for Hungary by subsidizing the German export to Hungary, the Bank rejected this German project.

Thus in 1941 it was already obvious that Germany could not maintain the equilibrium of payments in the merchandise traffic and she wanted Hungary to grant credit for the trade balance.

All these issues caused a constant increase of the clearing balance "in favor" of Hungary, the financing of which was enforced by the Germans more and more. In July 1942 the Bank had already refused to finance the clearing surplus and also declined to agree to the raising of credit of the commercial banks over 200 million RM. So the Treasury was obliged to carry on the financing of the clearing balance. However, the refinancing of the RM amounts taken over by the Hungarian Treasury could only be effected by the Bank therefore the Bank utilized all possible means to enforce the decrease of the RM incomes and to press the Germans to deliver securities and other valuables in turn for the Hungarian exports. The Bank thought to achieve this by the following means:

a. The amounts transferred in the clearing had to undergo a sharp examination by the Bank before paying them out. Only amounts were permitted to be paid out for when the goods passed the border and this fact was certified by the Customs houses. The Bank did not accept advances upon exports in the clearing because this would have facilitated German purchases in the country. The purpose of these measures was, that German firms should not dispose of cash-money in Hungary; as the Hungarian exporters wanted payment in advance or at least cash contracts of shipments and settlement of the payments was made difficult for the Germans. The examination of the amounts before paying them out involved a certain amount of time and delays in the remittance to the exporters. The Bank almost constantly was criticized by the Germans for these sharp checking of the payments from Germany it made the merchants dissatisfied to make trade and in general hampered the export to Germany.

b. The Bank did not authorize the Hungarian commercial banks to grant credits to German banks or firms for the purpose of purchases in Hungary. The consequence of this was that the German importer in order to have pengős at the time when he had to pay the sales price of the goods was obliged to pay the due amount several months before the delivery has taken place. This attitude of the Bank was also criticized by the Germans because it retarded the German purchases on a large scale.

c. As to directing exports to other countries than Germany the Bank sacrificed large amounts to subsidize the export of Hungarian goods to other countries and to make exports to Germany less attractive. Such countries were in the first place the countries with free currency such as Switzerland and Sweden, and such countries from which valuable goods could be bought such as Slovakia, Turkey etc. The Bank constantly opposed the export of such goods to Germany, which could be sold also in other countries even with sacrifices and protested against the import of such goods from other countries, which could be bought in Germany.

In the session of March 1943 Hungary succeeded in getting released a quota of 50 million RM for shipments to other countries.

The Bank laid such a great stress upon directing exports to countries that when the idea was raised that Germany should pay for Hungarian goods with gold, the Bank did not insist obstinately be paid in gold, but preferred to decrease German contingent quotas in favor of other countries.

d. Repurchasing chiefly Hungarian securities in German hands.

e. To enforce the transfer of German claims from Hungary to Germany, the Bank laid great stress upon clearing out German dues from exports to Hungary by diminishing the clearing balances and preventing the accumulation of German capital for penetration or other purposes. Therefore, the Bank kept strictly on file the imports from Germany, registering them from import licenses checked by the Customs Houses. This registration involved the value of the imported goods and the payments made for in the clearing. The importers being in arrears were asked by the Bank to explain the delay and if the answer was not satisfactory, the importer was summoned to transfer his debt immediately to Germany.

f. The Bank opposed most obstinately the German project to separate the payments for deliveries and services of war importance, for example subcontracts, Verlagerungsauftrage from the clearing and to book them on special accounts. The realization of this project would have facilitated the German purchases in Hungary through the clearing and would have excluded the complicated clearing machinery as a hindering factor for a considerable part of the payments. This was not desired by the Bank because the payments of "war importance" increased the clearing balance very considerably and the waiting period for the exporter of other "normal" commodities became proportionally much longer. If the exports of "war importance" would have been booked on special accounts, the waiting period would have been shortened, which would have had a stimulating effect upon exports to Germany.

But also another viewpoint induced the Bank to a resisting attitude. On this question it considered the whole clearing balance as a commercial indebtedness of Germany, which must be repaid by commercial deliveries. This character of the German debts would become disputable for the part of the debt separated from the clearing. How important it was for the Germans to realize this project was shown by the fact that immediately after the occupation of Hungary they put it into effect. See the "Finanzierungsabkommen" enclosed.

II. Payments beyond the merchandise traffic.

Throughout the progress of the war Germany needed more and more money in Hungary for various investment purposes, expenses of the Legation etc. Germany strived to settle these payments through the clearing because the German assets in Hungary were utilized and blocked for other or similar purposes and could not be released. On this question there was again sharp controversy between the Bank's viewpoint and the German aspirations because the Bank's principle was that these kinds of payments do not belong to the clearing and Germany should utilize her capital claims in Hungary for these purposes. From this point of view the Bank pursued the following aims:

1. German capital stock in Hungary should not be increased.

2. The clearing balance should not be increased by these payments and so the financing and refinancing of the amounts should not be necessary.

The Bank succeeded in stipulating that the German capital claims have to be utilized in the first place to decrease the clearing balance and in the second place only to investments and other purposes. This stipulation aimed also to prevent invasion of German capital to Hungary.

The capital payments were settled through the Girokonto of the Reichsbank with the Bank. To this account about 12 million pengős were paid in Hungary for dividends, repayments on loans, heritages etc. and this amount was paid out to Hungary for the settlement of Hungarian claims of the same character; therefore Germany did not dispose at free amounts on this account. This is why the Bank insisted that these payments – if they were licensed at all should be settled through the Girokonto. As in the Girokonto the balance was never sufficient for these payments. It was necessary to provide special arrangements for additional payments to this account in Hungary, which of course again made it difficult for the Germans in the achievement of their aims and delayed the settlement of the affairs. The Bank's standpoint is also by the following part of the exchange of letters between of the Commissions. (See the whole letter enclosed under Nr.)

Beyond the merchandise traffic the Germans pushed payments in the clearing chiefly for the following purposes:

a. This question was handled by the Bank with the greatest antipathy. The Bank whenever possible balked at the emigration of the workers to Germany. Also the Bank, in refusing to permit the transfer of the savings of the "illegal" workers, compelled a large number of these workers to come or escape back to Hungary.

b. For "educational and cultural" purposes of the German minority in Hungary considerable amounts were wanted by the Germans to be transferred to Hungary. Chiefly, building of schools and other cultural purposes were indicated by the Germans and the transfers were directed to the "German House" in Budapest, but the actual utilization of the amounts, of course, could not be checked.

Knowing the Bank's aversive attitude in such questions the Germans did not approach the Bank for giving its consent to such transfers, they preferred to apply directly to the Premier who determined the extent of the amounts to be transferred. The Bank permitted these payments also through the Girokonto, but of course, as there was always a deficiency of pengős, the transfers could only be affected by installments and with great delays. Just these difficulties induced the Germans to shift these payments to the clearing and they succeeded in July 1943 when upon intervention of the Premier, the Bank accepted the payments in the clearing.

c. Support for the families of the members of the Waffen SS enlisted from the German minority in Hungary. This question was subject to special agreements between both Governments owing to which the Bank was obliged to follow the stipulations of these agreements and accept these payments in the clearing. The amount to be transferred was about 2 million RM monthly, but undoubtedly the whole amount was not paid out because the administering officer of the Waffen SS, as later it was disclosed, accumulated considerable reserves.

d. Similarly by virtue of a special agreement between the Governments the costs of care in Hungary of German children from areas subject to air raids were transferred to the clearing. The costs for 10.000 children amounted to 1.2 million RM monthly.

III. Central Clearing

The Bank performed also in this question a hard resistance because it was convinced that this project could only serve German interest, and would give the possibility to Germany the control of the economic relations of Hungary with other countries.

MEDALS FOR DISTINGUISHED SERVICE

Our father received the following two distinguished awards for his work in economics from the governments of Sweden and Yugoslavia in 1939. The Serbian medal of St. Sava was the same one given to Helen Keller, who received her Ph.D. and was known around the world for her work with the blind.

—ɯ—

Figure 8: Medal awarded to our Father from Serbia for distinguished service as Foreign Exchange and Clearing representative for the MNB.

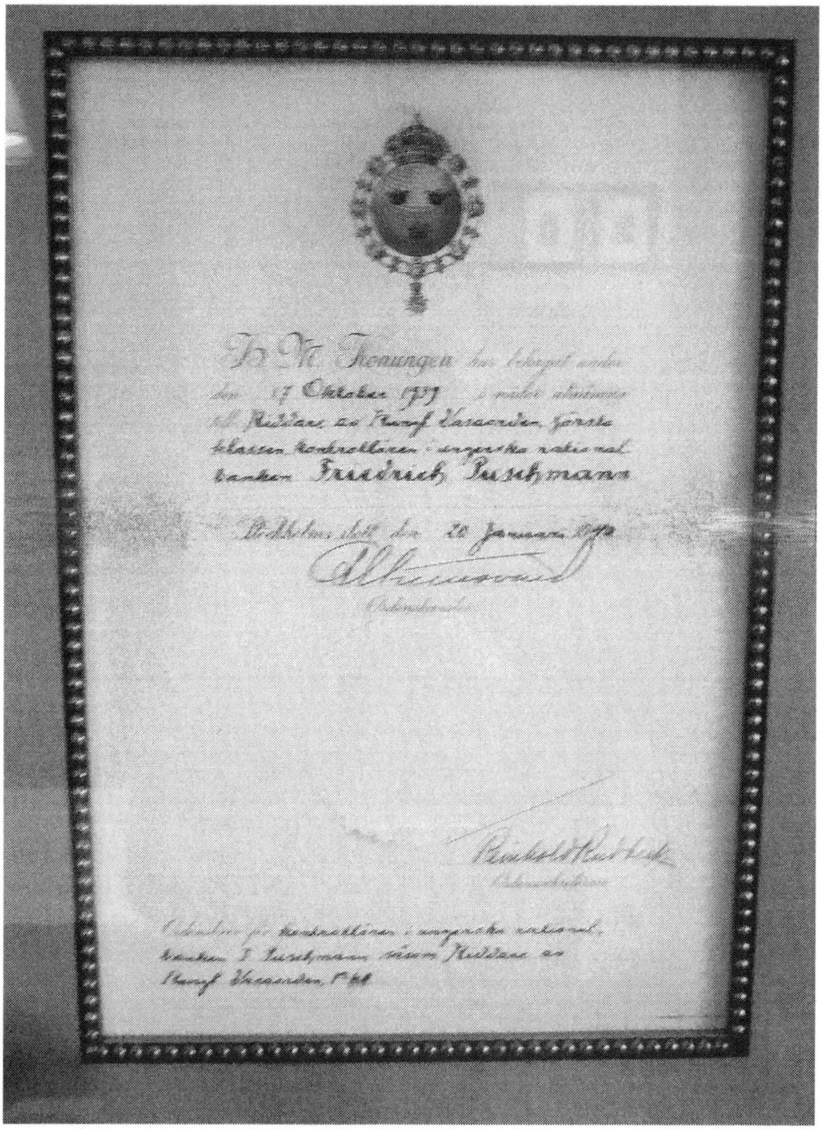

Figure 9: October 17, 1939, Commendation document from Serbia for excellence in service with the MNB

Figure 10: January 30, 1940 Medal received by our father from Sweden for distinguished service as the Foreign Exchange and Clearing representative for the MNB.

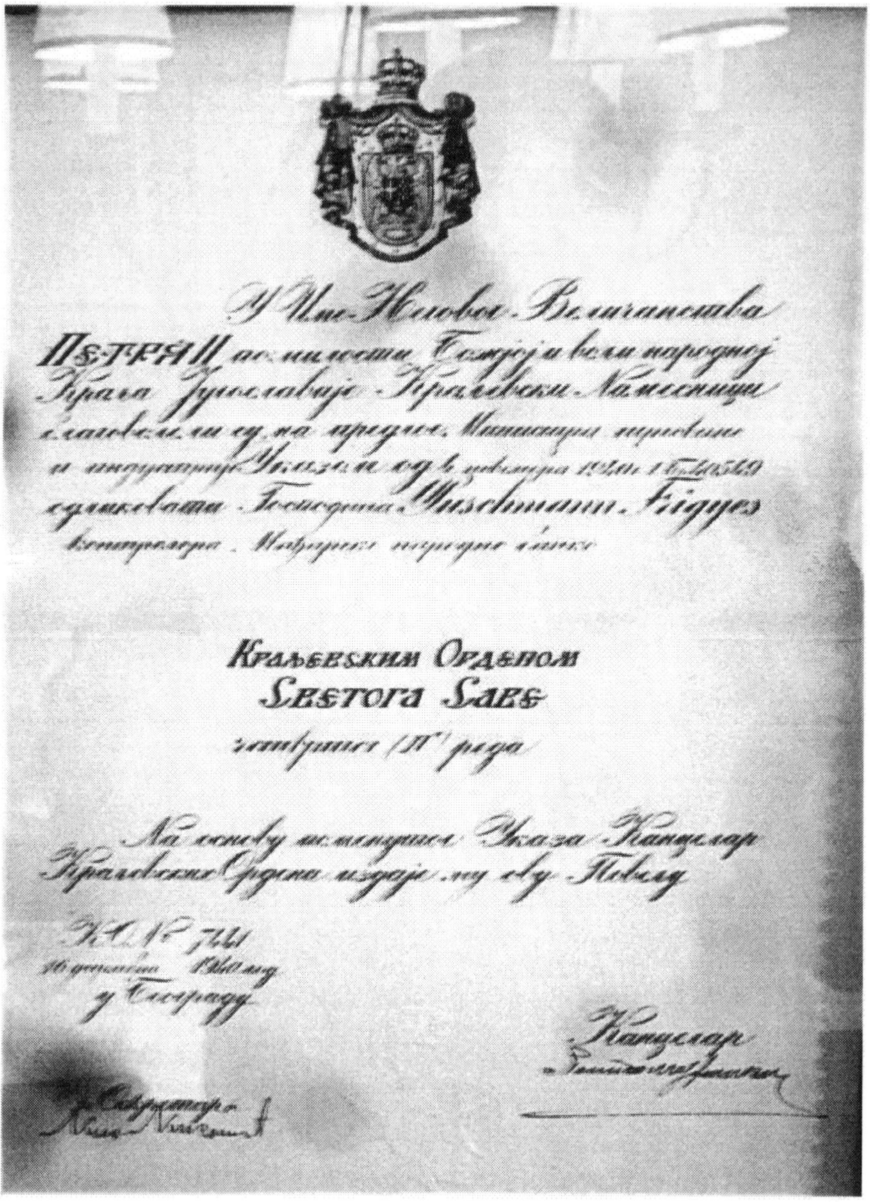
У Име Његовог Величанства
Петра II по милости Божјој и вољи народној
Краља Југославије Краљевски Намесници

Краљевским Орденом
Светога Саве
четвртог (IV) реда

На основу поменутог Указа Канцелар
Краљевских Ордена издаје му ову Повељу

К.О. № 741
у Београду

Канцелар

Figure 11: January 30, 1940 Commendation to our father from Sweden for distinguished service.

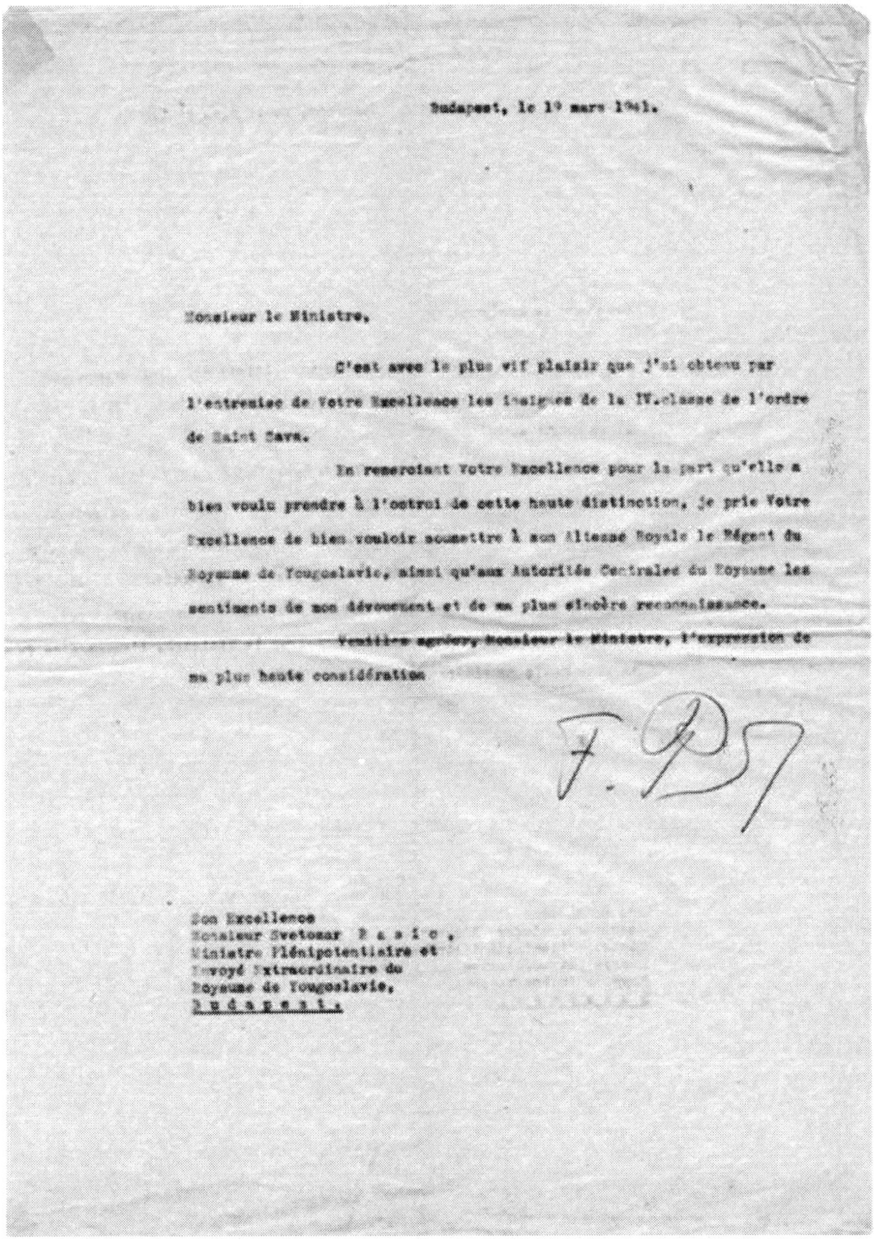

Budapest, le 19 mars 1941.

Monsieur le Ministre,

C'est avec le plus vif plaisir que j'ai obtenu par l'entremise de Votre Excellence les insignes de la IV.classe de l'ordre de Saint Sava.

En remerciant Votre Excellence pour la part qu'elle a bien voulu prendre à l'octroi de cette haute distinction, je prie Votre Excellence de bien vouloir soumettre à son Altesse Royale le Régent du Royaume de Yougoslavie, ainsi qu'aux Autorités Centrales du Royaume les sentiments de mon dévouement et de ma plus sincère reconnaissance.

Veuillez agréer, Monsieur le Ministre, l'expression de ma plus haute considération

Son Excellence
Monsieur Svetozar R a s i c ,
Ministre Plénipotentiaire et
Envoyé Extraordinaire du
Royaume de Yougoslavie,
B u d a p e s t.

Figure 12: March 19, 1941, Our father's acceptance letter of the Order of St. Sava from Yugoslavia (Written in French)

Budapest 19 March 1941

Your Excellency Mr. Minister

It is with great pleasure that I received through Your Excellency the Crest of the Order of St. Sava, IV Class

Thanking Your Excellency for the part he was willing to take to award this prestigious distinction and I beg Your Excellency to submit to his High Royal Regent of the Kingdom of Yugoslavia, as well as the Royal Central Authorities the expressions of my devotion, and my most sincere gratitude.

Please accept, Mr. Minister, the assurances of my highest consideration.

His Excellency
Mr. Svetozar Rasic
Minister Plenipotentiary and
Envoy Extraordinary
Kingdom of Yugoslavia
Budapest

Figure 13: Award acceptance letter translated into English by Fred B. Tarnay

THE HUNGARIAN NATIONAL BANK DURING THE WAR
(*FRED E. TARNAY, CONTINUED*)

For the protection of its treasures, the National Bank of Hungary started building underground shelters and vaults in 1938 since the tensions in international affairs left no doubt that sooner or later a war will come. In these massively built modern shelters, the Bank could continue its business operations without being interrupted by alarms and air raids. One of these huge shelters was built in Budapest on the Western side of the Danube in the so-called Tower Hill District, the oldest part of the city... Uri Street 72. Inside of this hill there are plenty of natural caves and caverns used as shelters and hideouts way back during the Turkish Wars 400 years ago. In World War II the various Government agencies located in the Tower District built their air raid shatters in these caverns. Some of them had been adjusted to public shelters and served as last refuge for the starving and horrible suffering population during the long-lasting siege of the Tower by the Russians. The second and even larger shelter was built in the city of Veszprém situated in the mid-western part of the country close to the Lake Balaton (Jokai Street, 31 Veszprém). It was equipped with modern printing machines and with all facilities to secure the function of the Bank during a war.

—◊◊◊—

To use the words of the U.S. Ambassador, J.F. Montgomery, Hungary was an "unwilling satellite" of the Axis Powers in World War II. As a small country, squeezed in between two big totalitarian adversaries, Germany and the Soviet Union, it had not too much chance to keep out of the war. For four years it managed to escape the German occupation, but in 1944 when Rumania was about to surrender to the Red Army, Hitler did not want to take the same chance with Hungary and overran the country on March 19th, 1944.

Technically Hungary was still an ally of the Axis, but de facto it was a prisoner of the Germans, a prisoner who was not enthusiastic at all to be liberated by the Red Army.

The ideal solution for Hungary would have been an invasion and liberation by the Western Powers from the Balkan Peninsula, yet the Yalta agreement killed this idea and along with it the hope of 100 million people (the Poles, Czechs, Slovaks , Hungarians, Romanians, Bulgarian and Baltic Nations) to be really liberated, was gone.

Figure 14: The MNB train route went approximately 350 miles from Budapest to Spital am Pyhrn, Austria. The route from Veszprém to Fertőboz took 3 days. Traveling at night, we stopped and zigzagged to avoid a chance of robbery and the advancing Russians. Fertőboz to Spital am Pyhrn in Austria was a direct route of several days duration.
(Scale: Sopron to Linz= 112 miles)
Route drawn by Eszter Rekassy
Map Source: "Historische Landkarten / Wappen (1880-1898): Österreich-Ungarn - Politische Einteilung." Historical Geographical Encyclopedia of the World 1880-1898. N. pag. www.hicleones.com. Web. 27 July 2013.

FREDERICK ELMER TARNAY AND KATHERINE TARNAY

CHAPTER 1:
"THE TERRIBLE REALITY THAT THE LAST ACT HAD ARRIVED"

Révfülöp
June, 1944 to December 6, 1944

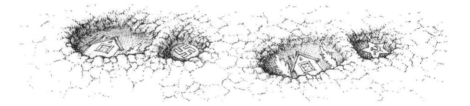

Our father always seemed to know when there was an important event that should be documented for future references. October 15th, 1944 was one of the most significant in Hungary's history. He wrote a lengthy diary that fateful day of the Nazi Arrow Cross takeover of Hungary.

During the last six months of the war in Hungary, Hitler put everything he had left into holding on to Hungary against the Russians and their new found ally, the Romanians.

We were in Révfülöp at our grandparents place at Balaton Lake when he heard the news on the radio. We had moved from Budapest because the Siege of Budapest had already started and the bombing was especially heavy where we lived in Castle Hill. The Siege of Budapest became one of the war's cruelest and bloodiest battles. As it turned out, we heard our home was bombed out.

—⁓—

Figure 15: View from our family's former apartment on Hunyadi János Ut. 15. The steps are The Jesuit Steps and lead to the old site of the Jesuit Monastery on Castle Hill (Presently the Hilton Hotel) and Matthias Church, steeple in the background. (Picture by Geher Ferenc)

MIKLÓS HORTHY

Figure 16: Miklós Horthy crossing the Chain Bridge on his way to Castle Hill. (Photo late 1920s or early 1930s) Miklós Horthy was regent of the Kingdom of Hungary between World Wars I and throughout most of World War II, from March 1, 1920 to October 15, 1944. Diary of Frederick Tarnay, October 15, 1944 "Our Homeland...Its Most Bleeding Days"

On Sunday, as almost every Sunday I spend my time with my family in Révfülöp at Lake Balaton. By now the trains cannot be counted on and it is a very inconvenient situation. The one day of getting away from the depressing mood of the war in Budapest felt very good and gives a man's chased nerves a rest.

Figure 17: Our father riding in the Danube near Mosonmagyarovar in the early 1920s

It was a beautiful fall sunny day. The vineyard surrounded our villa lying along the hillside where the vintage mood of Lake Balaton reigned giving no sign that our homeland is going through its most bleeding days of its life.

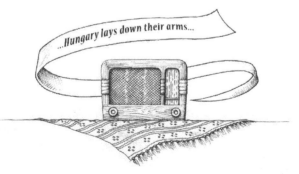

...*Hungary lays down their arms*...

But, yes! The radio… This little dear cabinet that doesn't know who is listening to it and brings the winds of war everywhere. One can forget about the terrible war in the peacefulness of the country, but soon is reminded by the droning, feeling-less machine sounds, as if this was a natural part of this world, informing us that here come the air raids.

I despise this situation from the bottom of my heart and this was probably the reason why I disconnected from it at noon. Let them fly over, if they are over us, we noticed and that they are only on their way across the countryside to somewhere else.

This is the way we passed the time while listening to President Miklós Horthy on the radio when he announced that Hungary will put down its weapons. But just as I went out into the garden, the neighbor yelled out the window said jokingly, "Now there is peace!" after which I knew that he was inclined to be a little bit out of this world. He even said that he wants to write a very beautiful novel, after he had a little Balaton Riesling wine to help with Sunday lunch.

I thought he was teasing or heard something on the radio, which he told us he would like us to hear. I realized when he began to speak in a shaky voice about what was said on the radio, that perhaps something important really did happen and I began to pay attention to the neighbor. Interestingly enough, nobody here at the house was listening to the radio and by chance I only realized later what was really happening.

Although these events were expected, it still shook the nation with the terrible reality that the last act has arrived. We irretrievably fell into the terrible Red arms. And what ensued was exactly what Hungary was most afraid of. What the nation already tried once and because of that the country was uncontrollably pulled into this war: and because of this the country became the prey of the eastern front.

This Nation has for a thousand years, shown its bright light towards the Christian West and for this has shed much of its blood. Then for naught, the Christian West, with the stroke of a pen, threw this Nation to the eastern Red executioners.

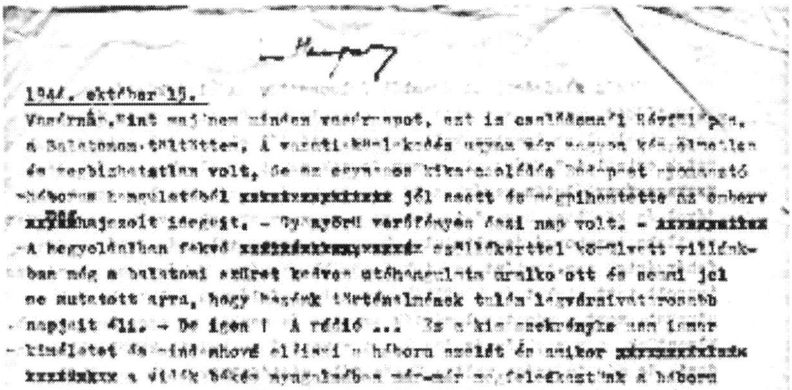

—⁓—

Figure 18: The beginning of our father's diary on October 15, 1944 when the Nazi Arrow Cross overtook Hungary

I remember what Kozma Andor[1] wrote in *Nyergeljetek*... If he wouldn't have written it then, than surely he would have written it now. Everything came to my mind and the question came that came now "What do I have to do now?" Somehow I felt that I need to go to Budapest as soon as possible. Our fate will be decided there as to what the Germans will do.

I feel that things are not going to go very smoothly. In the afternoon a good friend cartographer came by with his car and said he is also going to Budapest and asked if I would also like to go with him. I joined him right away and we took off toward the unknown and insecure journey.

Nothing unusual happened until we reached Fehérvar. At Fehérvar the soldiers checked our ID and said that we cannot go any further to Budapest because the Germans closed the road and they don't let anybody through. We went to a flight-lieutenant friend of ours. He couldn't give us any more information, but he already had knowledge of the Red radio conversations which nobody else knew anything about.

We went out to the lieutenant's sister-in-laws, a princess whose husband was at the front and we didn't want to leave her alone in her castle. We had dinner and everybody gathered afterwards around the radio. If I remember right, they repeated the declaration of Vörös János and then came Szálasi's proclamation of the Arrow Cross takeover of the country.

It was interesting to observe the reaction of the people about the news. The soldiers' attitude, in particular the cartographer friend of mine fanatically hated the Reds and believed in the power struggle to the last drop of blood. Later I learned that he voluntarily left his mapping job and joined the fighting force. The battalion he was in at the final battle was completely wiped out by the Russians and he fell there protecting his homeland. This is the way I have to write it.

Many people probably considered it a crime even today to fight against the Russians, but this young man's deep feeling of patriotism and protection of his homeland, valiantly gave his life for his country, leaving behind his wife and two small children. I still have the letter to his mother today, which I should have forwarded to her, but did not find her.

When I found the letter a year later among my writings and read the letter, I was not able to destroy it because this letter from her son and his homeland is a beautiful manifestation of his feelings to his very loving and protective Hungarian mother.

His little countess wife expressed her thoughts in short concise words: "Why this wretched government" was her remark. Unfortunately she did not know then that her young husband had died. He fell during the fight against the Russians (we already knew this, but .... [*The next page is missing*]

---

1 *Kozma Andor (1861-1933) A well-known nationalist conservative during this period.*

1944, "MY LITTLE RED GLIDER FLEW OVER THE PEACEFUL VINEYARD AND CRASHED." BY FRED B. TARNAY (SON)

Révfülöp is the most peaceful place I remember. When we left, I was six years old and I have always thought of it as the home where I grew up. The setting by Lake Balaton with the vineyard sloping down to the water; the peach, apricot and almond trees in fruit and the grapes ready for harvest; the house with the large glass enclosed veranda looking over the sun rising on the water, it still warms my heart. It is still home for me. It was our grandparents' place, 8 acres of land first settled by my grandmother's ancestors (Tótth) who built the house and planted the vineyard. Grandfather made changes and added to the maintenance building as well as planting the fruit orchards.

Figure 19: The Tótth (Tarnay) Villa, 1908. The villa had over 6 hectares of mostly vineyard. The Tarnay family had its own registered winery. (Révfülöp City Archives)

Figure 20: In 1944, looking over the vineyard towards Lake Balaton from the Tarnay Villa in Révfülöp.

Badacsonyi borvidék

Rizling

DR. TARNAY KÁLMÁN RÉVFÜLÖPI PINCÉJÉBŐL.

Figure 21: The Rizling wine label from the Tarnay wine cellar in Révfülöp

Because of the war and the danger in the cities, our parents took us out of Budapest to live there 60 miles west of the city. I had started school in Budapest, but things were so unsettled that I was enrolled in the grammar school in Révfülöp. Not sure what grade it was, but I remember making the number 4 hundreds of times it seemed on my slate pad.

Father took the train or drove to the city, but sometimes stayed in our Budapest flat during the work week and came out on the weekends....

Figure 22: In 1938, our parents at Lake Balaton near our grandparents' villa in Révfülöp. Many weekends and summer vacations were spent there.

Father came home one weekend and brought me a red glider. We launched it from the veranda stairs and it flew over the vineyard, but eventually crashed so badly it couldn't be fixed.

NOVEMBER 1944, SAFEGUARDING THE CROWN OF ST. STEPHEN

In November 1944.... Because of these almost permanent alarms and air raids, the Bank moved into the first underground shelter in the Tower Hill. But not for long. When Marshall Tolbukhin's army crossed the Danube in the South and the danger that Budapest might be encircled became imminent, the Bank decided to move to its second and last shelter in Veszprém.

Our gold reserves (32 tons) and all other assets were already stored there. We had to safeguard not only our own valuables, but also the masterpieces of the Museum of Arts, the treasures of the Historic Museum and even the most sacred relic of the nation, the thousand year old Holy Crown, an award of Pope Sylvester II to King St. Stephen for the conversion of the pagan Magyars to Christianity, was hidden there.

"I DID NOT WANT TO SHARE THE BLESSINGS OF A COMMUNIST STATE"

…The story of my family's flight before the Russian invasion is told in my article. I did not want to stay in Hungary because; 1) I did not want to see my wife raped to death by Red soldiers and myself wind up somewhere in Siberia; 2) Everyone with a little common sense could figure out that under Soviet military occupation and under the terms of the shameful Paris Peace Treaty that sooner or later, Hungary must go Communist… and I did not want to share the blessings of a communist state. (F.E. Tarnay)

Our Mother's Letters:
Sailing in the Winds of War

Figure 23: Mother

Our mother, Kati wrote frequently to our father, Frici. He still lived in Budapest, worked at the MNB, and came to Révfülöp on the weekends.

This collection of our mother's letters shows her courage, the steel springs of a woman who kept bouncing back from the obstacles of the war. At the same time, she kept working for the MNB at a distance. With our father away on business, our mother cared for us three boys "Pityi" (Little Frici) aged 6, István (Steven) aged 4, and "Hapsi" (Matt) aged 3. She kept the fire burning in the steam engine of our family.

Our mother always wrote about us, her children. She enjoyed us. She said we kept her busy and focused on what was important even though war was all around us.

NOVEMBER 11, 1944, "I CANNOT CRY ANYMORE"

People experienced deep sadness, fear, and uncertainty during the Soviet invasion. Our aunt Zsuzsanna was also working in Budapest at the time with the MNB. Our mother and we were in Révfülöp at our grandparents' villa next to Lake Balaton. Our mother worried about the Russians cutting off the road between Budapest and Révfülöp and leaving our father stranded and not being able to come back to Révfülöp.

Gonga and Julsca were our nannies and helpers for the family. Each family was allowed one pig for themselves and the other pigs went to the army to feed the soldiers.

—⚏—

My Dear Frici,

It was a nice little picture you drew of what the war in Budapest looks like and you could imagine what kind of feelings I have that you are still there in the middle of the war. It worries me that you have to walk across to the Pest side every day and not to the bank building in the Vár (Castle Hill) which is so close to you.

I could hardly imagine with my timid nature how you could put up with this, even though I got used to this, but still I have to think of all the dangers that you have to live through every day.

I am ashamed of myself for that and I always think, maybe I will also have a part of that war at some point being that close to it. My mother is very sad that Zsuzsi also has to go through it and maybe she could come closer to us here. One minute she is at peace because we are at least together and the other minute she is worried the Russians will cut us off so you couldn't get back to us. Mother also asks that you think about that. I don't know what Zsuzsi is planning and Mother also doesn't know what to tell her.

My mother only says now that she would like to see Zsuzsi at least one more time. Today she just lay around all day. I can't even cry anymore because I try to put away the sad thoughts. I'm scared that it will be even worse for my mother if she sees me crying. I am envious of Maczi because she sits high on her horse and takes it all in stride and this also gives me confidence in myself. Maybe I can once more be happy to finally be together with you again.

There is lots to write about now and would like to write a little about our fate if there is time. My dear Frici, when you come from Budapest, bring the yellow down cover, the kids need it, otherwise I can only give them a warm blanket or two. You can send all the family papers anytime, if you don't need them anymore. It's a very bad feeling that there is nothing with me that I can identify myself with.

The other day in a crazy moment I asked you to get me dresses. Don't buy them! I already made another one and God forbid that we spend money on things like that during these times.

I pretty much have finished the packing and sorted things out. I don't know what you think about all the baggage and how much we should take: 1 chest full of food, 2 sacks of clothes for the kids, and bed linen sewn up. We put all your things in your leather suitcase and put in your mother's large leather suitcase some bed covers, undergarments and your leftover clothes and my clothes.

I would like to also take another large basket, but this packing together for 5 people and all their needs is already more than I thought we can handle. I would still need about a half a day to finish packing if we suddenly get word that we have to leave.

I am afraid that with so much baggage and with four of us and five with the cart driver, we may not fit on the horse cart, or that we would have to go so slow because of the heavy load that the kids would not be able to handle it. I would gladly go with the cart by myself, but who would go with the kids and how would they go? Of course they would endure the trip if they really have to, but I can't reduce the size of the baggage if everything is going to go as I think it will with this journey.

So far I have said that you shouldn't take advantage of anything, but now that you are staying there, my feeling is if you can, take advantage of everything that will make things easier for you. I don't even dare to suggest, but you can imagine how happy I would be if you could come here and we can go to Veszprém together. Think how it would be for me to be alone there and not be able to hear any news from you. It's terrible here too, but at least we are home.

If I am with strangers and being cut off from you, I can't even imagine that.

We already give you enough to think about, but I'm sure you think about that however helpless I may sound. My dear Frici, you know that I will do everything for the kids so nothing will happen to them before you get there. I would love to have the kids travel with a car, but I cannot depend on anything the way things are nowadays. Things change from day to day.

Mother had her birthday today. I gave her 1000 pengős so she could have some money for herself, because my father is now tight with the money since he hasn't received his pension. I thought we will slaughter our pig this Monday or Tuesday. It has been growing nicely, but isn't 100 kg yet and would just be good for meat, but not much fat. It will be 2 weeks until it cures and we can take some of the meat with us. If we leave, my mother can't keep the other pig because they are only allotted one.

I know you also can't see ahead, but do you think we still have 1 or 2 weeks here? If you could give me an answer soon, so we could slaughter the pig which will be the best way. I can pick up the mail at the post office.

Figure 24: About 1944 at the Tarnay Villa in Révfülöp. Little Fred is sitting on Uncle Ödi's lap next to our mother and grandmother.

The kids are doing fine. I asked the doctor to come and see István. He has tonsillitis. He was already without any fever, but today he was jumping around all day and he had a fever in the afternoon. It is worrisome that he has been in bed for 5 days already, I'm afraid he will have a hard time to get used to being normal. I will watch him very closely tomorrow, but his throat is swelled up and that will take time to come down.

He is a sweet little sick kid. He is somewhat calm, just like you. He loves the medicine and he takes his own temperature conscientiously. Pityi (Fred) has been unfortunately left to himself lately because we haven't had time to spend with him and it showed. He is very agitated. I could hardly handle him today. I will speak with Csonak tomorrow and even if he goes over to see her once or twice it still would be good for him, at least she can go through the printed ABC's with little Fred so he could learn how to read. Maybe he will have an easier time to keeping himself occupied.

The other day he showed some rare perseverance when he helped Grandpa in the cellar all morning. Grandpa didn't even have to bend down once. It looks like a man's work is more to his liking. But there is a weakness in him among the women. Gizike had a headache yesterday and little Fred conscientiously ran home to get some medicine and brought back Steve's vitamins for her. He also has some indigestion now, but handles it well and looks good.

With Hapsi there is no competition with the other two, he again has a double chin and tonight at the big table after dinner he ate everything he saw that was left on the table. His vocabulary multiplies with food words like pastries, preserves and similar nice recipes that spin around in his language. Marsi made a statement about how grateful he is to you and how much you have helped him to bring himself together. He said as a man he will stand beside us all the time. I hope we don't get to the helpless point where we would need his help.

You can imagine with what sad heart I listened how you helped others, unselfishly, as always. I must be a big idealist who believes that God will in time recognize this characteristic of yours.

It is true, our conscience is clear and honest, but in today's ugly world the people are selfish and they fish in troubled waters and I feel so alone amongst them. I think you also think this way and it is all the more important that we get together and then I would be able to easier handle everything else. You promised to come from Budapest in time and I believe you will, and you wouldn't consider it your duty to help others if it would do harm to yourself. I know that I know you and this does not look like a disgrace, but the contact I made with Marsi brought to mind the difference between the headless man and the type that you are who the work was always first. We will see which one will go farther, but one thing is for sure, I would not trade you for anything and what you think will always be the best for me.

I hear that the Bank is only working on the rescuing efforts and as the deputy of the vice president your turn will come about soon. The local inactivity and crazy insecurity feeling would probably be worse for you here and I know you would not bear it very well, especially together with everything else. The cutting off the Danube I can also see as being a logical point the Russians would do and this is what I am afraid of most. I hope the Bank president is also taking this as a priority in the evacuation plan.

I would like to know what will happen to the library, if they will keep Zsuzsi there till the last minute, or they just need her to help with the evacuation. I worry about that she isn't considered that important that she would be able to come in a car and this way you may not be able to stay together.

Figure 25: Our mother and aunt Zsuzsa looking out over the Tarnay Villa veranda window across the vineyard to Lake Balaton in Révfülöp.

I hope you are not mad at me for all these things I'm thinking about. I don't have much else to do and this is the way I keep busy. Take care of yourself and together with Zsuzsi write if you can or at least come and see us sometimes. I will write every-day now, even if it is just a few words. I will send this letter with Zoltan if he comes soon and you can write to me the same way.

Hugs and kisses to both of you with lots of love.
November 11, 1944

NOVEMBER 21, 1944, "WE ARE CARRYING WITH US THIS DEEP HURT THAT WE MAY NEVER SEE OUR HOMELAND AGAIN"

Our father was still in Budapest and we were in Révfülöp. The Russian front was coming closer. The situation in Veszprém was chaotic. The bank personnel were running around in a panic trying to find train wagons so they could leave before the Russians came. There were sounds of air raid sirens and airplanes in dog fights over Balaton Lake.

—✀—

In November 1944 the situation became critical in Budapest, the capital of Hungary. The Red Army stood before the outskirts of the city and if you felt so inclined, you could take the street car to have a ride to the battle lines. Budapest had seven huge, beautiful bridges across the Danube. All of them were undermined, ready to be blown up by the Germans in case they had to retreat to the West bank of the river. I felt not a bit at ease when every day I had to cross one of these bridges to get to my office. It was not more encouraging at all when one morning one of the mines went off by accident and in the heaviest traffic jammed street cars, horsed teams, automobiles and hundreds of passengers fell in the cold waves of the Danube. In the beautiful and once so happy streets of Budapest, guns, tanks and all kinds of equipments were moving into position and at nights you could see the flashing of gunfire from the battle lines. And on top of this every day and night the efficient visits of the US Air Force, the crazy barking of the anti-aircraft guns and the thunder from the hits of the bomb loads.

—◆—

Nov. 21, 1944

Dear Frici,

I received this morning the clothes, your letter and the paprika. Thank you very much for the clothes, although it is not the best material. I know you didn't have time to look around and besides it cost a lot of money. You know how much of a Scotch I am, that when I put on such expensive clothes, the price always comes to mind, but you know me, I cannot save when it comes to myself. You know how thrifty I am. Anyway, it is going to serve me well and it is not that fine a cloth that I need to take extra care of and I can wear it valiantly.

It was very difficult for me that you could not be here on Sunday.

Let us hope that one day we will benefit from the fact that you have been working so hard and were always modest. Try to think of it this way-if someone does an honest job and yet fails to reap the reward, they still have a clear conscience, ant that is worth more than anything else.

You wouldn't feel comfortable if you had to hang around here or if you were in Veszprém where there are just a few people who are running around with their heads off. This way in Budapest you will at least know if there is something really serious and important going on and you can make appropriate intelligent decisions for yourself. This is the only way I can console myself and anyway, people have little more than hope these days.

The Sunday bombing was from a distance. Saturday afternoon there was a short period that we felt much more because above us there were dog fights.

You wrote that you sent the skis. I don't know how you figured out that we can take these. You can bring the children's sled from the attic. If it snows here, they would be useful to get around with. I will leave it up to you as to what is best. I thought that tomorrow will be a good time to slaughter the pig. If we stay here any longer, it will be good to have whether it's the meat or the little fat that comes from the pig. If we leave I will figure out how to take it with us. There will be fresh hurka and sausage when you arrive Saturday. We can smoke the ham at Otta's. My father was of course against it. He tried to slow down the preparations to leave, because he didn't want us to go away. On the other hand, if I have to go through with this moving with my father and without you being here, I would not be able to endure it.

They are sleeping in the dining room. This new arrangement is working well. I am living in two rooms that are divided according to conserving the heating, but my room is not that cold that I can't do something or work in it. Even now as I am writing this letter in the room, it is very comfortable. This is also good for my mother because she can work in the morning in the room and not be bothered by father's constant calling for something. I just have to get our things arranged in the rooms.

Yesterday I ran out of my bed to wake up Zsuzsi and I was lucky that little Frici woke me up at 4:30 because he wanted a toothpick. Of course I was mad, but then I was also happy because he woke me up just in time for me to get up to wake up Zsuzsi.

I got a good cold from the running around in the cold with only my night gown, but today I am somewhat better and taking care of myself. Yesterday the kids were walking in the rain and wind and they had no problem.

I wanted to send something to Julsca along with the packages, but in the hurry, it stayed here. I will send it with you. She is a very neat woman and not only her work, but for her intelligence and her faithfulness. She is worth everything. I only have one shoe sole. The other I have used on your shoe this summer. This is easy to pack and will be useful.

The idea that we could get there right away would give us many advantages since you know a lot of people there and you even speak Swabian [German dialect]. You know, everybody, including you and me, are in our hearts really hoping to stay here.

We are preparing ourselves for the future with our instinct for survival and carrying with us this deep hurt that we may never see our homeland again.

With lots of love, hugs and kisses

Kati
You see, my father is already losing patience.

—⁓—

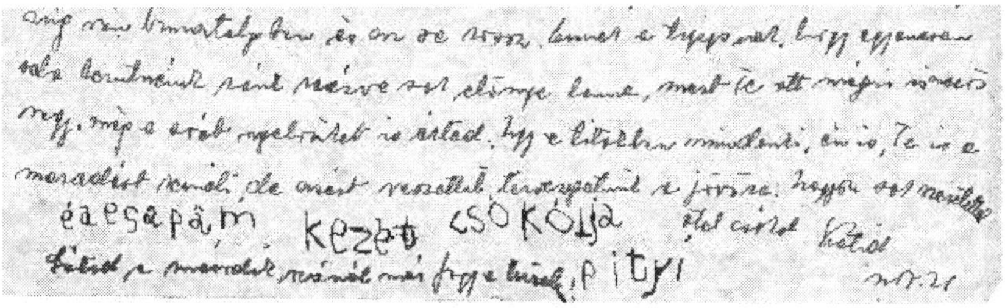

Figure 26: The ending of the letter with Little Frici at 6 years old greeting and signing the letter to his father.

NOVEMBER 24, 1944, "I AM CALMER NOW... USED TO THE CONSTANT NOISE OF WAR"

My Dear Frici,

I just received the cigarettes from Marika. They arrived just in time because I finished off the last of them; in fact I was without for half day. I don't know why, but I am much calmer now than before and I don't smoke as much. I think it is because I gained some weight in the last week and I feel the effects.

I don't have any particular reason for being calmer, maybe perhaps because I have gotten tired and used to the constant noise of the War. Today I heard some wild war stories from Galek and Maczi. Of course, the war is not close by, but is still at a distance and coming our way. T. Bela was here at home yesterday and they already went west and they discussed what they should do.

We talked a lot and in the dark because of the air raids yesterday evening and about how they were able to make it through to get here. Nothing has changed here. We are living like before.

I try to get everything together that we might possibly need. The kids, especially little Frici's and my soles are wearing through. I was silly that I didn't have my soles done earlier because the shoemaker has already left.

We have to give the people here something. Do you have time to find Kutko? My mother is very afraid that the cold will affect Julsca and that she may not be able to get enough food. If she is willing to come live with us, it may be the best for her. Mother says that as long as we are here, she can handle this many people at the house and I have some warm clothes here that I can give her. I don't know how things are in Budapest, but she may be able to live better there. It would be up to her to make the decision. Were you able to get her some snow boots?

Julsca probably can't go home anymore and if there a battle, then it is better for her to be in Budapest than home with us here. I consider her to be part of the family already and we will take care of her as long as we can. If nothing else, we can give her food.

István is getting so much better and tomorrow I'll still keep him in bed to be sure he will be all right. Little Frici will be starting to study with Cseke and Hilda, the three of them together. The group studies well together and it helps him to be more serious.

The teacher is asking 3 pengős per person per hour, but it is all right because I am very happy that they are studying. They are waiting for my letter (the letter carriers) and I'm trying to hurry. Actually they are not expecting for us, maybe next week. We haven't received any news from Zsuzsi. You write her, too, when you will be going. Together with the kids we send you lots of loving hugs.

Nov. 24
Your Kati

NOVEMBER 28, 1944, "DAZED HUNGARIAN SOLDIERS"

My Dear Frici,

I received your letter and there is really no good news in it, but I was relieved anyway because I received some news about you. Now fortunately we are separated in only three different directions. If only if you could be in Veszprém by now. I am guessing Laci (Lászlo) Jánkovics will be going down to see his family and his place is very close to Benedict, about 5 km. I will write to him in Veszprém, but that won't be too bad of a situation for you. Maybe I will bring your bicycle so it will be there for you. That's why I would like to bring everything over there.

Benedict mentioned that the road is full of wondering soldiers asking for something and they are drunk.

You can say that that the security here is not very good these days. Everybody has their problems and they don't have time to care about anybody else. Mrs. Takacs was deciding today whether she was going to go or stay. Her husband is in the west and came back to her to make a decision. If they go, I will try to go with them and Mother said it would be nice if you can come too with us, especially the way the road travel is so unpredictable with the war.

I think we will be slaughtering the pig on Monday. I told Kati that you are moving to Veszprém and if they take you from there that we have to go with you. I cannot be on my mother's back with three kids. I will make sure my parents are well packed with everything they need here. At least there will be somebody in the neighborhood that will look after them and from whom they can get some news. Mother cried a lot about us leaving, especially about Hapsi who is her favorite.

It's so terrible the world around us is swarming in war.

There is terrible news and we still are living alone here and there is no immediate help available. I am sitting here in the veranda without heat on a beautiful fall sunset day and writing a letter.

I would like to write about something else than what we have to do in this beautiful, quiet and peaceful time, but only dark, sad thoughts came to my mind.

I'm afraid of the good bye, the road ahead, and the whole future. I also am afraid that we will wind up in the biggest turmoil if we start too late.

The many Hungarian soldiers retreating are very depressed. They no longer have a home and unfortunately they are not welcomed by the German soldiers. What will we do with all these soldiers? Can we trust them? Can we feed them?

My dear Frici, I don't want to torment you any longer about my concerns. Overall we are all right. István is getting better. I hope to see you in a week. Give the leftover wine to Godolls if they are still there. The chest would be better if you leave it with them. Tell Benedict what there is in their cellar. If Julsca stays, leave a bunch of food from the Bank with her and give her the wood. She can store it in her room. Look after her and yourself, too.

With lots of loving hugs,
Your Kati

NOVEMBER 29, 1944, "THE RADIO IS TELLING THE HORRORS THE RUSSIANS ARE DOING..."

The family is still in Révfülöp. Everyone is packing and getting ready to leave. In the midst of it all, Mother is trying to plan something for the kids to make a Christmas.

—∞—

My Dear Frici,

It is very late now. I knitted for a long time, but I will not have time tomorrow and I won't feel good if I don't write you a letter before I go to bed. Today of course, the situation is very bad, since the Russians are in Pecs and the front is getting closer.

Already last week, particularly since you left, I hardly did any packing, but today the news shook me up a little bit and I started to pack the food. The people living here have gone to Budapest so at least I don't disturb anybody with my packing. What were my little problems are now my biggest problems, so I won't be late. If you write or come I will be ready to leave. Don't be upset that in the last letter I asked you so many questions. This is still from the optimistic view, but today I don't get close to that.

Even the swallows are leaving.

Takacs family has already packed everything. Yesterday the old man telephoned and they are only waiting for a car to take them. I'm going down to see them tomorrow to see how they packed everything and maybe I can learn something from them. I warmly recommended Maczia to them and if it is possible, they can take her to Vasarosmis where her husband is at the present time. And I would like to ask Terus if he has any children's toys. I would gladly take them. They brought these things with them here. I wouldn't be able to buy anything for the kids and we may be spending Christmas here.

My father is preoccupied with how to dress mother for Christmas. It's too bad I didn't bring a Santa Claus mask. The mask is in Budapest along with the Christmas things. I would like that the old ones would be able to enjoy this Christmas. They are already upset. Mother decided that when we go she will stay in the dining room. She can't stand the white room where the kids staying.

The radio is now telling the horrors that the Russians are doing. Mother is very afraid of them. I feel very sorry for them, but I cannot think of any escape route for them. Maybe if they gather up all the things I will leave here, they can manage with them.

If there won't be a strong theater of war here, maybe the orphan home can help them out a little. They can't depend on their pension very long. My mother thought again that maybe they should go to Budapest. I talked her out of it, because it would be even harder for them there. I will tell Maczi this before she leaves to see her husband and if she happens to stay here I will get her together with my parents.

I spoke with the teacher, Mrs. Csonka and she said she is very satisfied with Pityi. He has really changed a lot. The gentlemanly children have a good effect on him. Today as he came home, he immediately went to do his homework. Hapsi learned a new word, "ugly," and he goes around saying it to everybody. Of course the others like what he is doing and have fun telling him this word.

Pityi already knows about Santa Claus and he teaches István some Christmas songs when I turn off the lights. They were very sweet and I eavesdropped and listened to them for a long time and enjoyed them.

I hope you are all right. I am waiting for your letter and I have a little hope that you would be able to come down to visit on Saturday.

Now I'm terribly sleepy, I cannot write anymore. Many kisses and hugs from me and the kids.

Your Kati
Write me if you know something about the travel plans.

NOVEMBER 29, 1944, "IF HE SEES A GROUP OF COLD, SHIVERING SOLDIERS, HE INVITES THEM TO HAVE SOME WINE."

Pest was in ruins. The bombing and the Siege of Budapest was continuing. Our father was with the German Commissioner Leopold Scheffler, a reliable source of information since he had direct connection with the Germans.

Our mother was referring to Scheffler when she said, "I'm glad you have someone that can give you reliable news." She may not have used Scheffler's name because she was sending the letters by messenger.

—⚏—

November 29, 1944

My Dear Frici,

I'm sending you this letter with Nessi. I'm so lucky these days to find somebody to take letters to you. You will get them so much faster. I received a long letter from you today which made me very happy, even though it wasn't good news, at least I heard from you. I am glad to hear that you have someone that can give you reliable news. Even with this uncertainty it is good to know that perhaps we can stay where we are a little longer. You know it still would be ideal to be like this even in this cold weather and to deal with my father's spicy nervousness.

Don't think I don't want to be with you, but first of all, that Pest is in ruins and possibly our home there, too. Secondly, the children would be affected by the difference in the food, the different schedules, the war situation there and all the unknowns that would come up. It would be unrealistic to think that things would be like they used to be. Now life is giving us many difficult problems, but it is comforting to know that it could be much worse. I think the Nessies are also very discouraged. Maybe they wish Erno would have gone to Veszprém. However, when he got frightened, he soon went there quickly.

Maybe I'm not as discouraged now because I quickly got tired of crying about everything that's happened to us and I'm looking for the good in everything.

You know how I'm always planning and during these times it's very useful. Other times I remember you got upset about it. I already left out in the last two letters the thought of you talking to Born about the defense protection (how to use a gun). Maczia brought it up to me about why don't I do it also. I always wanted to write you, but nowadays there are such bad situations here right now that in this mess we have here, it escaped my mind. I was happy and also especially for my mother.

My father has many fearful moments and this gave him some peace. I had a serious talk with my father today about everything that can be done if you have the will.

He looked at me as if he never heard that before. For the last two days he has been complaining all day, of course about nothing, mostly because we had to go sometimes to the cellar or someplace safe because of air raid warnings. My mother responds to every complaint of my father and she spoils him that way.

Now my father has a goodwill passionate pastime. If he sees a group of cold shivering soldiers, he invites them to have some wine and they soon become familiar with his invitation.

Everything would be all right if only we had enough wood. Today we are just heating the dining room and its 4 o'clock in the afternoon. I sleep in the white room with the kids. My mother and father moved into the dining room. Tomorrow in the morning we will see how this new arrangement worked out. It is possible that I can heat the small room for myself.

Believe this, I am washing myself in ice cold water in the bathroom, I tell myself that really it is not cold and everything is ok.

István is already better and all three of them are tough and handle everything very well. We usually only heat during the evening. Of course the kids are well dressed up during the day. The schooling of little Frici is going well, but unfortunately the other mothers, especially Buci, consider taking the kids down to school every day a little too much work and now they just go three times a week. This is stupid because the kids can really be taught in school. I told them the reason was that when the Russians come the kids wouldn't be going to school anyway. Until then at least they finish the important parts of their schooling.

The other day, Cseke confronted me about this, but in a way it was funny. That's why he was so mad in the first place, because he had to wait till the end of the hour. I thought it would be nice and he would enjoy it and he could take time from his work and he could take your eldest son to school. The other day his mother-in-law confronted me and asked me "What are we doing?"

I said, "I am going to where they are making plans."

"Where to?"

"To the West."

"But how?"

They did not say, everybody decided to stay and finally she left. I didn't tell her anything. I'm a little tired of them. See, I'm gossiping a little, you are probably tired of this, no?

Yesterday Zsuzsi and I had a good talk. We talked about the past and it was good to hear about you and what was going on in Pest with everybody. I am very happy that Zsuzsi is with us here, although probably it would be better if she was with mother, but she is right, our mother can better handle father if she is alone with him. I wrote down a bunch of things. I would like to ask you if you can get some straps from the Bank or someplace for the trip. I'm not sure, maybe I already wrote you about this.

With many hugs and kisses with the kids together with love,

Your Kati
Nov. 29, 1944

DECEMBER 1, 1944, "I CAN HARDLY BELIEVE IT NOW, EVEN THOUGH MY MIND IS NORMAL."

Evacuations of towns and villages were in process as the Russian Front was coming closer. People prepared to flee. Midst the chaos, Mother writes to Father and a son remembers.

—ɱ—

Dear Frici,

I couldn't write you every day now because with this heating problem we had to gather together to keep warm and the time just went by. I hardly had any room to do anything. I stand around a lot every day. Always thinking of some wonderful way to take care of things, but the days just pass by without accomplishing anything. The little ones have a cold and I put them in their room. Maybe they will get better sooner that way. I'm pulling together the food, the clothes I already have packed and I already sent some of it away, then it won't be such a slow job. However, you can imagine this also takes lots of time.

Periodically we get frightened and we quickly put something more together before something more comes along.

Yesterday in Boglar they evacuated the civil population. I imagine they will do the same in Somogy like they did in Alfod and then really we wouldn't be able to stay here. I really got frightened yesterday evening thinking that the Russians will come much sooner here than in Budapest and that I wouldn't be able to meet with you. I slept on it and I'm a little better today, but we called up Zsuzsi yesterday and also talked to her today.

Actually Mother and Father worry the most, we of course are ready to go away, but they are very afraid to stay here as the Russians are getting closer. I'm also a little nervous about that. For instance, if they send Annu away, there will only be three old people left who can't take care of themselves alone, let alone be able to settle in by themselves.

My father is complaining to himself now as to why he didn't sell the wine. He would have had 10,000 or 15,000 pengős now and he could have gone to Budapest where at least there are more people like him and maybe he would get his pension easier than here. My mother says that we could kill a pig and stock up with food and there will be Julsca who would be able to help take care of us. I must say, it is not a bad idea.

Here I'm very afraid for them, because here life is very hard, especially for the old ones. But on the other hand, they wouldn't be able to bear a month long siege of Budapest and here it certainly wouldn't be so long. They will only go to Klari if they cannot go anywhere else. You know it is natural for them to feel so helpless if we go away. It is not any better for us either, but we cannot help with this.

I don't dare to console them, so they keep their spirits up.

I hope they keep trying to take care of things, so that if we come back there will be something to start with. You know I think Father thinks that if we don't take them with us, that he would save something here for us. They would do this anyway and wouldn't have any other goal in mind except to take care of themselves. I won't say anymore about this, you already know this and it won't help talking about it. I am so weird, what I have imagined up to now, what will be bad and hard.

I can hardly believe it now, even though I know my mind is still normal. I have become very used to the idea of separation from the lifestyle I was used to and live in an apathetic crazy frame of mind.

It would feel wonderful if you could come down and see us, but Zsuzsi said that you can't get away from your work right now. I haven't received a letter from you yet, but hope you are all right, as much as can be expected from the present war situation.

I feel cowardly that I don't go to see you, but I'm afraid to leave the kids here by themselves.

My parents are so nervous now. We can put up with this for the next two weeks and more if necessary. I would really like to hear some news. I think that probably you don't know any more than we do and probably nothing for certain.

Nobody is interested in renting the apartment, but at least we don't have to spend time dealing with strangers.

I received a bunch of toys from the Takacs family. Santa Claus will bring these to the kids. Pityi was very funny yesterday, He forgot to learn a poem for school and only remembered after he went to bed, but of course he forgot where he put the book. I told him he should tell the teacher that he forgot to do it and maybe he won't get punished too much.

"But I want to say something else so I won't get punished," he said anxiously.

I think he was pushed to be better probably by Zoltan's effect on him. I brought him to school today, so I can get him cleaned up. He was very anxious and wanted to go early so he can learn the poem before the teacher gets dressed for school. He met with little Zoltan and by the time he recited the poem two times, Pityi already knew it. Pityi was very happy and I didn't mind that he was so anxious for a little while. He is already learning the handwritten alphabet and it's not going very well especially when he has to put the letters together. The numbers he already knows well and likes to work with them.

The little ones are now very mischievous because they are locked up all day. By evening they are pretty ragged looking from beating and kicking each other all day. We laughed a lot over István yesterday. He wanted to throw a chair at Pityi, by the time we took one away from him another one flew by. He was very mad about something. He said to everybody, "terrible, ugly," to mother and also to Gonga, Kati, and the whole house. Finally he says "But I can't say anything to Julsca, I only like her."

Be sure to tell Julsca how much István values him. This is really strange, since it has been so long since they have seen each other. Zsuzsi calmed me down, when she said that she was sure that we will meet each other, I hope so too, because I won't be able to believe in anything anymore.

If once we are together I will not be afraid of anything anymore, maybe a little from you, but we will get used to each other again.

If you think we will be together again with the kids, I can't think of anything bad that can happen. Now that I have been here for two days, I realized that's why I was complaining all the time because you were not next to me and we feel so pitiful without you. If you think it is worthwhile for my parents to go to Budapest and if it still can be accomplished with all the transportation and war battles going on, write to me about this. Even if it is not possible, at least it will calm down my parents. At least they will know that they can still stay here.

With the kids together, we give you lots of hugs and kisses.

Your Kati
Révfülöp, Dec. 1, 1944

DECEMBER 3, 1944, "THE RUSSIANS WILL PUSH US INTO THE LAKE!"

The Russians were continuing their advance on Révfülöp. They threatened to surround us and cut off the escape routes to Veszprém and to our father in Budapest.

The time had come to leave Révfülöp for Veszprém and our mother showed how strong she could be. She took charge while everybody around was walking in a daze. Her attitude was that she could do anything. It was this iron quality our father knew our mother had and that she could handle the war situation with the three kids and grandparents while he was away.

Our father had to be with the German Commissioner and knew he could get the job done that would save the gold and the personnel from the Russians. Our father was determined and dedicated to his job, despite his wanting to quit when the Nazi Arrow Cross took over on October 15th.

Our mother's letter was probably never sent because it was only 3 days before we had to leave for Veszprém on December 6.

—⚏—

Dec. 3, 1944,

My Dear Frici,

My father just talked to the refugees from Kaposvár. The Russians are already there. Don't you think I should go to Veszprém with the baggage and the kids, because the Russians will cut us off and then we will surely not be able to meet? You probably won't know about these events till later in Budapest. I know it is an uncertain feeling and you may be looking at it from another perspective, but here on the main road the Russians can easily surround us.

I would gladly go now, I'm already packing like a steam engine, but it would be good if you come here or at least send me word confirming our departure. Nobody is holding the other side of the lake, I would guess the Russians will push us into the lake and that's not something that they will let them do. Please come or write as soon as possible.

THE SADNESS WENT THROUGH TO OUR BONES, FRED B. TARNAY (SON)

….One day a tall SS Captain showed up at our door in Révfülöp and announced (politely when he saw we spoke fluent German) that we were to 'loan' our car to the German army for a brief period. I still remember the shiny boots and impeccable uniform.

They took the Cabriolet as I think the other car was in Budapest at the Bank at the time. The promise was kept as the car was returned a month later in very good shape; but as the situation was getting worse, it was 'borrowed' again few months later and this time we never saw it again. Anyway it was 1944 and soon we would be packing to leave. Father was already working at the Bank moving the treasury to Veszprém. He would come home sometimes in the middle of the night looking very tired and would help us pack. Veszprem is just a few miles from Révfülöp.

It was decided to bury some of the family treasures, mostly the silver in a spot near the maintenance building. Mother and Zsuzsi later dug it up before Zsuzsi sold the property and I think all of us have some portion of it now. The silver was ok, but the steel of the knives was not stainless and had rusted away. The spoons, knives and forks had the T initials engraved that stood for Tótth as it came from our grandmother's side of the family.

And then everyone was packing. We packed everything from Budapest where most of our belongings still lay and everything from Révfülöp. I don't know how they did it and I and my brothers were kept out of the way. The other MNB families were doing the same and all the belongings were being gathered and loaded on the train. We were ready and just waiting to see if or how far the Soviet Communists were going to advance to take over our country, our homes, and our freedom.

We listened to the radio all day, every day as we sat with blank faces, which is what I remember the most. It was cold, winter was here and the sadness went through to our bones.

DECEMBER 5, 1944, JÁNKOVICS' MEMORANDUM, "URGENT THINGS TO DO"

General Manager of the MNB László Jánkovics wrote this Memorandum of MNB directive from his hospital bed in Budapest where he was recuperating from an illness. He wrote the memo after he received a letter from Veszprém from the Bank officials saying that the Russians were advancing rapidly and it was imperative to move the Bank to someplace safe across the border in Austria.

Jánkovics assigned Frici important responsibilities, especially in connection with the German Commissioner Leopold Scheffler. He was designated to arrange and coordinate the evacuation of the National treasures as well as the Bank personnel and their families. Jánkovics designated Frici as the lead acting Manager of the MNB from Veszprém to Spital am Pyhrn.

[Note: numbering is the same as the original, purpose unknown. Ed]

—w—

BUDAPEST 12-5-44

[*Translation*]

Urgent Things to Do

1. /Urgent things to do: Pro Memoria preparation (excerpt from original memo).

2. /Acting Managers Tornay Edgar and Tarnay Frigyes shall continually keep each other informed and cooperatively take the necessary steps to keep contact with the German Embassy. Tornay Edgar's contact shall be Magyarossy, the government trustee, and Tarnay Frigyes shall be the contact with Scheffler. Through a national leader, the President shall send this pro memoria to the Minister of Foreign Affairs due to diplomatic concerns. It is urgent that these two parties have a conference as quickly as possible.

3. / Director Fazekas should inquire from Director Porer if there is a possibility to acquire the needed trains through MAV (Hungarian Train Co.). At the same time, Tarnay Frigyes, acting manager is required to have a meeting with his German counterparts to inquire about filling these trains within 24 hours.

Section 5/C

In my opinion, Tarnay Frigyes should be put in contact with the Minister of Finance and I would have him strongly consider moving the entire Bank to Sopron.

13. / I would like to ask Superintendent Salmon that he put family members first on his list of priorities amongst the refugees. Tarnay Frigyes should speak to Scheffler to find out if these refugees should be evacuated immediately or not. If the answer is yes, he should consider how they should be transported. This is why the first 50 train cars are crucial on the Hungarian and German sides.

14. / Tarnay Frigyes should also consider in what currency the Bank employees should receive their pay.

18. / I would also like to ask Tarnay Frigyes to ask Scheffler how they can get a uniformed Party member that has full authority to arrange things in Vorau. Considering that the Gauleiter (territory leader) is under Hitler and he is 80 km from Graz, this is why we require a member that can always be trusted. The Bank shall be responsible for providing for this person.

19. / Tarnay Frigyes shall discuss with Scheffler about acquiring a hotel for us instead of staying in Vorau.

BUDAPEST, 1944, DECEMBER 5

As per instructed by: Jánkovics, Chief Director. Dictated in Budapest, OTBA Sanatorium, in the presence of Acting Manager Tornay Mészaros Zoltán and Superintendant Salamon Lászlo."

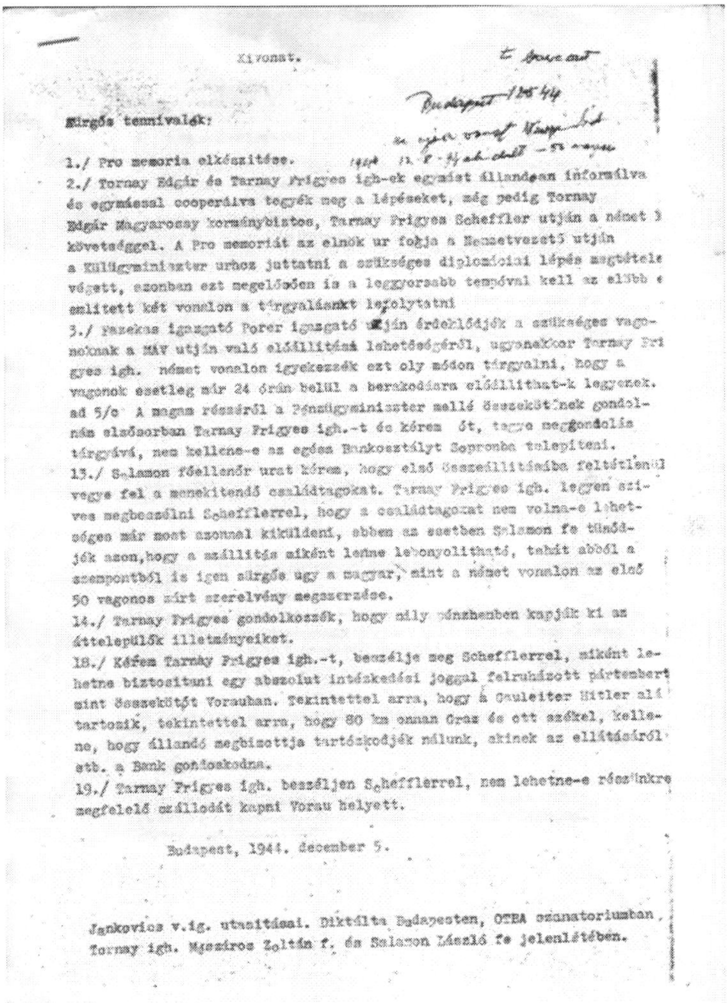

Kivonat.

Sürgős tennivalók:

1./ Pro memoria elkészitése.
2./ Tornay Edgár és Tarnay Frigyes igh-ek egymást állandóan informálva és egymással cooperálva tegyék meg a lépéseket, még pedig Tornay Edgár Magyarossy kormánybiztos, Tarnay Frigyes Scheffler utján a német követséggel. A Pro memoriát az elnök ur fogja a Nemzetvezető utján a Külügyminiszter urhoz juttatni a szükséges diplomáciai lépés megtétele végett, azonban ezt megelőzően is a leggyorsabb tempóval kell az előbb említett két vonalon a tárgyalásokat lefolytatni
3./ Fazekas igazgató Porer igazgató utján érdeklődjék a szükséges vagonoknak a MÁV utján való előállitásá lehetőségéről, ugyanakkor Tarnay Frigyes igh. német vonalon igyekezzék ezt oly módon tárgyalni, hogy a vagonok esetleg már 24 órán belül a berakodásra előállithat-k legyenek.
ad 5/c A magam részéről a Pénzügyminiszter mellé összekötőnek gondolnám elsősorban Tarnay Frigyes igh.-t és kérem őt, tegye megfontolás tárgyává, nem kellene-e az egész Bankosztályt Sopronba telepiteni.
13./ Salamon főellenőr urat kérem, hogy első összeállitásába feltétlenül vegye fel a menekitendő családtagokat. Tarnay Frigyes igh. legyen szives megbeszélni Schefflerrel, hogy a családtagokat nem volna-e lehetséges már most azonnal kiküldeni, ebben az esetben Salamon fe tüntődjék azon, hogy a szállitás miként lenne lebonyolitható, tehát abból a szempontból is igen sürgős ugy a magyar, mint a német vonalon az első 50 vagonos zárt szerelvény megszerzése.
14./ Tarnay Frigyes gondolkozzék, hogy mily pénzben kapják ki az áttelepülők illetményeiket.
18./ Kérem Tarnay Frigyes igh.-t, beszélje meg Schefflerrel, miként lehetne biztositani egy abszolut intézkedési joggal felruházott pártembert mint összekötőt Vorauban. Tekintettel arra, hogy a Gauleiter Hitler alá tartozik, tekintettel arra, hogy 80 km onnan Graz és ott székel, kellene, hogy állandó megbizottja tartózkodjék nálunk, akinek az ellátásáról etb. a Bank gondoskodna.
19./ Tarnay Frigyes igh. beszéljen Schefflerrel, nem lehetne-e részünkre megfelelő szállodát kapni Vorau helyett.

Budapest, 1944. december 5.

Jánkovics v.ig. utasitásai. Diktálta Budapesten, OTBA szanatoriumban, Tornay igh. Mészáros Zoltán f. és Salamon László fe jelenlétében.

Figure 27: Original letter from Lászlo Jánkovics MNB Manager

We left Budapest on December 5th, 1944, forming a small convoy of automobiles and tried to take the highway to Veszprém. We had no luck. It was already blocked and pounded by Russian gunfire and so we had to use the side and dirt roads filled with refugees and retreating German units. It was quite an experience and a hard test on the driver's skill. Imagine a traffic jam on a soft, muddy road churned up by tanks and heavy armored equipments, crowded with the largest variety of vehicles from wheelbarrows and oxen carts to Tiger tanks.

When we finally arrived in Veszprém, we had only a couple of days to get settled in our new quarters and offices. The military situation became so alarming that the families of the employees living scattered in villages and resort places at the Lake Balaton were picked up by trucks and brought to the shelter in order to have them ready to be moved out with the Bank in case the Russians should break through to the city.

—ɯ—

CHAPTER 2:
"WE MUST GO"

Veszprém and Fertőboz
December 6, 1944

Almost all the railway system was under German army control. The German Commissioner Leopold Scheffler was the only one that was able to get railway cars for the Bank with his authority. The Bank personnel were working around the clock loading the train cars and Veszprém looked like a hen house with a fox in it.

Our family had arrived from Révfülöp and boarded the train that left Veszprém on December 8th. When the train finally left Veszprém it zigzagged its way through the countryside at night to avoid detection by the enemy.

—⁓—

"I WAS GLUED TO THE RADIO" BY FRED B. TARNAY

I remember that last day; we were gathered in the family room, I was glued to the radio reporting/repeating every bit of news which I'm sure did not help. It was mid morning and then Grandfather finally said, "We must go." Everyone's face was ashen as we tearfully said a last goodbye to our grandparents. A MNB truck was coming to pick us up with whatever else we could carry with us. Zsuzsi came along as well to help and returned later somehow. The roads were busy, not sure why, but I think people were on their way to the Austrian border. The truck slid down an embankment sideways as it tried to pass the traffic, but did not overturn. The next thing I remember we were settling in one of the railroad cars with our mother arranging the horsehair mattresses on top of the gold bullion boxes.

DECEMBER 6, 1944, "WITH A HEAVY HEART I LEFT MY PARENTS THERE"

My Dear Frici,

We are here in Veszprém and luckily we arrived without any big problems. It was getting pretty bad at Révfülöp already when we left and I was totally ready to travel by the time Zsuzsi arrived.

With a heavy heart I left my parents there, but you know that everything about Révfülöp is still with me.

I said goodbye to them last night, because I had so much to do that I didn't have time to talk to them today. Annu's father arrived, the old man from Szeged already is living here and they helped us tie up all the luggage and bring it out.

The house was so full of wonderful people and it made me much calmer that my parents are not alone for the moment. Mother is also helping a lot with the packing and the old man dug out the toilet pits last night and does the heavy work. Annus said she will stay as long as she can and they figured that if they cleared out Révfülöp, Annus will go home. Her father will come the next day through Pulan with the Benedeks with a long cart to pick up my parents. They will stay in Pulan as long as they can then come back to Révfülöp if they can, but I think that plan will probably change a number of times.

We tried to make sure as much as we could to leave them some money. The old man from Szeged is proudly wearing your coat and I gave him some of your underclothes also. He also wants to go with my parents, but I don't know how they will arrange that. He now tries to attach himself to someone, but I don't know what the outcome of that will be.

My dear Frici, I received today a desperate letter from Julsca. She is not staying any longer in Budapest and I just don't know what the end of that will be for her. She doesn't want to go to anybody, neither to Fanni or Benedeks. She would rather go out on the street; she can't stand it anymore there. Dear Frici, the first thing I must do is to think about Julsca and I wrote her to be sure she leaves some food there for herself and the firewood is also there for her.

We have been hearing gunfire all day for the last 3 days. The windows rattle all day and night.

I would be very happy if we leave even tomorrow. It is close enough to the last moment. If Zsuzsi doesn't come today, I already reserved a car for tomorrow afternoon to Pula and from there Benedek would have taken us to Veszprém. I tried to bring everything that you mentioned in your letter like the bucket and so on. It is already packed up.

I have a feeling that I may not see you until we are in Vorau. I only ask you that you take very good care of yourself and don't be late in your travels. I will take care of the kids and luckily I know that Zsuzsi is also registered in Vorau as an employee and she would be able to help me there. There is no work to be done for the Bank anyway. I am very happy that we are leaving soon, just so it's for real. If once we have to start it is best if we go right away, so there wouldn't be so much to do with the kids. They are all doing fine and took the trip very well. Pityi enjoyed the change and the new adventure.

István said to me not to come here anymore and in the evening he wanted to sleep next to his grandmother.

He is the only one that knows and feels what is happening to him, because he isn't enjoying himself like Pityi. Hapsi also shouted, "Mother!" when I put them to bed.

My dear Frici, I ask you please take care of Julsca. I will also write to her. I can't give any other advice than for her to go live with her mother, if she wants to be independent. I'm not nervous now I even left my medicine with my father.

I know what awaits for me and I look courageously ahead. I look at everything with the worst possible outcome. That way it will be better to endure when it is better after all. If we will be together, nothing can go wrong. That is for sure, because I do not have any pretensions and you may be calm for that. And I come out all right with people, also.

Embraces kisses from one who loves you very much.

Your Kati
Dec. 6.
Please leave some money with Julsca before you leave.

—∞—

On December 9th, 1944, we received the bad news that the Red Army reached Lake Balaton and was no farther than 16 miles from the City. A wild panic broke loose. The gold and valuables were still sitting in the vaults and no sufficient trucks or railroad cars were at our disposal for their transportation. We had to get railroad cars by all means if we wanted to leave the danger zone. Our efforts to obtain them from the State Railways and from the Hungarian Transportation Center were futile, for the whole railroad system was under the control of the German Army.

Fortunately, I must say, the Bank had a German Commissioner delegated by the German Government to supervise the operations of the Bank since the country was occupied by the Germans. I informed him about the situation and within a few hours we could start loading 1 coach car and 7 freight cars.

That night the whole personnel of the Bank were feverishly working to load the cars and get them out of the city as quickly as possible. 32 tons of gold, representing a value of 33 million dollars packed in wood boxes weighing 110 lbs each, were placed on the floor of three plain 15 ton box cars. Their capacity marked as "for 40 men or 6 horses," but gold being known as heavy stuff there was still plenty of space left for 2 guards and their families to live on this precious carpet during two long winter months.

The women and children were squeezed in the coach car. Finally, at midnight the train carrying hundred millions of dollars and a desperate crowd of crying and worrying women and children left the city with the orders to pull as close as possible to the Western border, but not to cross it until further instructions.

—ᴍ—

A unit of the Royal Hungarian Gendarmes was attached to guard the valuables during this voyage of uncertain destination. The men had to stay and load the cars we expected to get from the Germans the following days. There was a great shortage in railroad cars and we had to take any type of freight cars, open or covered ones, available. For instance, we had to put 100 tons of silver ingots safeguarded by us for the Royal Treasury in seven open hoppers just like a dumped load of coal.

Fortunately, the Russian offensive had been stopped and a German counteroffensive had thrown them back to a safe distance from Veszprém.

One day, I even tried to make a business trip back to Budapest, but after 20 miles of driving 3 Russian fighter planes appeared above our car and started firing. In no time, I took to the bushes on the roadside. One of the shells hit the ground close to me, but when they passed and kept on firing, I saw that their target was a train standing at a small village station loaded with German tanks.

The planes made several circles over the train and kept it under permanent fire. They did it undisturbed, because the Germans did not return the fire either from the ground or from the air. Nevertheless, not one of the cars or tanks was hit, but a good lot of the houses in the village caught fire from the shells. They sure were poor flyers and gunners. This incident and the information I gathered from drivers coming from the direction of Budapest made me give up my plan and return to Veszprém.

By the German counteroffensive, we gained time enough to load everything we wished to take along. Successively, we had about 80 cars loaded and assembled into a train at a small station named Fertőboz near the city of Sopron and the Lake Fertő on the Western border.

About 500 people, among them my family, lived in this train during the two cold winter months.

DECEMBER 1944, THE GHOST TRAIN

In early December 1944 as the Russians were rapidly advancing, the MNB decided to move all the banking business activities from Veszprém to Sopron, which was only a few kilometers from where the train was waiting to cross the border at the Fertőboz train station.

There are few letters between Father and Mother at this time because of the danger. The train and personnel needed to be invisible… A Ghost Train. There was no modern communication and the families lived in isolation. Constant air raids forced the families into hiding in the forest.

—⁓—

DECEMBER 10, 1944, "HIDE IN THE DITCHES AND BUSHES"

The greatest problem however was to find a safe place for these immense valuables loaded on plain freight cars and exposed to the daily air raids of the US Air Force. You have to realize that main targets of the air raids were the strategically important railroad tracks, bridges and highways, in order to cut off the supply lines of the Germans. Thus, a railroad station was the worst place we could keep our treasures and families.

Every time an air raid came, the women and children had to leave the train and hide in the ditches and bushes as far as they had time to run. Another reason to leave the station as soon as possible was that the Station had only one restroom and one well for 500 people. The sanitary conditions became unbearable

We knew that not before long we had to move somewhere in Germany, for there was no doubt that pretty soon Hungary would be occupied by the Red Army.

We were determined to stick stubbornly to the idea that the valuables and personnel with their families were inseparable and composed an indivisible body in which the employees and their families formed a protective wall around the gold and the treasures.

Therefore, our first objective was to find and get an appropriate location where the treasures and the staff with their families as a community could be resettled and sheltered. Then, before we could leave the country, we had to arrive at an Agreement with the German Government bearing the guarantee that we may move and stay together with our treasures. We may guard them ourselves even on German territory and independence and integrity will be secured during our stay in Germany.

DECEMBER 14, 1944, "HE PROVED TO BE VERY COURAGEOUS DURING THE RUSSIAN ATTACK TODAY"

Scheffler put his life in danger, for if the Nazis found out he was helping the MNB, he would have been arrested and probably killed for treason. Frici also had to keep this close col-

laboration with Scheffler under cover from the MNB officials. This was necessary for fear of his appearing to collaborate with Germans.

The following letter from Frici shows the close professional relationship between Frici and Scheffler. That became the key to the eventual saving of the gold and Bank personnel. They roomed together during their business travels in Budapest. They even stayed at Révfülöp at our grandparents' villa.

The train had already left Veszprém on December and was in the Fertőboz train station. Meanwhile, Frici was traveling with Scheffler from Veszprém, Budapest and Sopron. They were making arrangements so the train could continue to Spital am Pyhrn.

—ꝏ—

Figure 28: Around 1925, our father in army uniform. He received several distinguished medals during his service in the Hungarian Army. Unfortunately, they were lost in a robbery of our mother's apartment in the U.S.A.

Thursday, Dec. 14th, 1944

My Little Kati,

Tomorrow, a truck is taking Ladányi and the Bank department to Sopron. I have to go to Budapest with Scheffler and so I will only arrive in Sopron later. Probably on Sunday or Monday. The main reason is because we are going to Budapest so the President could decide whether we should go to Vorau, or if we should find some other place for the Bank personnel and their families.

It would be better to provide you with some normal place, because Vorau will not be very pleasant, especially since nothing has been prepared. I am staying here with Scheffler, because they took away everything from my room.

Everything would be all right, but I do not have undergarments. You left nothing here. You could have at least left Lajoska's suitcase that had everything that I needed packed in it. Leave something in Sopron if you can, or I will be in quite an impossible situation because of my undergarments.

I do not know if we will meet in Sopron, because it may well be that you will leave before I arrive. I will return to Veszprém with Scheffler and will continue to Sopron from there. If we can, we will stop to see Révfülöp. I would like to see what our poor elders are doing.

Ladányi told me you were fairly well-lodged. I am sorry I did not come to meet you at the train, but with all the kids and suitcases it was not possible at the last minute. Maybe it is better that you are there, because the front is quite close here and if it falls, there will be immediate danger. I would really like to see you all. How did the children handle the trip?

I will finish now, because Scheffler wants to add something, and we will have to go to bed, since we will be up early tomorrow.

Zsuzsi's shoe is here, though without a sole.

I send my loving kisses to all of you.

Frici

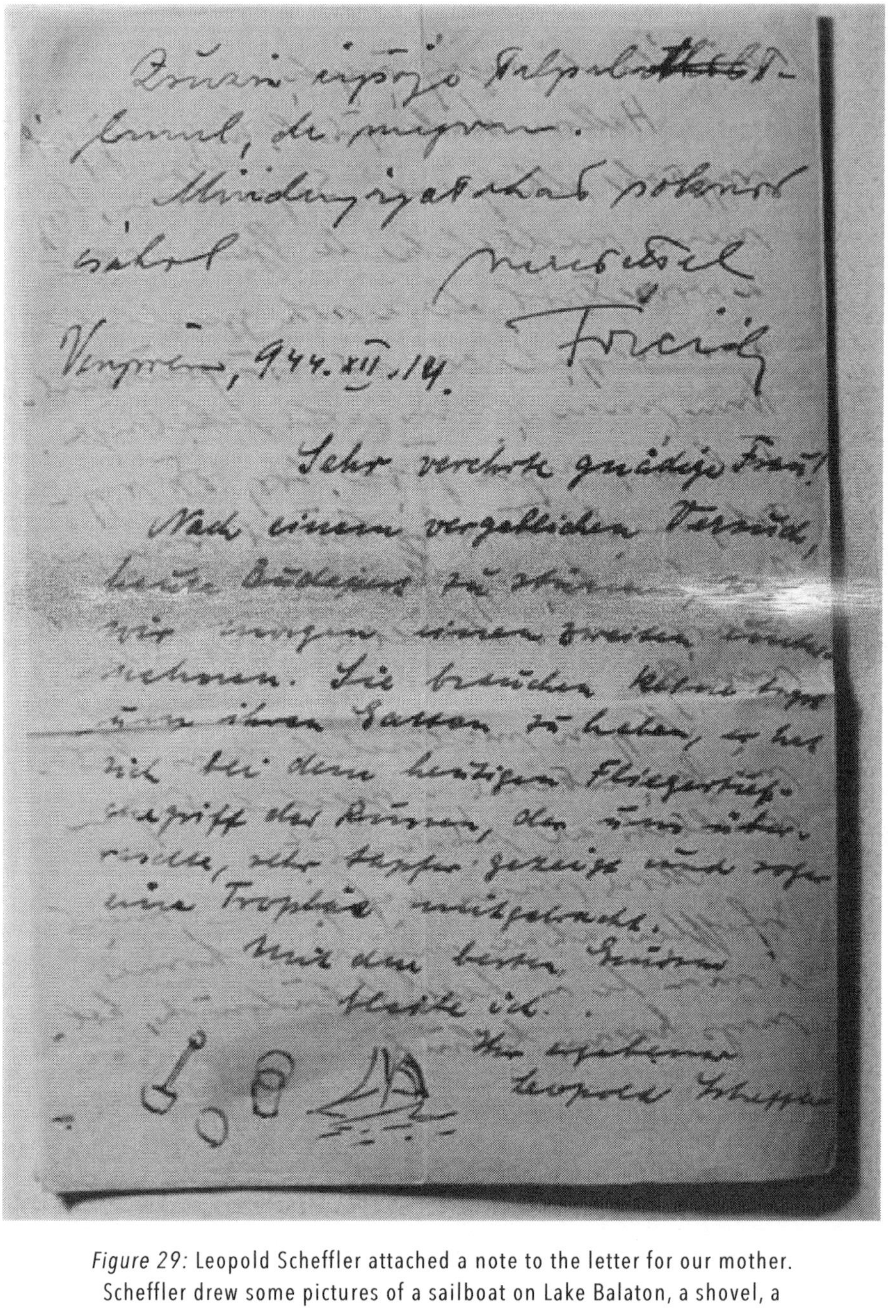

Figure 29: Leopold Scheffler attached a note to the letter for our mother.
Scheffler drew some pictures of a sailboat on Lake Balaton, a shovel, a
bucket, and a ball for us three kids.

[TRANSLATION] VESZPRÉM, 12/14/44

After an unsuccessful attempt to take Budapest today, we will try again a second time tomorrow. You don't have to be anxious about your husband. He proved to be very courageous during the Russian attack today, which caught us by surprise, and he even brought back a souvenir.

With best wishes,
Sincerely Yours,
Leopold Scheffler

Figure 30: Frici's Auto Union car at the Révfülöp Villa. It may have been the MNB car Frici and Scheffler travelled in together. Little Frici and István play around the car. The car was an F5 front wheel drive, 2 cylinder-2 cycle engine. The three-speed transmission had a top speed of 50 miles per hour.

DECEMBER 22, 1944, THE SIEGE OF CASTLE HILL, "THEY RAN OVER THE CROWDS WITH TANKS."

Our father was in Budapest and not able to mail or deliver the December 14th letter to our mother. He kept the letter and this note until he saw us, after he and Scheffler escaped from the Siege of Budapest.

Our father wanted to share with our mother this very sad, emotional moment during the last days he was in Budapest, before he had to leave ahead of the Soviet advance.

The note is put into verse "The Siege of Castle Hill" to describe the helplessness of the Hungarian civilians. They were caught between the Romanian and Russian forces and the occupying German forces as they battled each other during the Siege.

———※———

Figure 31: December 22, 1944. This is the original note written by our father to our mother on December 22, 1944. He was on Castle Hill at the time.

THE SIEGE OF CASTLE HILL

- They pray for us at every Mass,
  they ring the bells –
    they think of us –
There are black flags everywhere –
    for sure the news will spread.
We do not know –
    how many have died,
      they ran over the crowd with tanks.
There is no need to worry–
    it will not spread,
There will be no bloodshed elsewhere–
    there will be an end,

It cannot last long–

1944, Dec. 22   FRED TARNAY

Figure 32: This is our father's note translated and put in verse by Steven
Tarnay

FERTŐBOZ, THE RED TAPE AND COURAGE

About 500 people, among them my family, lived in this train during the two cold winter months. An almost insoluble problem was how to heat these cars. The coach had steam radiators, but there was no locomotive to supply the steam. The freight cars were not equipped with heaters of course. We needed stoves desperately, but it was impossible to get them. The stores were closed and practically empty anyway.

What saved us in this case, believe it or not, was the so much scolded red tape. When one day we went to the railroad station to load the cars assigned to us, to our great surprise, we found one of them filled with stoves. Just the kind of camp stoves we could use for our railroad cars. Nevertheless, we honestly reported this fact to the railroad official and asked for replacement. He, however, ignored our apparently bothering and under the prevailing circumstances, I admit, ridiculous complaint. He declared that according to his records, that car is empty. Thus it must be empty and he is not going to give us another car.

Seeing that he stubbornly stuck to his infallible records, we did not insist further. We closed the door of the car and sent it as it was after our families to Fertőboz. The problem of the fuel to heat the stoves was solved, too.

Along the tracks of the station where our train was standing was a little forest of young trees. Too big a temptation for men with freezing families to leave them unharmed and let them grow bigger. Two months later when the train left the station, the owner's only worry was how to replant his forest.

FRED B. TARNAY (SON) "ROASTED GREEN APPLES"

The train moved in short increments and it seemed we spent most of the time stopped somewhere for various reasons. The atmosphere was one of mixed boredom, fear, anxiety and a general apprehension about what would happen to us. We didn't know if we were going to make it safely and it seemed some mishap or accident was a daily part of our existence. It was still winter and it was cold. Each car had one small wood stove. It was also incredibly cramped. We were all, each family in one little compartment, sitting or lying down on mattresses on top of the strongboxes of gold bullion and surrounded by our belongings.

I don't know how long we were underway, but it seemed like months. We were also on top of our neighbors. At times people had a hard time getting along with each other, especially those with kids. We children had no outlet for exercise and we were antsy all day. There was also little food. We often left the train to go into farmers' fields and orchards to gather whatever we could to survive. We had roasted green apples often. We just put them on top of the wooden stove in each car. We were always hungry. I remember looking at my hands and the joints were all popping out, because we were so thin.

Apparently a car was lost once and had to be found and retrieved. We had to find a new locomotive once. We came under attack from Russian fighter planes and had to run and hide in the forest. The pilots were poor shots as my father recalls in his memoirs. We would have been safer in the train than outside. We lay in the woods as we heard bullets whiz by and hit the branches above us, while my mother covered us with her body. What I remember was my mother doing always what had to be done. She put her fears and feelings aside. The survival of her family came first.

JANUARY 15, 1945, THE AGREEMENT, "YOU FOLKS ARE GOING TO BE FAMOUS."

The German Commissioner, Leopold Scheffler received orders from Berlin to separate the gold from the Bank personnel and take the gold to Germany. With Frici's collaboration, he ignored those orders. The Commissioner stood by the MNB officials' insistence to keep control of the Bank's assets and personnel before crossing the border into Austria. Scheffler convinced other German officials to sign an Agreement with the MNB. This would allow the train to cross the border into German occupied Austria.

—⁓—

The attempts of a special delegate of the Bank and our efforts through the diplomatic channels to obtain an adequate location from the German Government having failed, I was instructed to get in touch with the German Commissioner and solve the problem as quickly as possible.

An urgent solution was imperative, for in case of a rapid Russian advance, the Germans would have evacuated our treasures even by force to Germany. They would not have cared what happened with the personnel. I was present when a telephone call came from Berlin for the German Commissioner suggesting that the gold be put into vaults of the Reichsbank in Vienna, the silver be shipped to Magdeburg, and the treasures of the Museums to Berlin. And as to the personnel … well, they could take refuge in the Province Upper Austria (at that time called Upper Danube) like other Hungarian refugees. This would have meant the complete loss of control over our assets.

Fortunately, the German Commissioner shared our idea of indivisibility and ignored these instructions. When he finished his talk with Berlin and saw how upset I was about those "suggestions" from Berlin, he told me not to worry. He reassured me that, "We'll find something for our treasures, but we have to go ahead immediately." And so we did.

Our idea was to pick one of the old cloisters in Upper Austria, at that time [*the cloisters were*] confiscated from the religious orders. We gathered information about old monasteries, studied the maps, and then went to the Gauleiter (governor) of the Province Upper Danube with our request and suggestions.

We did not anticipate having an easy job, because the Governor's Province was already flooded with refugees. Our application for sheltering our valuables and our personnel was just another headache for him. Yet, to our surprise, he was very cooperative, and although he could not assign to us the place we chose, he assured us that we are going to have even better shelter in an abandoned cloister in the village named Spital am Pyhrn.

He called the bürgermeister, mayor of the village right away. When he could not get him, he interrogated the switch board girl of the local post office about the conditions in the cloister. He left a message for the bürgermeister that the gold of Hungary will be sheltered in his village and he would receive more instructions next day. "You folks are going to be famous," he finished his talk to the switch board girl in his broad Upper Austrian accent.

So, finally we knew where we were going to be settled. By having a definite destination point, our hottest problem seemed to be solved for a while at least. We would have preferred a location farther West, but Upper Austria was assigned to Hungarian refugees and it would have taken longer to get something in another Province. The Governor authorized us to get in touch with the mayor and work out the details of our resettlement in the village.

As soon as the agreement with the German Government was signed and our new quarters in the village were prepared, the green light was turned on for our train to leave the little village station in Hungary and cross the border to Austria.

—⁂—

This Agreement was worked out between the MNB and Germany while the train was stationed in Fertőboz for over 8 weeks during the middle of winter. Frici worked with German Commissioner Leopold Scheffler who signed the Agreement as "Reichsbank director" representing Germany. Leopold Scheffler's signature clearly identifies him as the person in charge of the train. The Agreement kept the Bank personnel and families together and formed a protective shield in keeping the gold from the Nazi SS.

—⁂—

AGREEMENT 1

The moving of the Hungarian National Bank to Germany

At the request of the Royal Hungarian Government, the German Government is willing have all the valuables and the bank personnel and families pass into Germany and allow their return to Hungary.

1. The moving of the Hungarian National Bank will be on the basis of general rules upon which the Hungarian and German government agree to in the future. The agreement would provide for the migration of valuables and the personnel and families and funding for provisions needed by them.

2. The German Government will avail itself to finding accommodations in Germany, particularly in securing the valuables and help in the eventual return of the valuables to Hungary.

3. The moving of the valuables in no way changes their ownership by the MNB. The German Government considers the Hungarian National Bank as the agent to conduct business affairs.

Sopron, 1945 January 15
Finance Minister (signed: Prof. Remenyi-Schneller)
Economic Minister (Signature): Boden
Sopron, 12 February 1945 I.A.
(signed)Leopold Scheffler, Reichsbank Director[2]

---

2 Cottely, Stephen. "The Hungarian Gold Reserve of the Second World War." Trans. K. Páffy.Hungaria Magazine,Széchenyi Könyvtár Library, Budapest, Hungary. Document 1992/11 1992: 82-97. Print (Translated into English by Steven Tarnay)

JANUARY 20, 1945, CLASSIFIED SECRET

It was Commissioner Leopold Scheffler, representing the German government, whose signature gave the order for the trains stationed in Fertőboz to cross the Hungarian Austrian border. Scheffler's priority was the safety of the Bank's personnel. He used a secret classified message and provided assistance so the train could sneak through the dangerous war zone to reach Spital am Pyhrn.

—⚡—

Sopron, January 20, 1945
The Commissioner Representing the Official German Government of Hungary
Budapest, IV. Maria Valeria Street.
(Carlton Hotel) Tel 188-970

CLASSIFIED SECRET
ORDER FOR THE TRAIN TO START TO SPITAL AM PYHRN

As agreed to between the German Government and the Hungarian Government, The Hungarian National Bank will immediately move all the valuables and personnel to Spital am Pyhrn. The German train number 117,437 will be under the direction of Hungarian Bank Manager Stephen Cottely and the cargo guarded by the Hungarian gendarmes.

The shipment will include the gold reserves of the Hungarian National Bank.

We ask that all German and Hungarian officials help in the protection of the train. Mainly to insure that there would be no difficulties and the shipment would be without delay through the danger zones through the shortest route to the destination.

STAMP OF THE GERMAN ECONOMIC REPRESENTATIVE
I.A.
Leopold Scheffler m.p.
Reichsbank Director

—⚡—

As soon as the agreement with the German government was signed and our new quarters in the village were prepared, the green light was turned on for our train to leave the little village station in Hungary and cross the border to Austria. One half of the train with banknotes and food left on January 17th, 1945. The second half carrying the gold and the other treasures, as well as the personnel and their families, left Hungary a week later. On their way to Spital am Pyhrn, they lost a "gold" car at a ranging station. Otherwise they arrived safely. There was "some" excitement about the loss of that car, but it was quickly recovered and joined the train a couple of days later in Spital am Pyhrn.

—◊—

[Early January, 1945] I was ordered to stay in Hungary with our branch office in the city of Sopron on the Western border. I stayed there until the Russians took that city too. Frankly, I do not know why, because I spent most of my time either in the basement of our office building, or when the air raid alarm warned us in time, I drove to the surrounding forests where we felt much safer than in the basement of our one story office building. If these smaller buildings got a direct hit, the cellars and basements usually turned into your grave. Besides that, I had to take turns in digging fox holes and tank traps in the snow-covered frozen ground around the city…

—◊—

FREDERICK ELMER TARNAY AND KATHERINE TARNAY

CHAPTER 3:
THE RACE ACROSS ENEMY LINES

Spital Am Pyhrn and Frankfurt
January 22, 1945 to November 1946

This little village nestled in the alpine mountains of Austria became home for the MNB for almost a year, from January 1945 to December of 1945, when the Bank returned to Budapest. Life in Spital am Pyhrn was relatively comfortable considering the turmoil of war and the refugee situation. The Bank personnel worked together to survive and to create a new life away from their homeland. It was here that the gold was hidden safely away in the crypts of an ancient church.

Spital am Pyhrn became a safe haven and refugee center of the Bank personnel and their families for several years after the war.

—⁂—

The village of Spital am Pyhrn is situated in the southern part of Upper Austria at the foot of the Alpine Pass of Pyhrn alongside a road of strategic and commercial importance dating back to the Roman times. In the early Middle Ages this road and the Pyhrn Pass were used by the crusaders and the pilgrims on their way to the Holy Land. They took shelter in a hospital at the site of the present village. Hence the name Spital, which means "hospital" in German. In the 12th century, a church was erected here which of course underwent several renovations and alterations during the centuries. It was rebuilt in the 18th century in its present beautiful Baroque style.

THE HARMLESS AND SILENT COMPANY OF THE SKELETONS OF THE DEAD

Figure 33: 1945, Stack of bones and skulls of people buried in the crypt under the Church in Spital am Pyhrn where the gold was hidden.

Figure 34: The gold was hidden in the crypts of this church in Spital am Pyhrn.

The basement of the church forms a large crypt where the priests and dignitaries of the village were buried. Now it is not used anymore. Almost all tombs and vaults for the coffins are empty and the skulls and the bones of the buried are removed and piled up in a separate consecrated room of the crypt.

Figure 35: The entrance to the crypt underneath the church. Firewood was stacked in front of the entrance to hide it. The gold was put into the crypt through a square hole next to the steps. Then the hole was cemented in to hide it.

The gold was placed into the crypt and shared the harmless and silent company of the skeletons of the dead. It was closed in by a thick wall of banknote crates, a poor substitute for the steel walls of an armored vault. The other valuables were put into the premises of the cloister, a huge old building with plenty of rooms and storage spaces. These rooms and the crypt however were by far not the ideal storage spaces for our treasures and assets. Under ordinary circumstances, any expert would have been horrified at a suggestion to put these tremendous valuables behind a plain rusted iron door with a simple padlock like that of the crypt.

Figure 36: Around April 1945, Bank Manager László Jánkovics entering
the crypt through an iron door with only two padlocks whose keys were
entrusted to two bank officials.

No armored steel vaults… no automatic alarm equipments… no combination
locks… unless you call a combination of regular door locks with padlocks a combination lock. By entrusting the keys of this very primitive form of combination locks
to two officials in charge, we had the dubious satisfaction of having complied with the
safeguarding rules of the Bank, or at least we did our best to do so.

Figure 37: Page from our father's story "Gold Rush from Hungary"
showing entrance to crypt of the Church.

Figure 38: Page from our father's story showing the courtyard of the
cloister. Lászlo Jánkovics in white overcoat.

Figure 39: Page from our father's story showing rooms in the cloister
were the Bank kept records and valuables.

The crypt was almost permanently flooded with ground water, which soaked a great part of our banknotes, but of course did not do any harm to the gold. Although we tried to make these storage rooms as safe as we could, much could not be done in this respect. We had to depend foremost on the alertness and trustworthiness of a gendarme unit of 34 men armed with only plain repeating army rifles. Not a single machine pistol was in the whole unit that guarded the treasures day and night.

Figure 40: Three MNB bank officials of the special guards (Csendörök)
protecting the gold. László Jánkovics in the white coat and another MNB
manager on the far right. In Spital am Pyhrn, 1945.

The office rooms of the Bank were in the cloister. The quarters of the employees were with families in hotels, inns and private houses of the village. The single men and women had two separated dormitories in the cloister. The families got one room each in which they had to cook, live and sleep. Yet, it was a relief after the much more rugged camping life in the railroad cars. The men had to fell trees and cut the wood rationed by the German authorities. In addition to the official rations, we were allowed to go to the forests and pick fallen dead wood.

Figure 41: The entrance to the courtyard of the cloister next to the
church, where the Bank set up its offices.

As the time passed, food became scarcer. As long as we had some reserves from
Hungary the situation was not so bad, but when they were gone it was hard. When
the war was over, the misery became even worse. You could really say the rations were
not enough to live on, but too much to let you die. Only the American food supplies
saved us from starving to death.

And—it would be unfair not to dedicate some words of commemoration to the "unknown" Hungarian horses. These poor animals pulled out thousands of wagons loaded to the utmost with refugees and their belongings from Hungary. Then when the war was over, they were ridden by American GI-s for pleasure. Because there was no fodder to feed them and no food to feed the people, they made their last contribution: they were slaughtered and their meat was distributed among the starving refugees and the Austrian population.

FEBRUARY 25, 1945, "IF YOU WOULD ONLY BE HERE WITH ME"

We were living in Spital and Father was still working in Sopron. We were in the Post Hotel with the higher officials of the Bank and their families. Commissioner Scheffler and his family were two doors down from our room until he moved to the Rohrauer Hof Hotel.

The Post Hotel was a central point of activity for the Bank and was located across from the Cloister where the offices were set up next to the Church.

—ɯ—

Figure 42: Spital am Pyhrn Post Hotel where most of the bank officials lived. Two of the MNB managers are standing in front. The one on the right is Jánkovics Lászlo.

Figure 43: In 1945, setting for a festive dinner, probably at the Post Hotel

—⁓—

Feb. 1945

Dear Frici,

One of the soldiers protecting the gold is traveling and I'm sending this letter with him. Today Is Hapsi's name day and I remembered just this morning. Nobody else could remind me. We celebrated with a double portion of canned fruit during dinner.

I can tell you now that everything is somewhat in order with us. Yesterday with a helper I scrubbed and cleaned and re-did the floor and now I have the cleanest floor in the Post Hotel. Did you send the yellow paint? I used the kid's watercolors instead, but it wasn't enough. There was a lot of moving furniture during the floor cleaning. We put everything in the hallway, but unfortunately the floor did not completely dry. It could have been nicer, but it now doesn't get dirty easily.

It was a different day. I was without shoes and very dirty when, at 6 o'clock, Mrs. Tornay came in and asked if I am going to the dinner. It turned out that there was a big dinner in honor of the mayor to which he had invited me, but her husband Edgar forgot to tell me. That's why he sent his wife to tell me. You can imagine how tired I was from the big cleaning, moving furniture, and everything, but I was very angry and determined to go to the dinner because of that.

Figure 44: Our mother Kati at the Révfülöp Villa, approximately 1936

It's been a long time since I hurried so fast. At 7 o'clock, we were still moving things back to our room from the hallway and we were brushing the floor. By 8 o'clock I was clean, dressed, and sitting at the table for dinner. I even had the beds made.

I told a couple of people that I came in only because they invited me so late. I'm sure they thought Kati had been getting ready and doing her hair all afternoon. I sat there till 11:30 and I was in a very good mood.

It was very interesting to see and be among all the people that were living in the Post Hotel, whom I usually only meet wearing a bathrobe. After that, I socialized with Zsuzsi for a good hour. The sister-in-law took the Mayor home; both of them were very nice people. I didn't talk to them, but after dinner everybody got together to socialize and sing songs (I did, too.)

What I enjoyed most is that I was clean and I sat there and having some time without the kids. We ate and were served a very good hot meal, and even had time for a couple of cigarettes. As you can see, we are comfortable and are enjoying the time here in Spital.

I was sitting at the end of the table next to Emil and I tried to find out something about when you will be coming back, but I wasn't able find out any news from you. The person that will be carrying the mail will soon leave. I found out from him that Scheffler and his family will move from the Post to the Rohrauer Hof Hotel and will have a nice room. I wanted to immediately go there to see it, but there was someone still living there.

With the cleaning I also had a little time without the kids. Frici [*son*] went to school, István goes to preschool. The wife of Biber Andráss is his teacher. She tried to talk me out of putting István there because he was too young, but I insisted. She is a wonderful teacher, at least from the first hour I was there, and she is at a much higher level than at Révfülöp.

Frici is very ambitious when he starts out to school. He runs to school without breakfast and without combing his hair. He writes his lessons much faster and not so correctly than when he is at home. He picks up his teacher Cottely's way of speaking, because they are with the kids so much, and the older ones imitate her Italian accent. We have a lot of good laughs about that.

He is getting more serious and independent and you can imagine that I am very satisfied with him. The preschool that István goes to may be not so good, but I don't want to send him to the Austrian school for fear they may get mad.

I picked a whole bunch of willows. Easter is still far away. I don't think I will be able to stand it if I don't see you. Have you been to Pozsony? Any news from your mother?

We didn't have time this week to look for a house. Next week, we will be getting ready with Zsuzsi. I'm thinking about whether I'm going to have enough baggage to be comfortable. Maybe they will bring some wine with them. Wine is becoming a treasure here with us now. They were happy to tell me that you brought 14 hectoliters of wine.

Frici, I haven't asked anything from you, but now I do. I could use Hungarian stamps, yellow Victoria floor wax for the brushing, and lots of buttons for the clothes. I bought the rain jackets at a store on Matyas Kiraly Street and there were lots of buttons there. The name of the store was something Frigyes. For instance, the pillow covers that you sent need to be a little bigger and with smaller buttons. My wish is to make clothes like the mayor's and you know there were antler buttons on it. See, I can be used to being home very quickly, if you would only be here with me.

I would even go to the end of the world, but I would only go on from here if you were with me. This is my last time that I let myself feel locked up.

Zsuzsi is very mad now and I will go to bed, considering it's already 3 o'clock.

Bring the kids some paint brushes, watercolors, color pencils and a bunch of school paper for Pityi (Frici). It doesn't matter what kind, even if you can't find lined paper. Some glue and color paper is also useful.

With hugs and kisses, lots of love
Your Kati
Feb. 25, 1945

MARCH 30, 1945, "MY MAN WAS GONE."

After the fall of Budapest in February 1945, the Russians launched a new and successful offensive moving closer and closer to the Western border of the country. Good Friday, March 30th, 1945, found the last strip of Hungary taken by the Red Army.

Consummatum Est....

The Russian attack on the City of Sopron came as a surprise. The evacuation of our branch office was a panicky 50 mile run up to the Austrian village Reichenau in the high Eastern Alps, where we thought we could take a breath and then move farther to our headquarters. Very soon we realized that we had not run far enough.

The Russians kept on coming with unexpected speed. Since the truck sent to our rescue from our headquarters was seized by the German Army, we had to abandon a broken truck loaded with Hungarian currency as well as our business records and all our personal belongings. The personnel and families fled walking and hitch-hiking to Spital a/p carrying 200,000 Dollars worth of foreign currency stock stuffed in their pockets....

The Russian invasion of Austria was stopped by the Germans for a couple of weeks in the Eastern Alps. This was the last effective resistance of the German Army. When it was ground up, the danger grew from day to day that the Russians would catch us before the Americans would reach our village. Some attempts were made to move the treasures westward to a safer location, but the Governor, who was plenipotentiary Commander-in-Chief on our territory, suppressed the slightest initiative to pull out of his Province. "*Abhauen gibt's net*" (no desertion) was his brief and resolute answer to our suggestions.

In the second half of April, the situation became desperate. It was evident that the final collapse and the end of the Third German Reich, established by Hitler for at least 1000 coming years, was only a question of a few days.

The road winding from the Pyhrn Pass through Spital a/p became very busy. Retreating German units and refugees were moving down the village and pulling westward. Long columns of convicts in their striped clothes and Jews from concentration and forced labor camps were driven on the road.

I'll never forget the look of a Jewish man in a column which stopped right in front of our window. He lifted his eyes toward me and pointed to his mouth indicating that he was hungry. I picked up some bread and hurried from the second floor down to the street, but the column was already moving again and my man was gone. I only saw the end of the column, the guards urging the sick and the weak ones supported or pushed on wheelbarrows by their campmates.

MAY 4, 1945, SALZBURG, "I HAVE TO GET THROUGH THE GERMAN LINES"

It was only a couple of weeks before the end of the war. It was an intense time in Spital with Allies, the Russians, and the Germans maneuvering to take advantage of the end of the war. The Russians were 3 miles away and the Americans over 70 miles away near Salzburg. The Germans were still scattered everywhere.

—⁓—

This commotion on the roads was a sign that the Russians were rapidly moving ahead and the situation was getting chaotic. In the vicinity, everybody knew of the gold being hidden in the crypt of the Church. We feared an assault of the mob, of irregular troops, or gangs of escaped prisoners who would take advantage of the last tumultuous days of the war to plunder the cloister and the crypt. The other hazard was the Russians taking the village ahead of the Americans and everything becoming a prey of the Red Army. So the crucial question was who will reach the village and the gold first? The Russians or the Americans? We had to act.

A group of the staff decided to contact the American Army as soon as possible. We sent two couriers to Kirchdorf, a town only 25 miles north of Spital a/p. Their instructions were to stay there until the town was taken by the Americans. Then, hand over a letter notifying the US Forces of our location and asking for urgent protection for our treasures.

I volunteered to go to Salzburg and try to contact the American Forces there. This meant that somehow, I have to get through the German lines. I needed papers from a German authority to pass the check-points of the German lines with a car. I disclosed our plan to the German Commissioner and asked him to get the necessary papers for one of my colleagues, the chauffeur, and myself.

Although to a German this sounded like instigation to conspiracy (treason), I personally knew him well enough to be sure that he'd not denounce us and would not refuse this last request. I was right! He willingly agreed and next day I had the passes.

The purpose of the rite (negotiations with the German Legation) given in the passes was of course a phony one, but the papers worked all right. Almost in every town, our car was stopped by German military police for checking our papers.

It was not a comfortable feeling to know that in case they would searched my body and found the letter to the US Forces, they would have shot us on the spot for high treason. But we were lucky and reached safely the outskirts of the city of Salzburg. Here we found the road blocked by German Police.

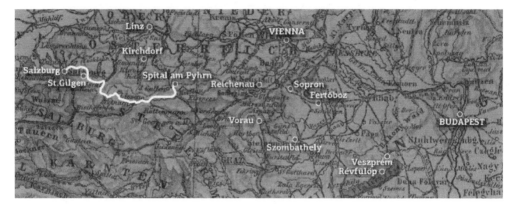

Figure 45: The route Frici took from Spital am Pyhrn to the American
Army in Salzburg
(Salzburg to Linz 68 miles or 109 km)
Route drawn by Eszter Rekassy, Map Source: "Historische Landkarten
/ Wappen (1880-1898): Österreich-Ungarn - Politische Einteilung."
Historical Geographical Encyclopedia of the World 1880-1898. N. pag.
Www.hicleones.com. Web. 27 July 2013.

TARNAY DIARY, "THE SS SUSPICIOUSLY GLARED AT US..."

The following is the personal diary our father wrote during his 70 mile journey through German lines to make contact with the Americans in Salzburg. He accomplished his mission with the help of a letter from the German Commissioner, Leopold Scheffler, with which he was able to get through the German check points.

—⁓—

MAY 4, 1945

We started out about 7 o'clock in the morning, Toboly Sipos, and me, with the big Steyrral. We had with us the passage letter that the German Commissioner (Scheffler) wrote so that we could get through the German checkpoints. The letter said that we were Hungarian diplomats going to Salzburg to negotiate with the Germans. With this letter we were able to very smoothly go past all the checkpoints and places on our journey.

We stopped at St. Gilgen at Tuboly's brother's place for a little rest and wondered about what lies ahead. The news indicated that the Americans are at the edge of the city and the city will probably surrender without a fight. The SS was preparing a defensive resistance at St. Gilgen and we observed on the road to Salzburg that they actually mined the road. When we ask about the road situation, they said that if we wanted to come back this way to come back within an hour, because they plan to soon blow up the road with the mines.

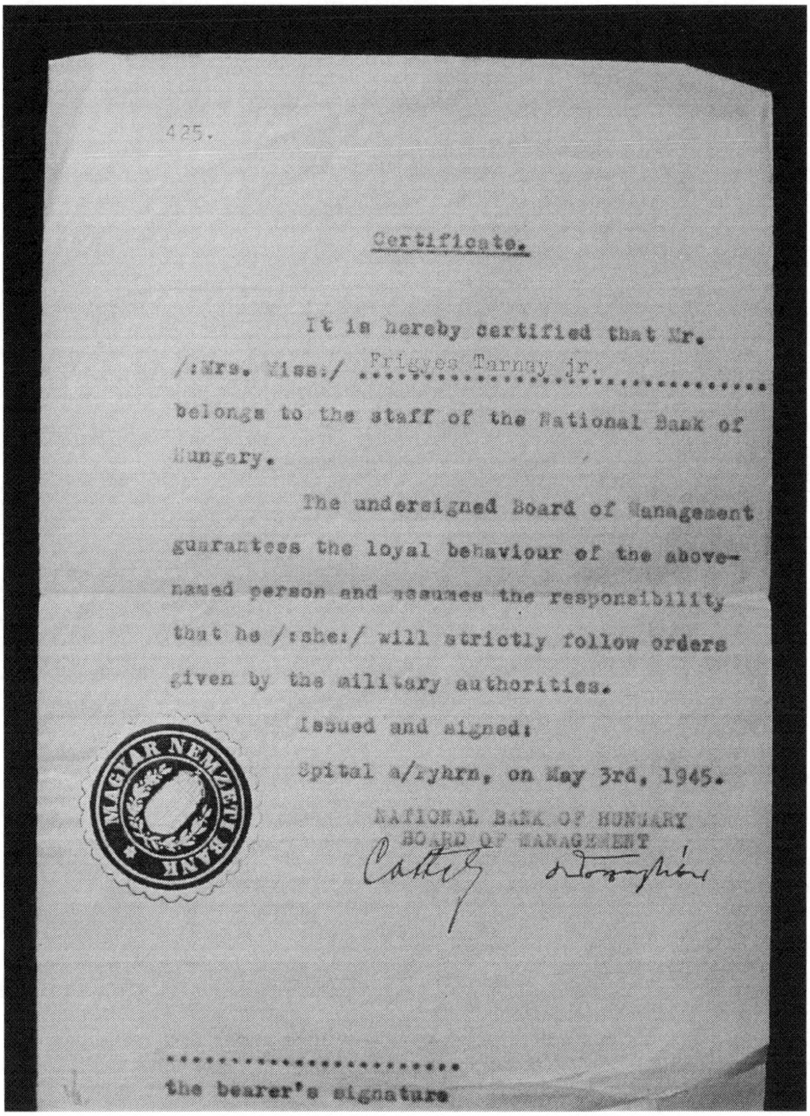

425.

Certificate.

It is hereby certified that Mr.
/:Mrs. Miss:/ Frigyes Tarnay jr. ....
belongs to the staff of the National Bank of Hungary.

The undersigned Board of Management guarantees the loyal behaviour of the above-named person and assumes the responsibility that he /:she:/ will strictly follow orders given by the military authorities.

Issued and signed:
Spital a/Pyhrn, on May 3rd, 1945.

MAGYAR NEMZETI BANK

NATIONAL BANK OF HUNGARY
BOARD OF MANAGEMENT

....
the bearer's signature

Figure 46: Copy of the certificate signed by Cottely and Torzsay-Biber saying that our father belonged to the MNB. Our father carried this certificate with him when he contacted the Americans.

About 2-3 kilometers before the city, we met a group of SS soldiers sitting in front of a restaurant. We asked them if they knew whether we can go into the city. They said we could still possibly get in. The city is in the process of being occupied (by the Americans). After that they became suspicious as to why we wanted to go to Salzburg and suspiciously glared at us. With this sign we quickly got into the car and drove toward the city.

At 1:30 p.m. we were at the city limits and the German police would not let us go into the city. I looked for someplace where we can relieve some of our tension.

I found a train station house where I made myself comfortable. I sent Toboly Sipos back with the car before the roads are blown up and closed by the SS. I tried to get into the city as soon as possible, but this was only possible around 4 p.m. when the first American tank stopped on the street in front of the house.

I started to converse with the tank crew. They were very friendly and immediately gave me Chesterfield cigarettes.

Figure 47: The original 1945 Chesterfield pack of cigarettes given to our father by the American tank crew

I went into the city, but I wasn't able to find and connect with the Division Commander.

The city was full of Austrian colored flags and white flags, not from the people's spontaneous enthusiasm, but because the radio announcement said to do that. The people in the city were apathetic to the Americans. They were just happy that the war was over.

For now there was only mechanized equipment coming into the city. The soldiers were friendly and willing to talk, but they had a terrible American accent that was very hard to understand (probably southern American accent). I started to get somewhat used to the accent after a while when I was talking to the crews of about 200 tanks that were around the place I was staying. The conversational interest was very narrow. They were not even very interested where they were and a lot of them didn't even know that they were fighting in Austria. But they were always in good spirits. It was very hard to distinguish from their behavior who was an officer and who was a soldier or what his job was. They did not show any tension in their communication among themselves.

MAY 5

Even though they announced that the people in the city can only be out on the street between 11 a.m. and 1 p.m., I started out at 9 a.m. towards the city so I could find some officers to talk to. The streets were actually almost empty and only American army vehicles were running around and parked in the city. No soldiers or anybody bothered me as I went around the city.

I went into the Reichsbank to see some of my acquaintances and to see if they would be able to help me find some American commander or official that I could talk too. Hansemenn answered that they don't know anything. There has been no news and they also haven't had any contact with any officers.

After the bank, I went to the police headquarters – perhaps they can help me. On the way I saw a sign that said "military Government," and thought this would be a good place to go. An American soldier at the door said to wait outside, but two minutes later I went in and I gave the letter to an Austrian looking interpreter.

He gave the letter to the soldier next to him, who was very interested as he read the letter and he went to find somebody else. He handed over the letter to someone who looked like an officer. He also read the letter right away and said it is OK and asked me to show him where we are.

I told him. "We are 140 km from here and the area is not yet occupied by American forces and that's why I'm asking that you send this letter up the line to commanding officers or drive me to them."

He said to leave the letter with him and he will send it on further.

I told him, "This is why I'm asking for help like it says in the letter and the reason I want to leave it with you to pass it on."

He said it is not possible to make the urgency any faster.

I also reminded him of the urgency of the situation. I had an unsure feeling about whether he will send the letter further up the command and I wasn't sure he was going to do this very fast. So I went further to a police station to find the police chief. He had apparently already left, so I talked to his deputy. I told him what I wanted. He understood and asked me to come back tomorrow at 11 o'clock and meanwhile he will talk to an American intelligence officer and will bring him to meet you.

I also asked him how I can stay here and how I could get back to Spital, but he said, "We can only take care of this tomorrow when we speak to the intelligence officer."

After that I went to the German Red Cross to find out if there was an International Red Cross Commissioner there, but I found the offices empty.

(Note: quotation marks inserted above by editor for clarity)

MAY 6

On Sunday at 11 o'clock, I showed up at the police station. The new police chief, Grasslmayer was there and said that it would be best to talk to the intelligence officer, Cowles, who could be found at the City Hall. I went over to the City Hall and talked to him. He read the letter and said that it was not his area to deal with it because his was dealing with the soldiers, but since I came to him, he would take the responsibly to deal with it. He immediately hand copied the letter and got in a car and left.

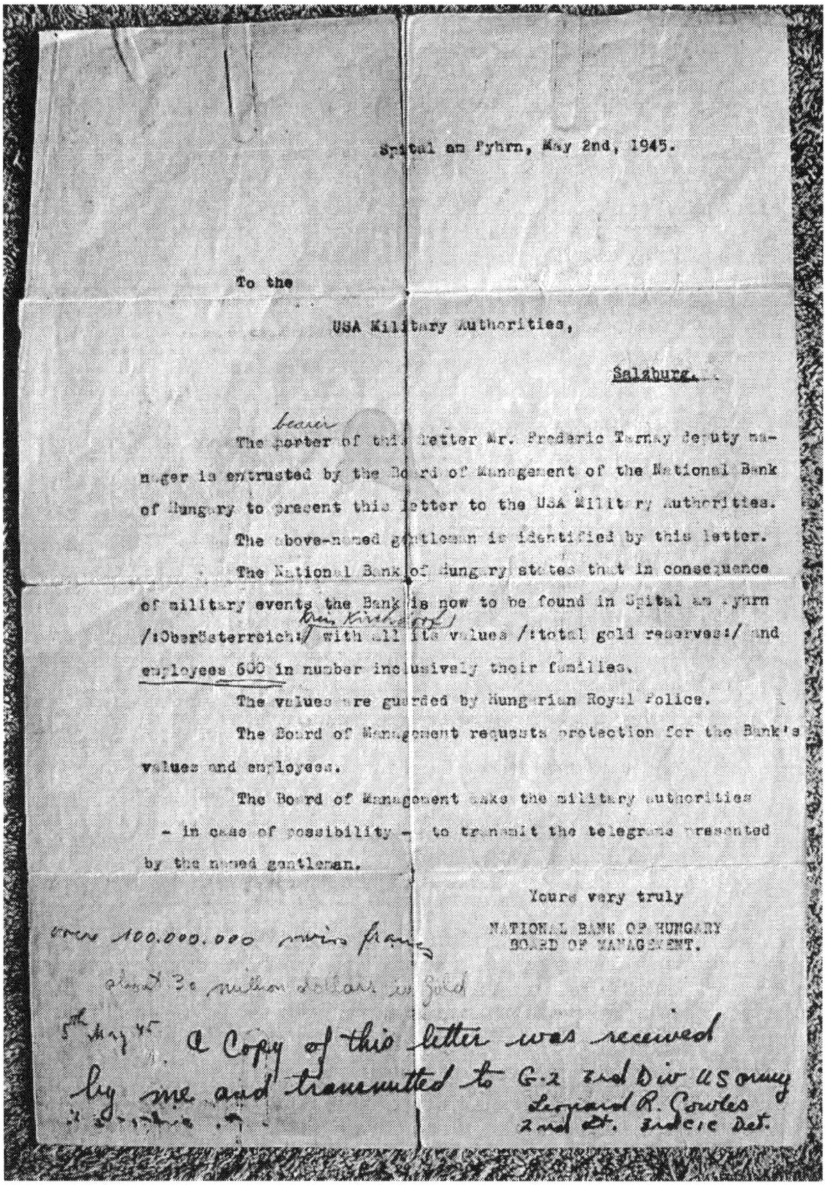

Spital am Pyhrn, May 2nd, 1945.

To the

USA Military Authorities,

Salzburg.

The ~~porter~~ bearer of this letter Mr. Frederic Tarnay deputy manager is entrusted by the Board of Management of the National Bank of Hungary to present this letter to the USA Military Authorities.

The above-named gentleman is identified by this letter.

The National Bank of Hungary states that in consequence of military events the Bank is now to be found in Spital am Pyhrn /:Oberösterreich:/ with all its values /:total gold reserves:/ and employees 600 in number inclusively their families.

The values are guarded by Hungarian Royal Police.

The Board of Management requests protection for the Bank's values and employees.

The Board of Management asks the military authorities – in case of possibility – to transmit the telegrams presented by the named gentleman.

Yours very truly

NATIONAL BANK OF HUNGARY
BOARD OF MANAGEMENT.

over 100.000.000 swiss francs

about 30 million dollars in gold

5th May 45. A Copy of this letter was received by me and transmitted to G-2 3rd Div US army

Leonard R. Cowles
2nd Lt. 3rd CIC Det.

Figure 48: Letter from the MNB carried by our father to the US Military in Salzburg. Second lieutenant Leonard R Cowles. US Army received the letter.

After this, I was satisfied and wandered home.

There were more and more soldiers to be seen around in the afternoon. They were looking to buy eggs and jam. Mrs. Hagen said that they wrote on the front of the door "Res. No. 6," but she erased it. My friendly tank crews disappeared, probably from the walking which was too much for them. In the morning the SS started shooting at the American soldiers. Two were killed and one wounded.

There was a lot of activity on the road as the front moved ahead (probably towards Spital).

At 6 o'clock in the evening, American soldiers came into the house and announced that while they were there, nobody could sleep or do anything in the house. They came into my room. One of them picked up my Finn knife and said, "This is mine" and put it in his pocket. They also curiously looked at my Belgian boots. They asked if they were in Austria and if I was German. When I told them that they are in Austria and that I'm Hungarian, they let me alone and let me take all my things out of the room.

I moved into the barn because I could not go into the city by then. Poor Hagens. They tried to save what they could. The soldiers slowly looked over everything they had and whatever food they found, like eggs and meat, they ate.

I asked them, "Why do they do this?" And they answered, because the Germans did just the same in France and that's why they do it. In Germany, a hundred of them killed 20 of the household. I tried to talk to them. They were a little uneasy about their behavior, but most of them went ahead and took many things. I don't think the Hagens had much left after the soldiers departed.

At night they put sentries in front of the barn where we were sleeping. They were so afraid of an attack. They kept asking whether Hagen's son was an SS and asked if they have any guns or cameras in the house.

MAY 7

In the morning, I went to the Reichsbank to ask Hansmann for a place to stay. He offered his servant room at his place. I settled in into my new place 3 km away in the afternoon with my heavy backpack and suitcase.

Before noon, I went to see Cowles to ask him what he did with my letter. He said he sent it further up the line.

FROM THE GOLD RUSH

The following is Frici's recollection of the events above written at a later date.

—⁓—

Here we found the road blocked by German Police. They told me the city surrendered to the Americans and the occupation of the town was already going on. This was good news for me. All I have to do, I thought, is to stay here and wait until the first American tank shows up. I sent back the car with my colleague and then with a heavy rucksack on my back, I stayed close to the road and kept on watching.

Finally after two hours of waiting, an American tank rolled up and stopped in front of me. The crew was very friendly and the first thing they did when they heard me speaking a little English, was to give me a package of American cigarettes (Chesterfields) something I had not seen for a very long time. They made jokes and looked very happy.

This was the most for me. I had not seen happy faces since I did not know when. With us, everybody was worried and bored, everybody looked tired and worn out. These guys looked well fed, in high spirits, relaxed, and always ready to make jokes.

Upon advice of the tank crew, I went into the city to find the U.S. Military Government. Although a curfew for civilians was announced by the military loudspeaker car, I went around in the downtown section of the city, but could not find any military authority established yet and had to return to my room in the outskirts.

Next morning, German snipers fired at the crew of the tank and wounded a soldier. This incident could not stop me, however, from walking downtown again and looking for the Military Government.

I finally found it in the town house and succeeded in handing over my letter to an American officer. He read it and was immediately willing to go and have a look at our treasures, but when I told him that the village is 70 miles away and still occupied by the Germans, he looked disappointed and disinterested. He put the letter in his pocket and turned to another applicant. This attitude was not too encouraging and I decided to find somebody who shows more interest in my letter.

I went to the American Counter Intelligence Corps and presented the copy of the letter to a young second lieutenant of the U.S. Army. When he was through with reading he declared he is not in charge of this kind of cases, yet, since I happened to come to him with this important looking letter, he felt responsible and was going to take care of it.

Answering his questions, I told him the approximate value of our treasures and gave him the exact location of the village. He made some notes, copied the letter on his typewriter, and rushed out of the office uttering a "Come back tomorrow" to me. Next day, he informed me that the letter and his report have been wired to the G-2 3rd Div. of the U.S. Army and upon my request he confirmed this on the letter.

I felt great relief when I left the office room. My mission was carried out and no more could be done on my part. Now everything was up to the American Army.

Yet, I could not relax until I learned that Spital a/p was really taken by the Americans. I wanted to return immediately, but civilians were not allowed to leave the city and no means of communication were available for the public. Everything was still in the state of war although the war was technically over.

—ᴍᴍ—

Figure 49: An American jeep going past the Post Hotel as the Americans
entered Spital am Pyhrn on May 7, 1945

Two weeks later, the Bank sent a car for me with a special pass of the U.S. Army. It was good to see my family and my friends again. There I heard what happened during my absence and how dangerous the situation was in the last days before the Americans occupied the village.

The day after I left for Salzburg, a German military commission of 3 German officers entered the Bank and wished to talk to the management. The head of the delegation identified himself as the delegate of the 6th German Army and pointed out that his mission was to secure the treasures of the Bank before the American Army would occupy the village. To our objections, he answered that the treasures must be saved as long as there is the slightest chance to do so. However, we did not yield and the commission said that they would report to their commander and left the Bank.

Next day, the Governor of the province called us by phone and asked what were our intentions. The General Manager told him we want to stay where we were and to turn over everything to the Americans. He asked the General Manager to see him in the neighboring village. There he informed him that he agreed with our intentions, but was afraid that the Bank would be plundered by irregular German military gangs and wanted the Bank guarded by a strong German unit commanded by a reliable officer. The commander would be instructed to surrender to the Americans and to nobody else.

Indeed, within a few hours, a German unit of 25 soldiers and 5 officers, each one of them armed with machine pistols, joined our gendarmes and took their positions around the Church and the cloister. The commander presented the written order of the Governor which was in accordance with the promises made by him, so we had no doubt that the intentions of the Governor were all right.

Next day – it was May 7th 1945 – was a hot day. The situation was chaotic; nobody knew what was going on and what was going to happen in the next few hours. Words came that a resistance was prepared by the Germans in our narrow valley and they were going to blast roads and bridges. As the topographic conditions were suitable for a defensive operation, we feared the Germans would delay the occupation of the village by the Americans and in the last minute we would lose our treasures.

The delegates of the 6th German Army returned and informed us that the commander insisted that the gold be moved to a secure place at once and for this purpose there were 6 railroad cars at our disposal. We informed them about the orders of the Governor and called the commander of the German guard. He showed the written order of the Governor and told a captain of the commission that he wanted to talk to him confidentially.

When they left, the head of the delegation began to persuade the general manager that the gold had to be taken away. He reassured him that he arranged everything: The gold would be moved to a place where nobody would find it. He would care for it and that only the General Manager and he would know the location of the cache.

This was a pretty obscure proposition which, of course, could not be but refused by the General Manager. The situation was saved by the returning Commander of the Guard who declared that according to the orders of the Governor the treasures had to stay where they were. Then the delegates left in a hurry.

We suspected they went to the Governor to make him change his orders. The General Manager tried to call the Governor, but could not get him. Therefore, he wrote a protesting report to him. It was just finished when the screaming of sirens came from the street and the first American tanks were rolling through the village.

We were saved. The American Army won the race with a slight margin against the Russians who took the Pyhrn Pass, only 3 miles ride from the village.

The Americans disarmed the German unit. They left the rifles of the Hungarian Gendarmes and agreed that the Bank be guarded by them as before. For a couple of weeks, they gave reinforcement to the Hungarian unit, but later the Bank was guarded by the Royal Hungarian Gendarmes during 4 years following the end of the war.

So it happened that while the Kingdom was abolished long ago in Hungary, a small unit of the "Royal" Hungarian Gendarmes still existed and guarded Hungarian properties in the mountains of a foreign country.

—◊◊◊—

The discovery of our treasures was quite a sensation and "The Stars and Stripes" reported it under the headline, "Hungary's Gold Cache found in Alpine Village by 80th Division." Right after the village was taken by the Americans, even General Patton, Commander of the 3rd Army inspected our place and the treasures.

Then the Bank was ordered to turn over the gold to the U.S. Army. It was moved from the crypt of the Church and loaded on 3 American Army trucks. Accompanied by 2 tanks, the precious load was taken to Frankfort a/M and placed into the vaults of the Reichsbank, at that time the headquarters of the Finance Branch of the American Forces. So, after 5 months of being moved from one odd place to another, the gold finally landed from the vaults of the crypt to the definitely safer vaults of the Bank.

Four officials (among them myself) were working in the U.S. Headquarters in Frankfort a/M furnishing all information wanted by the U.S. authorities. Frankfort a/M is about 600 kilometers from Spital a/P. At that time no communication, not even mail services was established between Germany and Austria. So, for a couple of months we did not know anything about our families.

The boundaries of the occupation zones were not yet final and rumors went around that some parts of the American Zone would be turned over to the Russians. We wanted to be sure that nothing like this would happen with our families in Spital a/P and inquired in the competent department of the U.S. Headquarters (I wish we did not). An American major gave us the answer, which was one of the hardest blows in my life: The village Spital a/P will be turned over to the Russians within two weeks.

We do not remember how we got out of that office, but I know we all must have looked pale and pitifully helpless. Fortunately, this state of despair lasted only a couple of days and turned into rejoicing when an American Lt. Colonel informed us that Spital a/P was going to be connected to the British Zone.

This was not true either, but we could take it. The truth was that Spital a/P remained all the time in the American Zone, only these two American officers happened not to know it because from the three Spitals existing in Austria, one of them picked Spital am Semmerong in the Russian Zone, the other one looked at Spital a/ Drau in the British Zone on the map, and both of them missed our Spital a/Pyhrn in their own zone.

If these two gentlemen ever happen to read these lines, I herewith wish to assure them that we were fully aware of their good intentions and knew that they only wanted to help us with their information.

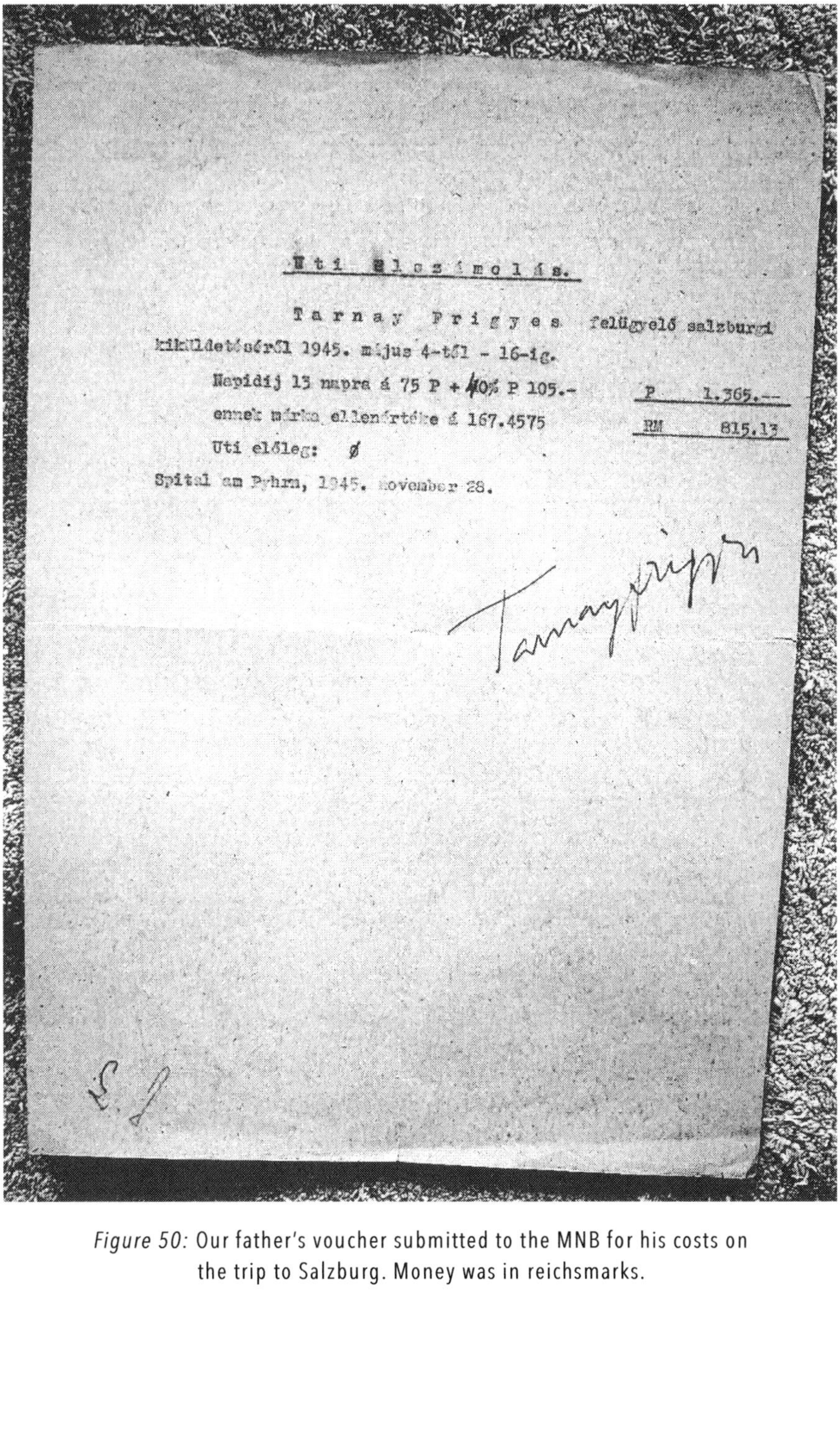

Uti Elszámolás.

Tarnay Frigyes felügyelő salzburgi kiküldetéséről 1945. május 4-től - 16-ig.

Napidij 13 napra á 75 P + 40% P 105.-	P	1.365.--
ennek márka ellenértéke á 167.4575	RM	815.13

Uti előleg: ø

Spital am Pyhrn, 1945. november 28.

Figure 50: Our father's voucher submitted to the MNB for his costs on the trip to Salzburg. Money was in reichsmarks.

MAY 8, 1945, THE WAR ENDS

WWII ended on May 8, 1945. The gold reserves and the National treasures were in the safe hands of the Americans. All the efforts were now directed to post war activities.

The Bank officials in Spital am Pyhrn were trying to figure out what to do with the MNB organization now that the gold was secured by the U.S. Army. Different factions emerged within the organization. One wanted to go back to Hungary and the other wanted to establish the Bank in Switzerland or Austria to protect the gold from "disappearing" under the Russian and Communist regime.

The Bank personnel had to re-focus to survive without the MNB. The Bank re-established their organization the way it was prior to the Arrow Cross take over in 1944 and made Torzsay-Biber their MNB manager. Frici was given back his position as head of the Foreign Exchange and Clearing Section of the MNB, however, it was meaningless considering the situation. His position did help his relationship with the Americans when the gold was transferred to Frankfurt.

—⁂—

Figure 51: The center of Spital am Pyhrn in 1945 during a celebration.
(Possibly at the end of WWII) Dignitaries sit in the foreground while
someone stands at the red podium.

Figure 52: 1945, Gathering for a celebration in Spital am Pyhrn. Notice a
band playing to the right.

MAY 15, 1945, SPITAL AM PYHRN, "GRANDMOTHER IS SINGING SONGS WITH THEM"

*Torzsay-Biber was an excellent bank manager, but the Bank leaders did not agree on a
course of action. There was a split between those who wanted to take the Bank back to Budapest and those who wanted to manage the Bank from outside the borders of Hungary.*

—ɷ—

Letter from our mother to our father in Frankfurt.
[This letter is missing the first 8 pages]

— The way things go here in Spital is that if I want to start housekeeping and put
things in order, it is certain something will come in between. For instance, if my parents would have moved from our apartment, then I would have had to move also. It
appears that this is the way it will be, but yet everything is not for sure.

I try to respond to everything that comes along the way and take things calmly as
they come along. It came to my mind that I would like to go back to working for the
Bank.

Gyula (Torzsay-Biber) will be speaking in private with Gossens when he arrives from Frankfurt. It is possible that he has some private matters to talk about, but it is also possible that he wants to talk about what the situation looks like here in Spital.

If you know that this is the case, I ask you to smooth things with Gossens before the meeting, because whatever the case, Gyula (Biber) is not popular here. He does not go out of his way to be popular and today the people make him so nervous that a war of words could easily start up.

Now, I'm finally writing about the kids. They are beautiful, healthy, and good too. Pityi (Little Fred) is a little more like Grandpa, but much less than he was in Révfül-öp. The sweetest now is Hapsi (Matt). You will just go crazy if you saw him now. He talks a lot and has an original sense of humor. István is starting to imitate him now.

Grandmother is singing songs with them. They like this very much and every evening there is a chorus of false notes. Hapsi starts the singing and keeps the beat. He crumples his pillow. This is his snail house. He lifts a piece of potato with his fork that hangs it down a little and says, "I'm fishing." His eating time is like a comedy theater. He makes faces and like a true Tarnay, likes to have people laugh at him.

István tends to get mad at him during this time. I could write a novel about Hapsi during this time, but I don't have time. István has a lot of trouble with his stomach now and is stubborn, but you know I cannot be mad at him. Pityi is starting to say thank you and is well behaved. It would be good to send him to school in the fall.

(The rest of the letter is missing. Note: "Pityi" means "little one" and could be applied to any of the sons when they were young.)

MAY 22,1945, STARS AND STRIPES, THE AMERICANS 'FOUND' THE GOLD

It was this false story that was the cause of the MNB personnel to be labeled gold robbers and essentially banished them from their country.

—⚍—

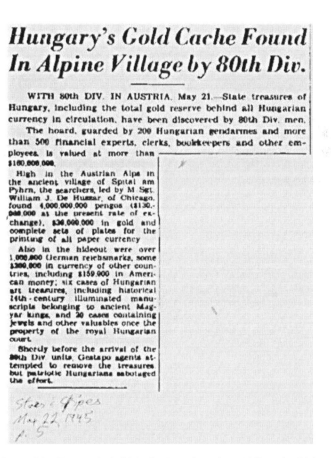

Figure 53: "Hungary's Gold Cache Found in Alpine Village by 80th Division." Stars and Stripes 22 May 1945, Paris ed.: 5. Print. (Courtesy of Humanities and Social Sciences Division, Library of Congress)

—⚍—

From the American Military newsletter *Stars and Stripes*, Paris Edition, Transcribed by Frederick Tarnay.

Hungary's Gold Cache found in Alpine Village by 80th Division.

With 80th Division in Austria, May 21.-

State treasures of Hungary including the total gold reserve behind all Hungarian currency in circulation, have been discovered by 80th Division men.

The hoard, guarded by 200 Hungarian gendarmes and more that 500 financial experts, clerks, bookkeepers and other employees is valued at more than $160,000,000.

High in the Austrian Alps in the ancient village of Spital am Pyhrn the searches led by M.Sgt William J. de Hussar of Chicago found 4 billion pengős/$130,000,000 at the present rate of exchange/$/30,000,000 in gold and complete sets of plates for the printing of all paper currency.

Also in the hideout were over 1,000,000 German reichsmark, some $200,000 in currency of other countries, including $159.000 in American money, 6 cases of Hungarian art treasures including historical 14th century, illuminated manuscripts belonging to ancient Magyar Kings and 20 cases containing jewels and other valuables once the property of the royal Hungarian court.

Shortly before the arrival of the 8th Division units, Gestapo agents attempted to remove the treasures, but patriotic Hungarians sabotaged the effort.

F. Tarnay, p.20

—◊◊—

Figure 54: 1945, In the basement of the Church is a large crypt where the priests and dignitaries of the village were buried. There, the cache of Hungary's gold reserves were held for 4 months. Notice the water and the break in to the crypts. The Americans did this because they thought the Bank was hiding gold and valuables in them.

JUNE 7, 1945, THE FRENCH CONNECTION

Within two weeks after the gold was saved, the Americans transferred the gold to Frankfurt to the vaults of the German bank. The transfer was made by a French transportation army unit accompanied by tanks.

This letter was translated from French to Hungarian by our mother as MNB president's secretary. This was a French Allied Transportation Company under U.S. Allied control. Our father was the head of the Frankfurt MNB delegation, along with former MNB manager Stephen Cottely.

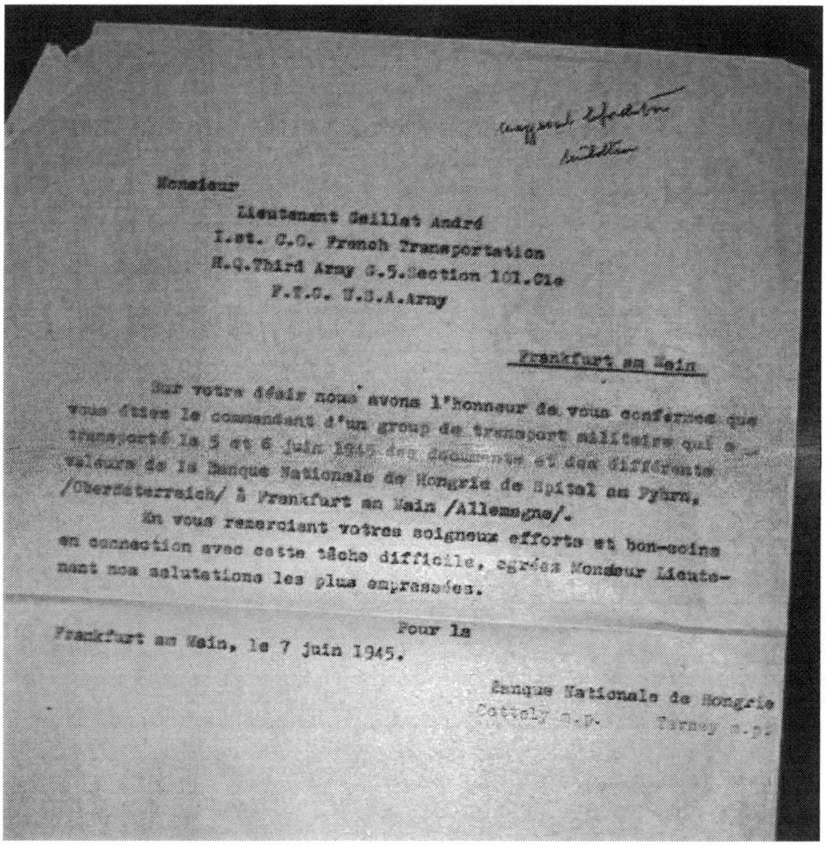

Monsieur

Lieutenant Gaillat André
I.st. C.O. French Transportation
H.Q.Third Army G.5.Section 101.Cie
F.T.C. U.S.A.Army

Frankfurt am Main

Sur votre désir nous avons l'honneur de vous confirmer que vous étiez le commandant d'un group de transport militaire qui a transporté le 5 et 6 juin 1945 des documents et des différents valeurs de la Banque Nationale de Hongrie de Spital am Pyhrn, /Oberösterreich/ à Frankfurt am Main /Allemagne/.

En vous remerciant votres soigneux efforts et bon-soins en connection avec cette tâche difficile, agréez Monsieur Lieutenant nos salutations les plus empressées.

Pour la

Frankfurt am Main, le 7 juin 1945.

Banque Nationale de Hongrie
Cottely m.p. Tarnay m.p.

Figure 55: Letter of Authorization to transport the MNB papers to Frankfurt

Lt. André Gaillat
I.st.c.o. French Transportation
H.Cr. Third Army G.5. Section 1O1. Cie
F.T.C. U.S.A. Army.

Frankfurt am Main.

The MNB has been very fortunate to have the French military transportation group under your command transport the MNB gold, its official papers and National treasures to Frankfurt, Germany from Spital am Pyhrn 6 in Lower Austria on June 5th and 6th, 1945.

We express our sincere thanks for this difficult task that you have undertaken and the care that you given to this important task for us. We express our greatest respect to you for your efforts.

Frankfurt am Main, June 7, 1945.
The Hungarian National Bank
Cottely s.k.; Tarnay s.k.

JULY 1, 1945, "THE BANK CAN'T ASK THAT AN EMPLOYEE LIVE AWAY FROM HIS FAMILY FOR MONTHS"

The officials, including our father, who went to Frankfurt to help with the inventory of the gold, were separated from their families. It was difficult to bear because there was no normal communications available between Germany and Austria except by carrier.

Our father wrote this to our mother in Spital. It was delivered by carrier.

—◊◊◊—

Via Gossen

The situation is turning out to be that we have to stay here for at least a month, but I think this will be more than that. That's why I would like to bring all of you here. I will ask Torzsay-Biber for a truck for you to be able to come here. The Bank can't ask that an employee live away from his family for months and from my viewpoint it is better for me to be here than in Spital in the big office. – It will be a difficult problem and question for your mother and Zsuzsi.

I don't know yet how I can find an apartment here and if we possibly move to Switzerland, we would not be able to take your parents and Zsuzsi with us. Zsuzsi would be no problem by herself because one more or less wouldn't make much difference and she is employable.

Please give Gossens my hunting rifle and my handgun. I asked him to keep them for me. Don't forget to bring the food from Freidrich and also the Maar girls' things, because you can bring it to them at Strasswalchemban on your way here.

Have Boci[3] send her American friend's address to me. I can send news to America from here.

Many kisses
Frici
1945, July 1, Frankfurt am Main

AUGUST 1, 1945, "THIS LETTER I JUST LET FLY IN THE WIND"

The letter shows the difficulties the bank personnel encountered from the lack of communications and the hardship of separation from their families. Our mother was desperately trying to go see our father in Frankfurt, but without communication and the inability to get a travel pass, she was not able to make the journey.

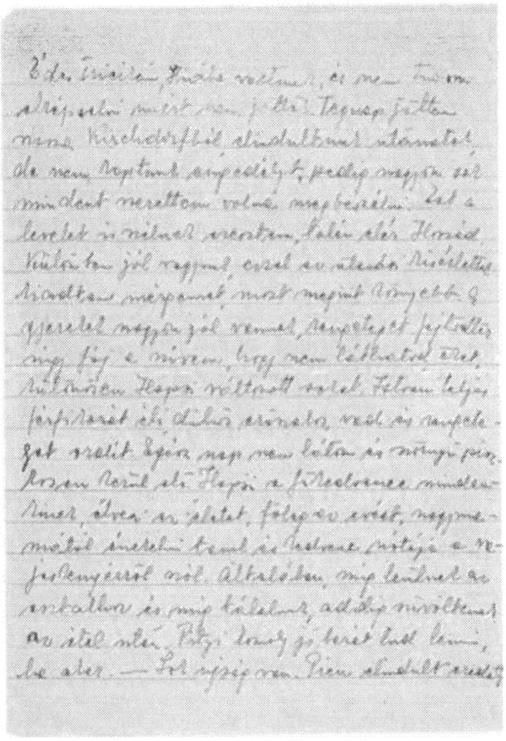

—⁓—

Figure 56: Letter from our mother in Spital to our father in Frankfurt

---

3 *Boci was the daughter of Bank manager Laszlo Jánkovics. She was sixteen at the time and wanted to write a letter to an American soldier she met in Spital am Pyhrn.*

My Dear Frici!

I waited needlessly and I cannot figure out why you haven't come. Yesterday, I came back from Kirchdorf. We started off after you, but we didn't get a permit and there was so much I wanted to talk over with you.

This letter I just let fly in the wind. Maybe it will reach you. Otherwise we are all right. This traveling to see you took the anger out of me. Now it is again a little easier.

The kids are doing very well. They have developed so much. Hapsi is the favorite of everybody. He loves life, especially eating. He is learning how to sing from Grandmother and his favorite tune is the buttered bread song. As always, they yell for the food until we finish serving the food out. Pityi can be a serious good friend if he wants to.

Gretta and Cica are still in Strasswachen. Greta is working as an interpreter and it is possible she will come back for their clothes. They are near Zella See. I only received a few words from them.

My parents finally found a place to settle in. It is a very nice place. It has a lot of problems, but they can put up with it because it is large enough. We also are doing quite well since they moved away and are living more normally by ourselves.

We miss you very much. There are lots of discomforts that are hurting my parents. We also lost a lot of things, others like Gundtnernel packages for example. I would like to talk over some things with you, but then afterwards I decided myself, maybe you will blame me when you come. I worry about how you are getting along a lot, but from the lack of newer news, I hope it is getting better.

One thing is for sure that I will never let you leave again by yourself!

The relationships among people here haven't changed very much. They are just as boring as before, but it is too bad that it is already the end of summer and it will be worse. I wait for some good news. Until then, the children and I send you kisses and hugs.

Your Kati
Aug.1, 1945

AUGUST 4, 1945, REGARDED AS ENEMIES

This letter was written by our father from Frankfurt to MNB Manager Torzsay-Biber in Spital.

Frici found out from the Americans that a Counter-Intelligence Corps officer received a promotion and a distinction for finding the gold. This is the origin of the gold robbers' story. The bank personnel were labeled criminals and could no longer return to their homeland. The few who braved returning to Hungary were imprisoned, died, or lived a beggar's life because they could not get employment.

At the end, some MNB officials accused our father of working with Scheffler against the Bank and we had to leave Spital early for Innsbruck.

—⁕—

Figure 57: In 1945, our father standing in the center with three Americans. He was the leader of the MNB group that was inventorying the gold. (From Fred E. Tarnay family file.)

During the Bank leadership by Torzsay-Biber, the Bank was in a chaotic state. Jánkovics had Torzsay-Biber jailed for treason. This exemplifies the lengths Jánkovics went to try to save the MNB. At the time my father wrote this, he did not know Biber had been jailed.

Jánkovics headed a group that wanted to return with the MNB to Hungary, but Torzsay-Biber and his group, with whom our father was a part, wanted to keep the Bank working in Austria or Switzerland. Torzsay-Biber felt that the Russians and Communists would plunder the gold and dismiss, jail or put to death all the Bank employees for robbing the gold.

Jánkovics eventually realized this and he also did not return to Hungary in fear for his life. He migrated to Sao Paul, Brazil, were he worked and sent back money to his family in Budapest. Jánkovics never saw his family again. He left his wife, two daughters and two grandsons. His daughter Rozalin (Boci) was the last in his family to pass away in June 2011.

—⁕—

In Memory of Rozalin Jánkovics (Boci)

Figure 58: The "Last Toast" with Boci in memory of the times in Spital am Pyhrn in Austria. Christmas 2010 in Budapest. Boci died June 11, 2011.

AUGUST 4, 1945, FRANKFORT, LETTER FROM FRED TARNAY TO MNB PRESIDENT TORZSAY-BIBER IN SPITAL AM PYHRN

[The rest of the letter is missing]

I was really waiting for your arrival, but I guess something must have come up because the time we had agreed upon has long since passed and you have still not come. Unfortunately our trip has been cancelled as well. Our last hope was that at least one of us would be allowed to go home for money because of our serious financial problems, but we have been transferred an advance payment through the Reichsbank. We withdrew 1,000 marks per person in two settlements.

We were given the hope that we would be sent home soon anyway and we would just have to wait while a committee inspects the gold reserve. We imagined a committee would come and together we would perform an inventory of the cases of gold. However, it seems they are inventorying the gold without us, since a civilian American has requested the books on the gold. He came back several times to ask some questions, from which we assumed they were inspecting the cases. Later they asked for reports concerning the crates of coins.

A week ago, we received a new commission when an official named Lathrop came to see us. He is an officer and a gentleman (I say "gentleman" because he is the first American from among the ones we met who has introduced himself and shook hands with us).

He asked us to compile a report on German clearing traffic. The next day, he asked for the same thing regarding the Swiss, Swedish, and Turkish clearing traffic and was particularly interested in whether we had bought any materials for the Germans from these countries.

This task will take us several weeks. We may need material from Spital and, using this as an excuse, might be able to see you for a couple days.

Otherwise the mood and the way they are treating us has not really changed. They regard us as enemies, but there is a difference between how they treat us and the Germans. These days they always bring a truckload of Germans into the bank to work around 10 am. The Germans have to work continuously until 4 p.m., after which they are taken back, but not before the whole lot is frisked. There is one familiar face among them, Ministerialdirigent Martini from the Reichswirtschafttsministerium.

We, on the other hand, enjoy total freedom of movement and work totally independently (the Germans work under supervision).

Yesterday, I saw Puhl, the Vice President of the Reichsbank. He was accompanied by an unarmed soldier. I found out he was brought here from Berlin and they plan to use him to establish some sort of an issuing institution based in Munich. Funk suspended Puhl six months before the collapse and it seems this is highly to his credit; anyway, everybody knew he was not a Nazi. He has never been looking so good and at first I was not even sure it was him. I did not recognize him.

We are under the impression that the Americans in general believe that we escaped, smuggled the gold out of the country, and then hid it in the mountains. This belief was probably strengthened by the reports given by those soldiers who, wanting to receive decorations, made it look like as if they had "found" the gold in some sort of a hiding place where a bunch of Nazis were sitting on it. For example, I learned that Huszár received five points and a decoration for finding us. I suggest to you that wherever possible, it should be spread that we did not go into hiding, but worked publicly in Spital, and that we informed the American authorities of our whereabouts.

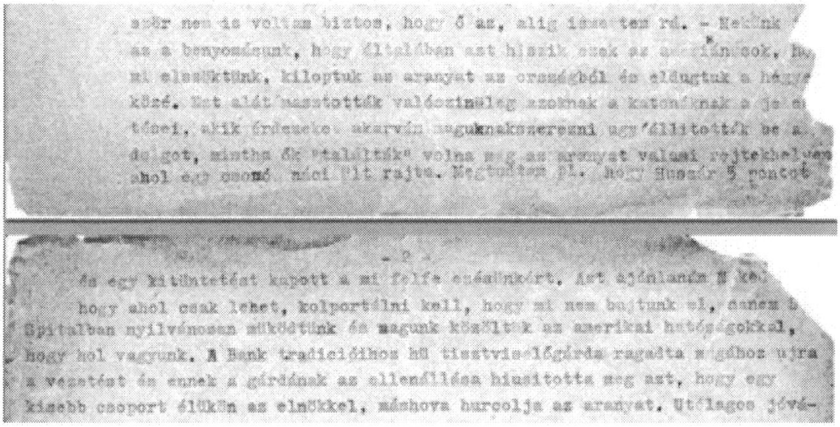
azér nem is voltam biztos, hogy ő az, alig ismertem rá. – Nekünk
az a benyomásunk, hogy általában azt hiszik ezek az amerikánusok, hogy
mi elszöktünk, kiloptuk az aranyat az országból és eldugtuk a hegyek
közé. Ezt alátámasztották valószinüleg azoknak a katonáknak a jelentései, akik érdemeket akarván maguknak szerezni ugy állitották be a
dolgot, mintha ők "találták" volna meg az aranyat valami rejtekhelyen
ahol egy csomó náci ült rajta. Megtudtam pl. hogy Huszár 5 pontot

– 2 –

és egy kitüntetést kapott a mi felfedezésünkért. Azt ajánlanám, hogy
hogy ahol csak lehet, kolportálni kell, hogy mi nem bujtunk el, hanem
Spitalban nyilvánosan működtünk és magunk közöltük az amerikai hatóságokkal,
hogy hol vagyunk. A Bank tradicióihoz hü tisztviselőgárda ragadta magához ujra
a vezetést és ennek a gárdának az ellenállása hiusitotta meg azt, hogy egy
kisebb csoport élükön az elnökkel, máshova hurcolja az aranyat. Utólagos jóvá-

Figure 59: Portion of letter to Torzsay-Biber from F. Tarnay from Frankfort during his detention by the Americans.

True to the traditions of the Bank, an official MNB unit regained leadership. It was the resistance of this unit that prevented a small group, with the Arrow Cross President at its head, from relocating the gold elsewhere.

Though we did not have your permission at the time, we made a correctional record and sent it to Joska Kelemen's older brother, who delivered it to Bruce in the best way possible and asked Bruce in his own name to aid us in dissipating these false rumors.

Unfortunately, we cannot provide you with a copy of this, because we sent the hand written copy through Gossen. We have already received an answer that they have forwarded it and will send a copy.

A major recently asked us whether we know the whereabouts of Quandt and a gentleman by the name of Sándor Szántó. American officers in Budapest requested him to locate these gentlemen. We informed him of the two latest clues we had, Thann and Hals, and asked him to notify us as well if he receives an answer.

Another major was inquiring about how many there are in Spital, how much food have, and how many cars we have. He kept stressing that we were in the English zone, a fact which we unfortunately had to rebut.

I have also been to the International Red Cross. I could not speak to Marty, the head of the delegation, because he was not there, but his deputy informed me that they could not be of assistance. Geneva received our letter and replied that we have to contact the Americans directly with our questions. We should contact the Swiss government through the Swiss consulate concerning our emigration to Switzerland. They could not aid us in our queries regarding food, either, because they are only permitted to deal with questions on supplying and caring for high officials.

The deputy admitted that their situation was very precarious, because the Americans pressured them into a very small area, and yet they must be glad they are tolerated. For example, it is a regulation that they are not allowed to provide assistance to citizens of enemy countries; can only employ Swiss citizens; and must fire citizens of other countries (even English citizens).

They have commissioned someone in Austria as well in the person of Dr. Mayer Moro, who is in Salzburg, but I am sure you were already aware of this fact. Gossen will make known the question of our immigrating to Belgium anyway.

Thank you for putting me on the list. I also want to thank you for helping arrange the transfer of our families here and for going to such trouble. I am attaching the certified copy of the SHAEF letter, in which there is no objection to our families being brought here. I think this will make it easier to get the necessary permits.

[*SHAEF – The Supreme Headquarters, Allied Expeditionary Forces*]

We are thin and weak, but otherwise healthy. I had a bad stomach disorder because we had to go to at least three different restaurants to eat enough of the muck that makes up one meal's worth, and so I had to be hospitalized. They got me feeling better in six days and I have been eating in the hospital with Vajkóczy and Kelemen since. At least the place is clean and they cook normally, even if they don't give us more than what we get with one ticket.

It is possible to make up for what one lacks on the black market, but that takes a lot of money. Since we have no more money, I am asking you to send at least 10,000 marks with Gossen, because who knows when you might have a chance to send money again.

We have been evicted out of the Officer's Hotel, since that was a transitional hotel and we could only have stayed a few days instead of the two months we spent there. Now they have issued us rented rooms. We all live separately, but not far from each other. I am attaching a note with our addresses. We have very nice rooms and I am glad of the switch.

We are not allowed to use our cars, since the traffic licenses have been revoked. I don't really mind, since they would have checked its use anyway and since the car has a license, they would have used it as well, and it would have ended up with them totally acquiring it. Our chauffeur has been transferred to Gossen, since they fired their Belgian chauffeur. He is very well off, since he is living on American food and was soon given an American uniform.

—ɯ—

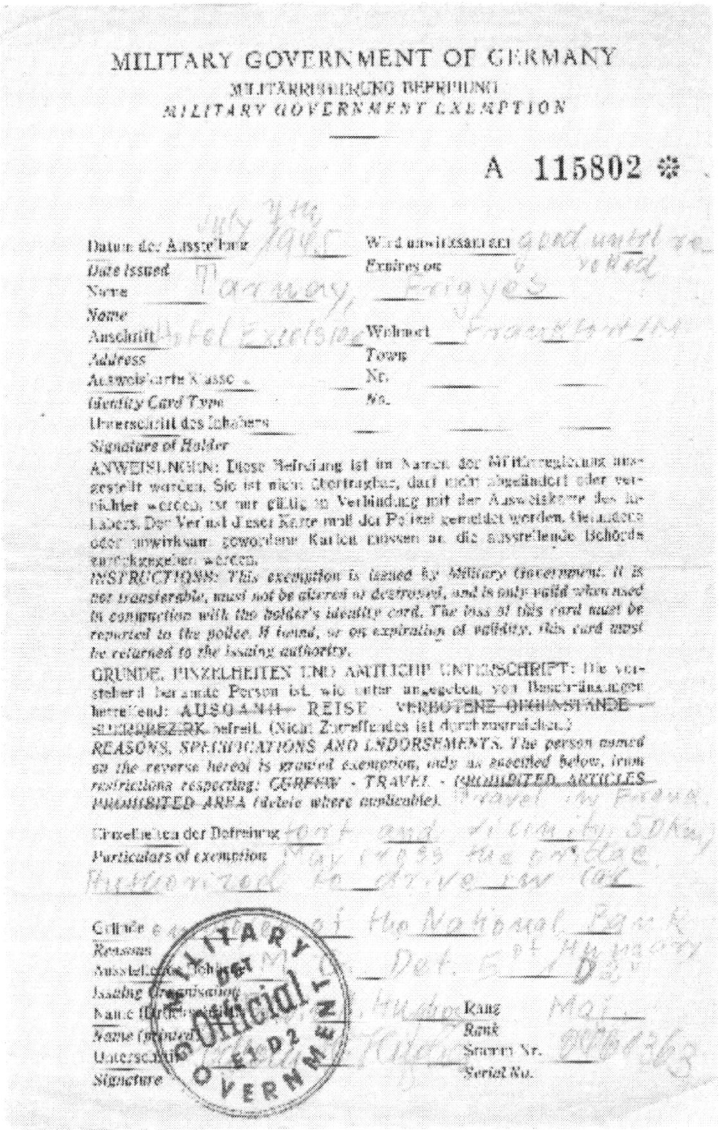

MILITARY GOVERNMENT OF GERMANY
MILITÄRREGIERUNG BEFREIUNG
MILITARY GOVERNMENT EXEMPTION

A 115802

Datum der Ausstellung / Date Issued: July 7th 1945
Wird unwirksam am / Expires on: good until revoked
Name / Name: Tarnay, Frigyes
Anschrift / Address: Hotel Excelsior
Wohnort / Town: Frankfurt/M
Ausweiskarte Klasse / Identity Card Type
Nr. / No.
Unterschrift des Inhabers / Signature of Holder

ANWEISUNGEN: Diese Befreiung ist im Namen der Militärregierung ausgestellt worden. Sie ist nicht übertragbar, darf nicht abgeändert oder vernichtet werden, ist nur gültig in Verbindung mit der Ausweiskarte des Inhabers. Der Verlust dieser Karte muß der Polizei gemeldet werden. Gefundene oder unwirksam gewordene Karten müssen an die ausstellende Behörde zurückgegeben werden.

INSTRUCTIONS: This exemption is issued by Military Government. It is not transferable, must not be altered or destroyed, and is only valid when used in connection with the holder's identity card. The loss of this card must be reported to the police. If found, or on expiration of validity, this card must be returned to the issuing authority.

GRÜNDE, EINZELHEITEN UND AMTLICHE UNTERSCHRIFT: Die vorstehend benannte Person ist, wie unten angegeben, von Beschränkungen betreffend: AUSGANG – REISE – VERBOTENE GEGENSTÄNDE – SPERRBEZIRK befreit. (Nicht Zutreffendes ist durchzustreichen.)

REASONS, SPECIFICATIONS AND ENDORSEMENTS. The person named on the reverse hereof is granted exemption, only as specified below, from restrictions respecting: CURFEW – TRAVEL – PROHIBITED ARTICLES – PROHIBITED AREA (delete where applicable).

Einzelheiten der Befreiung / Particulars of exemption

Gründe / Reasons

Ausstellende Behörde / Issuing Organisation

Name (Druckschrift) / Name (printed)

Rang / Rank: Maj.

Unterschrift / Signature

Stamm Nr. / Serial No.

MILITARY GOVERNMENT DET Official E1D2

Figure 60: August 7, 1945. Travel Permit authorization for "Frankfurt and vicinity" for Fred Tarnay while he was inventorying the gold.

August 3, Friday (Letter to Torzsay-Biber, Continued) Kelemen, Reuterweg 98. bei Keller

Cottely, Eppsteiner Str. 5. bei Schmitt.

Vajkóczy, Kronberger Str. 14.

Ferencz Nagy-György, Friedrich Str. 17/a

P.S. We just spoke to Kamarek and asked him how long they were going to keep us here, because we want to start taking the necessary measures to have our families brought to us. He could not give a definite answer. He does not intend on keeping us here permanently, but he cannot tell us the duration of our stay.

We also asked him whether they would keep the provided materials (books and such) for later, when there is no longer a need for them. Would they send them back to Spital? "I don't know," came the reply, "Decisions are made higher up." We tried to rephrase the question and asked him if we had to return to Spital when we were finished or if we had the option of staying here if we wished to do so. He could not answer this question, either. He would not give advice, since that would make him feel responsible, so it is for us to decide whether we should have our families transferred or not.

It is a difficult decision, since the peace talks are still very recent and could still bring about changes in our situation. They will doubtlessly be in need of MNB material and the question is where they wish to process it. Considering that the important Bank material is here, I feel it would be better to have our families here.

If you agree with me, please send them to us. I think it is possible to obtain the necessary permits with the attached SHAEF letter. I gave an authorized copy to the Gossens as well.

We could perhaps save some gasoline by having the truck come here and not make the return journey. If it has a paper saying that Spital belongs to the English zone, I am sure it would come to no harm. We would take care of that. If you need the truck, you can always order it back. There will always be that possibility through the military. If you manage to send them on their way, I also ask that you provide them with some food and enough money for several months.

Thank you in advance for your goodwill and the trouble you go to, in the hopes that somehow we will meet again, I send hugs, etc.

August 4, 1945

—⚍—

Editor's note:

The Americans were looking for Quandt, a Hungarian who joined the Hungarian Army and was imprisoned by the Americans the end of the war. With his experience in foreign trade and command of the English, Hungarian, and other languages, he was put into the American service and became the manager of the MNB in late 1945. He replaced Torzsay-Biber who was put in jail for not cooperating with the Red MNB in Budapest. Quandt resigned after moving the MNB back to Budapest and went into private business outside of Hungary.

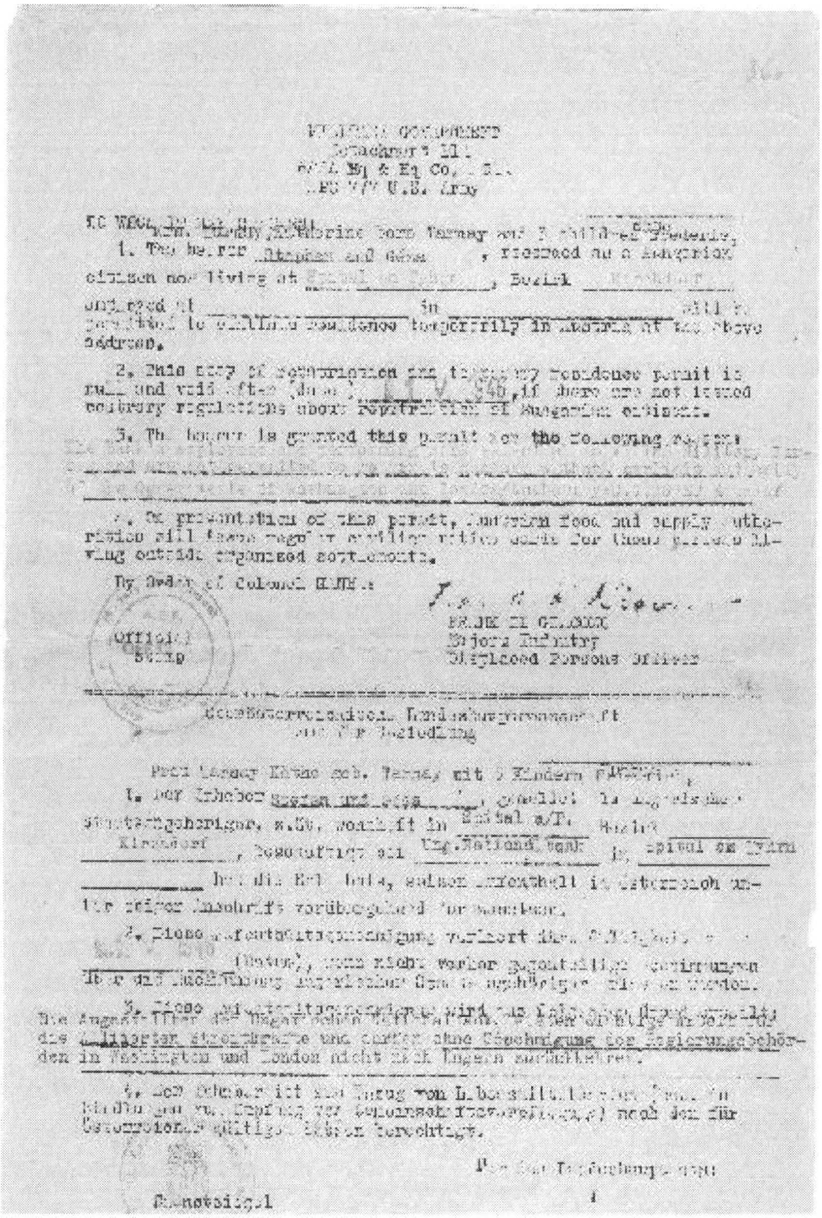

U.S. Army

1. The bearer Stephen and Géza

2. This copy of registration and temporary residence permit is null and void after (date)

3. The bearer is granted this permit for the following reasons:

By Order of Colonel

Official Stamp

Major, Infantry

Displaced Persons Officer

Ung. National Bank

Figure 61: May 5, 1945, this restricted our mother and children from returning to Hungary because our father was working for the Americans in Frankfort.

AUGUST 24, 1945, SMOKE FILLED MEETINGS IN OUR FLAT AT THE POST HOTEL

In Spital, the Bank personnel had a chance to take a breath after the end of the war. Our mother wrote this letter over several days. Our parents were in a unique position in Spital. Our father, mother and Aunt Zsuzsa were working for the bank. Our father's high position made him liaison officer with The German Commissioner, Leopold Scheffler. Our mother was Secretary for the MNB President and his staff.

Their meetings kept the MNB personnel informed and helped communication between MNB management and the 600 personnel and families in Spital. Our mother and Zsuzsi, her sister, were held in high esteem as advisors because they knew so much about what was going on. Those "smoke filled meetings" were held in our room in the Hotel.

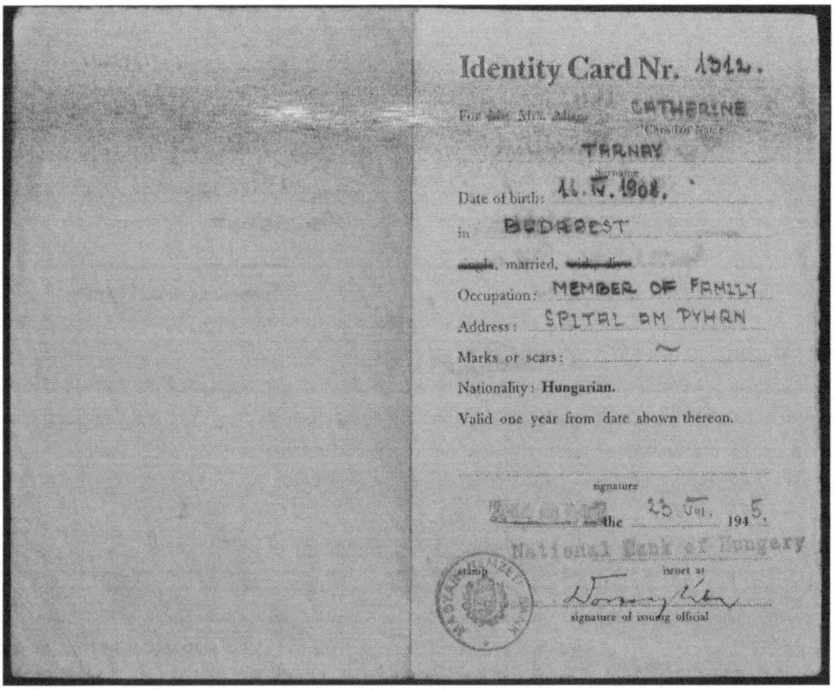

—w—

Figure 62: MNB identification card for our mother who was working in the Bank in Spital am Pyhrn. Written in English because of the American occupation. Signed by MNB manager, Torzsay-Biber, August 23, 1945.

—w—

Fred B. Tarnay, Son: Our one room was filled with people, all discussing events and plans. Everybody smoked and my bed was in the top bunk and I could see the thick layer of gray cigarette smoke that floated at about my bed height.

—⚬⚬⚬—

August 1945

My Sweet Frici,

I received from Biber the letter you sent him and I read it. It was really sad.

I feel and know that I need to be there beside you now and I feel so hopeless, sitting here in Spital thinking of a millions ways of how I could come and be next to you.

In the meantime I will tell you a little about how life is here with us. You know life here is still like it was under the Arrow Cross rule, where Zsuzsi and I were considered the "big boys" that knew everything that was going on. The only thing that can be deducted from this is that the bank organization here is at a low level. It was never like that at home.

People come to us for advice and to get refreshed.

Biber Györgyné, Elza, and Bébi came and together we were really immersed in our troubles. You know we see everything much differently here. You (in Frankfurt) hear very little from what is happening from home. We hear so much more being so close to the border and most of the people can hardly endure being here. Everybody wants to go home because first of all the food is terrible, and secondly because everybody lost so much weight that their clothes don't fit anymore.

The other day when Nitschmann went back home, everybody was in high fever. I was also caught up in homesickness a little, but I didn't let myself grieve over it.

Look, Frici, I know it wouldn't be good for us at home. You had plenty of trials working under the Arrow Cross and trying to keep your head together and now to do the same thing with the Communists? Maybe they will kick us back to them.

I heard today that Tibor Meszarovits is a supervisor and became one of the big boys. The Arrow Cross were also so "talented." It looks like this kind of change can also be going on at home. I believe you can't take anything seriously with this kind of people.

I would very much like to stay out for the sake of the kids schooling, so they could learn another language, because at home it wouldn't be possible because we wouldn't have the money for it. What will be our situation here, I don't know. In a way, it could be worse, but more depressing, like our cramped living quarters. I can hardly endure it sometimes. Again I have a lot of work to do, I am running all day.

AUGUST 24, "THIS FROG I HAVE TO SWALLOW..."

I'm always cooking. We don't have any wood. I have to beg to get a basket of branches. I can cook once with this. The heating wood would be even a bigger problem in the winter, although the Bank takes care of our needs for now. The big problem is the single room we live in is most miserable.

The daily rain, the constant mud, together with the dirt, the shoe cleaning and of course besides all the work, the handling of the kids… When it is raining they are more restless and can't move about and this makes more work for us, because they are always in the way in this situation. Believe me, it almost drives Zsuzsi and me crazy.

Today for instance, they were outside for a half hour and they came back with mud up to their necks. We had to give them a bath in hot water at 11 o'clock in the morning! Hapsi only had one pair of shoes and he was in the room the rest of the day.

There was a big drama yesterday. Mrs. Laci [*Jánkovics*] scolded all the kids (They were very mischievous in the corridor. I was cleaning and of course did not have time to look after them) and she came in and scolded me for not minding the kids. I told her, why doesn't she take care of the children? The poor kids don't know what to do with themselves. "You have two girls, why don't they take them for a walk?"

I reminded her when I cared for little Boci when Rozsi was sick. She became quiet and kind and promised she will handle the day care. To this I said that, "You just promise and don't do anything." I was very angry and also tired. She was so surprised that she wasn't even mad and just left.

I hate it when I have to say, "Why doesn't someone work?" because it is not my style. I got mad because here they are walking around all day doing nothing and then on top of that, they came over and criticize me. I don't raise my kids badly; I just don't have enough time to spend with them. They miss their father terribly and I am afraid that I can't handle them alone at some point in time. The children and your health are my biggest concern.

I know overall we don't have a bad situation here in Spital, but we, you and I, feel totally fleeced because of the Bank. If it looks like you have to stay longer, they shouldn't expect us here to bear the extra burdens associated with it.

Mrs. Jánkovics told me that here I have my parents and Zsuzsi who can help me. I know we can't ask for much more help from my parents. My mother also has a lot of things to do in the house. Twice a day, they scrape up something for lunch and dinner and she takes the kids twice a week. She is even now baking some pastry for us. I really can't ask any more from them than that.

It's also true that I have to spend time to help them, like to bring the vegetables and to deal with the million things Papa is requesting. In a way, they are here around my neck. They don't feel comfortable being here and always want to go home. I feel that I have to help for every one of their complaints, but because of all the work I have to do, it's impossible. Their discontent chews at one's insides, but they don't feel that I'm the cause of it.

Actually there are 5 kids that I have to mind. I asked Biber to let Zsuzsi stop working at the Bank. She is working in the kitchen three days at a time and you know her health is not that strong. She can only handle half as much as I can and she is not good at housekeeping type work because she is very unpractical. She doesn't sleep because of the kids and together we have to put back in order the daily mess they make.

Zsuzsa is also homesick, like all the other people that are preparing to go back, accepting what may be when they go home. Today 40 letters came from Pest and all of the letters from the Bank's people, without exception, said that we should stay and patiently wait. Biber did not let anybody go back, even Zsuzsi. Only if someone is dismissed from the Bank or if the Bank detachment goes back.

Zsuzsi also figures that she needs to go back to Révfülöp along with our parents. She is afraid that Papa will, without thinking, try to work at his job again (if by chance he gets it back) and try to sell whatever remains in the house. This is what she wants to keep from happening by going home with them, as well as to take care of them, help survive, maybe bring back the grapes.

This is how it is, but I'm afraid that she won't be able to handle it. One thing is for sure is that she is taking on a very big job. We cannot help them with anything at this point. We can neither give them money or things to take with them and, in fact, it is not sure that they can take all their own things.

Imagine how much they have to think about with Grandpa and of course me, too. It is fortunate that they are not leaving right away and there is time to contemplate My mother along with Takac's mother will leave together and I made reservations on the first train to leave. This was very nice of her. There is no reason for them to stay. The winter here will be harder for them.

Of course the departure will be difficult, but we have to bear through it. This frog I have to swallow. I see now that you and they would never get along very well. I resigned myself to this, but I just have to get used to it.

My Dear, I will now write about our living situation here. Much money is needed here. People are starting to bring many things. Flour is 45 schillings, sugar is 200-220, rice is 160, shoe sole is 220 a pair, butter is 120, baking soda is 180, cigarettes 1.7 for two. I was able to buy flour, fat, shoe soles and cigarettes (The latter, cigarettes, plenty because you know this is my only luxury).

We went with Zsuzsi into the hills to pick raspberries and cranberries, but we got tired and didn't pick enough to put aside to make preserves. Now some other things about living; what I bought I will trade and make preserves so I would have a little on hand and have some in proportion to the rest of the food. I'm drying mushrooms, carrots. If it is okay with you, I will use your leather gun case and have some shoes made for the kids and I have pants made for them by a Hungarian.

We even dressed Mother. Zsuzsi asked the bank for some shoes which she couldn't wear and I asked for some clothes, which we gave to them. We have now started to pack and with all the work we had to work at night, otherwise we didn't have time during the day to write letters.

I gave a German lady a pair of shoes that Hapsi outgrew and her children in return brought us as much coffee as we needed from the American kitchen. This of course is not as strong and we drink 8-10 cups daily. The coffee is brewing all day and Mother also has coffee. We couldn't give the leftovers to Biber Gyorgyne because she lives far away and doesn't come this way that often. Instead we give it to Takacs, the Geszner/ Gaszner kids, and B. Gyorgy. We got some mushrooms from Baba and wood from G kids and small favors from Vera, but the food is so little that it is hard to even look at.

We are together a lot now, mainly with coffee and cigarettes. We pass the time enjoying the little culture that Spital provides us. Buci is almost always eating with us, you know, he likes his stomach. On the other hand I make him work for the food. He brings raw materials. I sometimes send him for work, fruit, potatoes and he does some chores for us. We cook for him. I make pasta and wash dishes for him. It's like I found a home-helper and in the end we both are satisfied.

He even brings a few gossips and every night he sets up the radio and we have the best entertainment when his deep male voice frightens off the bored women that come in and out. I laugh a lot with Zsuzsi about this.

Buci is an interesting, good person. If there is a good dinner, he is moved and he even helps dry the dishes. I like his bachelorhood style, because you know he is like a good relative and sticks with us in times of trouble and likes to help us.

I think you know already that they stole our wine; at least we don't have to worry about it. I think our colleagues who like to drink are upset the most.

You know, I already take the losses we had much easier. I am getting used to the "it is lost" concept. Maybe you find it strange, but when many of them get the news about their home, whether they are still standing or what condition they are in, it does not even come to my mind about our home. It is so distant. I am too much involved with the present situation.

I have had so little time with you because you are away so much with work to enjoy a home life with you. I would be surprised when I have a home together with you.

Maybe you think I think so heedlessly, but believe me; I gave up on our home in Budapest. I am racking my brain about where we can find together another place where we can start building a new home.

I wrote you a letter the other day in which I wrote to you about going to Germany. Of course we would need Born's help for this.

This is so to say ——to myself, if you think about it, you will also see the advantages of it as well as the drawbacks. What do you think about it? I would very much like to know if you don't think so. Is my idea possible? Of course we would have to work towards it and that's okay with me! I feel now like I would want to just clean house and then brag a lot to you about what this crazy Spital environment does to me. But I know boasting has no merit, because the future does not look very stable with three mischievous little kids like ours.

The children are terribly sweet in their vivaciousness. István is now having a hard time. Alone he is an angel, but when the three of them are together, he is the center of the quarreling. He loves to work. Today for instance, he brought branches with Zsuzsi from the forest and Zsuzsi told how skillfully and persistently he worked. He can be a real help and he works wonderfully with people.

Sometimes I don't see him all day and all of a sudden he appears, sits up at the window, puts on a fake look, and stares out the window. I don't even notice that he is in the room. On the other hand, today he howled almost all day, no matter what we did with him. He is mama's boy. He is very proud about that and if he is not very angry, I can calm him down with that. It is interesting the other two don't envy him, as if they acknowledge this privilege. He still speaks softly as if he has the most need to be spoiled by mother.

Hapsi picks out his words when he speaks and likes to act as if he is important. I'm especially sorry you're not here to see him. The others you already know, but he is special. He is just like me, mischievous, notices everything, and is a very original kid.

We laughed a lot about the horse sausage joke. We get this fairly often and the kids like it very much, especially Hapsi. He likes food a lot and there is always a shout, "I also want some horse sausage".

The other day we were taking a walk with Zsuzsi and saw some horses grazing. Hapsi immediately started to rattle: "Auntie, do they make horse sausage from horses? And is it true that you can't make pasta from horses?" And also, "Can you make buttered bread from horses?"

As you see him, he always likes to eat. He is very smart, good-natured, and he likes when I whisper some secret to him. His habits are similar to Pityi (Fred) when he was smaller, but now he doesn't have to hold back. Of course as the third child, he developed his mind much easier and faster. He is not as unpredictable as Pityi and more self-assured.

Do you remember how naïve and surprised Pityi looked when he saw something new or heard something? Hapsi takes new things naturally. He stands closer to István in this way. We won't have very many problems with him. In fact, we have to watch that he doesn't get spoiled because he is so sweet now and he is the most popular when we are with other people.

It is interesting that István, since Hapsi's eyes opened and started to talk, became very reserved. People don't understand him very well and don't really like him that much. The kids his age, however, gladly play with him and he never falls out with anybody. They play much quieter around him.

The little Ossko Andras, who was a very natural rascally kid, likes István very much. There is a little leader kid, Gokocs Vince, who is his other good friend. The little Falussy kid acts a little older and is around grownups a lot and he rather runs after Little Frici. You know, István can be such a loyal and trustworthy friend. The two little Tarnay-natured kids on either side of him push him a lot, but he kicks back at them. Hapsi, growing like he is, will be a big kid. István's clothes already fit him and they can already use everything between them.

I'm writing about us a little now. I am looking well, of course very tired, sleepless, and my hair is not combed (I don't have time for that), but I gained some weight and keep myself up.

You know we cook for ourselves, mush for the kids, and we drink the coffee with sugar. There is a big rush for the food afterwards and because we are nervous and not knowing what to do with ourselves, we stuff ourselves.

Guess what? I sewed myself a very nice summer dress, of course with some help from Mother. Just in time, because the other one frayed on me. It was a little girlish. Long ago before Hapsi was born, I bought it when I was in a crazy mode. Nowadays, I'm very seldom so crazy. This Zsuzsi notices and I am aware of it now also, because people are taking me more seriously and I'm happy that they respect me very much now.

I wouldn't give much for the many experiences that this escape journey has given me, especially the long and constant absences from you that it brings.

I see people a little differently now, even though I still remain finicky the way I always was, but I can listen and hide the feeling that they bother me, especially when they are annoying. I hope that if ever we get into a decent environment this attitude will remain with me.

I spend a lot of time sitting at home, almost all day. It is too bad that I only go out to the Bank once in a while to take care of the many official things I have to do. The Bank doesn't have much for Zsuzsi to do. If something has to be done in the Bank and arranged quickly, I take a deep breath, get into it, and cry out all my complaints like a poor old grass[4] widow. This is really true and I tell people a lot about it. If I don't do it, nothing will get accomplished. I will really deserve some credit from the Bank for doing this. Besides, everyone will see that I am not lazy.

The kids are always good and this gives me time for the work at the Bank. I feel sorry for Zsuzsi now, the many jobs she does, because really we can only work at night. It doesn't do her health any good, although she is not skinny, but she does not look well.

Dudam, I will try to talk seriously with Biber tomorrow about coming to visit you. I'm sorry, but I just can't stand worrying about you and your health especially your stomach problems, etc. Biber is very good and understanding, but it sounds like he has other plans now. He told me he would like to bring you here, but he doesn't know

---

4 *Grass widow: a woman whose husband is often away from home*

whether if it is to stay or for just a short time and he would suggest to me to stay here. Besides, he said there is no gas or permits to travel, but I know there is gas and we can get it. I already looked into it.

I know that we need a special permit for one of the cars and the other doesn't need a permit, but the Bank needs that one. The traveling permits are a little more liberal now since the old Military government went away. The new one that replaced them is much more inclined to work with the Hungarians and in fact they go out of their way to help us and showed it the last 2 days. Laci Jánkovics and his family already received their permit to travel all of Austria. It is not good in W.G. [*West Germany*], but it is possible also.

I have got used to you handling our situation and I don't doubt that. That's why I would like to go, because you would like me to. But there are a couple of things to deal with here which I would like to take care of with you.

The Americans for the most part are leaving, but the locals are not willing to rent the rooms or apartments they had. Everywhere they are telling the bank employees to leave, partly because the mayor is not pressuring them to give out their rooms. Many of the men in the village are coming back after the war and a lot of the rooms like our parents' are only set up to live in during the summer. It is true that the Germans are going to leave in about 2 or 3 months and also among the Hungarians there will be some that will leave, but on the other hand there are a lot of refugees here.

If we have to come back, I won't be able to find a place like this where I can bring food, or a private place with our 3 kids. Here they would be very happy if there were fewer kids. This I ask you to insist on, because without water or a place to cook food, I won't be able to handle the work alone, especially in the winter. Of course, it would be better if my parents would come here, but that won't happen. Even if we leave a lot of our things here, it would still be questionable if we get our place back because there are so many that are without a place to live. I don't mind if it is rented until we come back, but make sure and make arrangement with them for that situation.

You know Dear Frici, that the interaction among people is the worst. This is the way it was on the train.

Biber promised when we first talked about leaving, that he would give us those things that are the Bank's. This is not much, but still something and we can bring the Bank things like the mattresses, pots etc. with us. We can save on the gas for the truck, if we don't have to bring it back right away. A vehicle like that is not being used here a lot of the time. It would be possible to send back the driver another way.

I'm looking at all the things we need to do. Since I don't have the travel permits yet, we will wait for your answer before we start out. By then you would be more sure about how much time is involved.

I miss you very much. Sometimes I feel that I can't go on with all the responsibility alone and really I can't even take one step more than what I'm doing now.

The situation here is absolutely terrible now. You have to admit that our bankers have a fairly nice situation. If one has a lot of money, you can even have enough food, but unfortunately it is not enough for the people. Gyula Biber has a big job now, but Laci [*Lászlo Jánkovics*] who used to be the MNB manager, keeps hounding him. They chide each other like in the bushes and of course Laci Jánkovics goes beyond reason. Now comes out the Magda-kind of friendship again. You know how Laci can be when he is mad and I am so careful not to come up in his conversation. Biber is more in the conversation now, but I am probably not far behind.

Biber was very impressed by the letter you sent him. He has a lot of respect for you.

Now I will say a few words about news from Hungary, which came from the 40 letters that were sent from Hungary. Edgar received a letter from her mother. They almost died of starvation. They lived through some terrible days during the Siege of Budapest (in Sashegy). Everything is very expensive. Everyone in the family is ok. Edgar should not come home. There are lots of enemies and people can't be trusted.

Buttykay Geza received a letter from his mother. The house is still standing (Rokk Szilard ut 29), but it received some damage from bombs. His brother engineer left his job and opened up a tin shop. He is doing very well with it. The Russians took his 52-year-old brother-in-law, but they did hear some news from him. They put him to work in an office in Przemysl and he will soon be sent home because his case was heard.

There were a lot of letters from the Bank. I will forward the letter that Maczi wrote Geza. The Bank is working. They certify the employees, but it is a very weak certification. In a sense, it is better for us to stay here and wait. In general, everybody writes that life is very difficult and they have to be very careful what they say. I know from somewhere else that Kiszta is in Switzerland.

You always mentioned that W.M. should go home and it looks like they are satisfied with that. Kato has been out since last fall and I have a suspicion that Kiszta is already out. Koszta doesn't hurriedly follow his own advice. Kesseru Pista has already been out, but was sent back from Switzerland to Bregenz, because a Hungarian committee opposed his stay as a Swiss resident. Kirchmann has left Spital.

I just received the letter from Maczi, it is to Geza. The letter came without a date.

[*To Geza from Maczi*]
>   My Dear Old Friend!

>   I will attempt the impossible and try to give you some news about Budapest. I worried a lot about all of you, especially about the little baby, who you know the baby the most, who I gave over to you long ago. May God help us get this world in order and the sooner the better for the people and this unfortunate defrauded nation.

But getting to the point – Babu will report about himself and I will report in short to you. Your mother and grandmother are luckily doing fine here. Erzsébet, little David, and Zenko are also doing fine. They are living in Pest, in what used to be the Phönix house.

Elizabeth's little baby, who was born after the Siege of Budapest, unfortunately died. Maria is OK, but she hasn't heard any news from her two sons. They took them to the west. Eva and her kids are also all right, they are getting ready to go back to Erdely in Romania.

Unfortunately your poor brother-in-law has died. He lived through the heavy hard times and after the Siege he went to Kolozsvár, so he can look after his place. There he met his last journey when he caught pneumonia and died.

Your flat is being lived in by the Körner family. The house is almost empty, because it was at one time a Budapest rental apartment house. This is how it is over the whole District I area.

I am alive and so is my family. My wife, children, and the whole Fráter family were near Pozsony at Bazin where they spent the difficult and heavy periods of the war. The women and the children are still there. I was with them recently and it was difficult for them to come home. My brother-in-law and I have big concerns. I can work at my former job. One of the brothers of Manci is in Regensburg and the other brother was arrested in the street and taken east.

Everything is so expensive here. Life is so very hard and sad here. I believe in a better distant future. I believe that my kids will have a better age to live through and this gives me a great deal of purpose in my life.

Your future place here would be very hard for you to imagine. Think through every step you take. I probably see everything on the dark side and different than how you see it from over there. For the present, coming back home in a way I cannot give any other opinion except TO WAIT, if it is at all possible. This applies to everybody. Your things are here, I am taking care of them, and of course there are some pieces that have been broken.

I am, My Dear Geza, the same old person and that's the way I will always be.

A number of the bank people died and a lot of them disappeared. W.Gy, the president and in his place was K.A. and Sz-S., the leaders who changed everything. There is no time or space to tell all the changes that have taken place. All the bridges are gone, Castle Hill is gone, and there are lots of things that are no more. My apartment is still there, but my valuables, my clothes and my collection of stamps were taken away by "who knows what" kind of people.

Now I'm finishing my things to do. If it's possible, send me some news from you. I send greetings to Salat, L.Bela. Please share this letter with them also. And also T.F. (Tarnay Fred) and Pt B. Ernö also says hello and he is in Szeged.

Your old and bonded friend embraces you and asks that you be sure you think about every step you take. Give Agi and the little ones many kisses.

Maczia and B. Tibor live in the country. They are well and have a little boy. The land reform took away most of the large landowner's land. They only left a 100 hold, but only if the landowner had 1000 or less hold. And the papers were underwritten by K.A. the Bank president!!!!!! Who came back to Budapest and apparently lost his job!

BUDAPEST AUG. 6, 1945.

I wrote about K.G before, but I will try to write you again.

Your mother and grandmother are living here and are doing fine. Erzsébet Zdenko and David are also OK, but they are in a new apartment because the old one was destroyed. Erzsébet's daughter Maria died after the Siege. He is working in place of Maria. Eva and the kids went home to Erdely Romania. Poor Gyurka, your sister died in Koloszvár from pneumonia.

Your house is still in a way there. The largest part of your furniture is in good shape. We are surviving. Babu is here and is working. Ivan is in Focsan and there is no news about the others. You will in time hear more about Maszárovits Tibor. My brother-in-law carried a letter to him.

There are a lot of changes here. It is a hard life here. We are hoping for a better future, a better fate for Hungary. I have a feeling that it is better if you stay there or can possibly go west somewhere.

I will hang on here in this poor country however I can. I send greetings to Fred Tarnay, T. Jozsi, Salat, Zsiga, and L. Bela. I also wish you well as well as Agi and your little boy and my present and future family says hello. Marce, Manci, Agi and kids are in Slovakia! I miss Geza. I wish the three of you well! Lots of love from the heart.

Maczi

—⁓—

My Dear Frici,

I think I don't need to comment on these letters. I was very moved by the first greeting, which was especially written to you from home. I especially was happy about Benedek Ernö. He is a very good friend that hasn't left you. I came to the conclusion from everything that what I have to do now is to come to you. I cannot stay here. Maybe there will be more possibilities arising for me there.

Here now the mood is just like it was when we left our home. People are starting to suspect each other and probing what kind of emotional state they are in.

Dear Frici, I don't long to go back home especially after all these depressing letters coming from there. It is very hard for me to let the old ones go back to Hungary.

It is so fortunate how strange people can be. We who are staying out are very depressed by this situation, but my parents on the contrary, see things in a more optimistic color.

I don't want to talk them out of going. I wish they would leave. We can't endure this many responsibilities.

Yesterday an engineer colleague of Friedrich went home. I wrote a few words to Toni. I was interested about the family, Edi, Fani. I wrote them that I am working with the MNB and that you are working in an official capacity for the MNB with the Americans. I addressed it to Kerteskör because I didn't know the Budapest address.

My Dear Frici, Zsuzsi says that if you took a raincoat with you that it is hers and please send it back somehow. I will send it to them; I will bring yours to you in its place.

I haven't spoken to Biber yet about the trip to see you. There is still time for that. Besides I cannot go right now anyway. I don't like to talk about it too much and I see that he also doesn't like to talk about it. I will wait for the right occasion to speak to him.

My Dear Frici, take very good care of yourself. I hope you still have some of the home supplements. If not, I can I can always send you some baked goods. The bacon is already gone. I hug you and kiss you many times."

Your loving Kati
Aug. 24, 1945

Figure 63: Letters that came from Hungary after the war were stamped "military censorship civil mails" by the Americans.

SEPTEMBER 1945, "OUR FATHER GOES AWAY ALL THE TIME."

This is a portion of a letter our mother wrote to Father when he was in Frankfurt. The family had the hardship of being separated because our father was always volunteering for important business trips. He felt he was needed because of his expertise and position at the Bank.

—⚬—

...Vera [wife of Torzsay-Biber] teaches with a personal touch. I enjoy it when Vera comes by and she talks about how the kids spent the time with them.

The other day they spoke about the swallows and how the papa swallow leaves for work and comes back with bugs and this is how it is with people too. Pityi replied to this by saying "Our papa goes away all the time."

But don't worry; I got my share of it too.

The other day Pityi was learning to read and in the book it said, "major frost." He didn't understand and when Vera explained it to him, he suddenly replied, "Just like when Mother comes through the door!" See how well they know us?

The amusing part of it is how he said it so seriously. You know the good thing about this type of learning is that it took away a lot of his inhibitions. I now send him everywhere by himself. He doesn't like it, but he does it and comes straight home afterwards. His handwriting is not as nice as when he went to the Arrow Cross school. There, they taught him handwriting, but on the other hand, here he advances in his reading.

He is becoming a teenager. He is talking back a lot. He whistles along and works with his hands more than before. He and Hapsi like each other very much and the little one imitates him a lot, especially when he talks back. The two small ones only get along when they play cooking or they pig out. István is the master of this. The newest is that they play with their portable potty. You can imagine how happy I am about that.

My Dear Frici, I already sent two letters to you since the one I sent with Gossensek. Stower took one of them. The other was sent by carrier through Roesti, an American banker in Linz.

Meanwhile I'm thinking about what the future has in store for us. For one, I'm not thinking about going back home to Hungary, because, you know, it will be not good for us, even though I became very home sick several times and I must say it was very traumatic.

The constant waiting for something doesn't help, but that's something that I can't do anything about. I wrote then and later I finished the thought. Maybe you should try to go through Baron to get some recommendations in Germany. If not any other way, then maybe in my name.

Now that I received your letter, my dreams cooled down a bit. I see we just have to wait and see what happens. The move to Frankfurt is getting less and less a possibility. At first the Americans took away the Bank automobiles and the Austrians took the gasoline. Now they somewhat gave them back, but only for within house use and for sure not for something like for moving to Frankfurt.

There is also a problem with the Bank's belongings and they don't even want to give the belongings in Vienna out. You also wrote, but I long since knew that there would be a problem in Frankfurt to find wood to heat with. Here at least they have cut down part of the forest and our heating is somewhat secure. If you could make this happen, then we can handle it ourselves.

I am now cooking, shopping, taking care of the kids and so on. Even now, if I cook, the whole housekeeping gets left behind and is untouched. If I send them to school and childcare or if I get a little help then I can handle it. But even then, you will have to be home for a half a day and not like Vajkoczy said… that you have to be working from 9 till 5:30 every day. My Dear, think about this.

All things put aside, it is terrible to be here, mainly because I am alone and also feel crushed with people around me. I really don't have time for anything.

Zsuzsi is going into the Bank. She needs the work and if she works hard they will put her to work in the kitchen. This will be even longer days and worse. She is now listening to the radio and it is interesting. We are receiving lots of news from home. Every day there is a letter to someone. By way of Roesti….

[*The other part of the letter is missing. Ed.*]

NOVEMBER 11, 1945, "ON YOUR NAME DAY"

Our father wrote to Mother while he was away in Frankfurt. Our mother's name day is November 25. It is a Hungarian custom to celebrate name days with flowers for women.

—m—

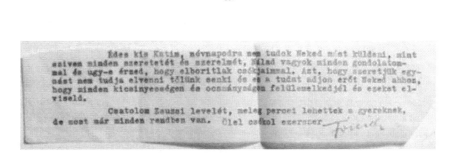

Figure 64: Father's note

My dear sweet Kati,

*On your name day I cannot send anything
except my heart's love with all its romantic
feelings.*

*I am with you in all my thoughts
And, yes, I can feel that I make you fall
apart with my kisses!*

*That we love each other—
Nobody can ever take that away from us!*

*And let this give you the strength
To lift yourself above every little thing -- so you
can bear them.*

I hug you with kisses a thousand times!

Nov. 11, 1945   *Your Frici*

Figure 65: Set to verse by Steven Tarnay

ON CHRISTMAS 1945, "HOW PAINFUL LOVE CAN BE"

It was a month before Christmas. Mrs. Torzsay-Biber's husband was accused of treason by the MNB officers. He was arrested and sent to the infamous Andrassy Street 60 secret police prison in Budapest. Today the prison is a museum called the Terror House.

The MNB did not always work smoothly and there were factions and disagreements especially with over 600 additional people cramped into a small village more than doubling its size. The MNB employees and families felt deserted, robbed of their livelihood, their families torn apart, trying to survive in the chaos of the war and its aftermath. It seemed as if once the gold was safely in the hands of the Americans, the MNB personnel fell apart. Their mission was accomplished and they had nothing to hang on to or to keep them together. Still, the personnel were heroic in their efforts and commitment.

This poem was written by Torzsay-Biber's wife Gyurika to our mother. Gyurika shared her feelings about her husband's imprisonment during this Christmas season.

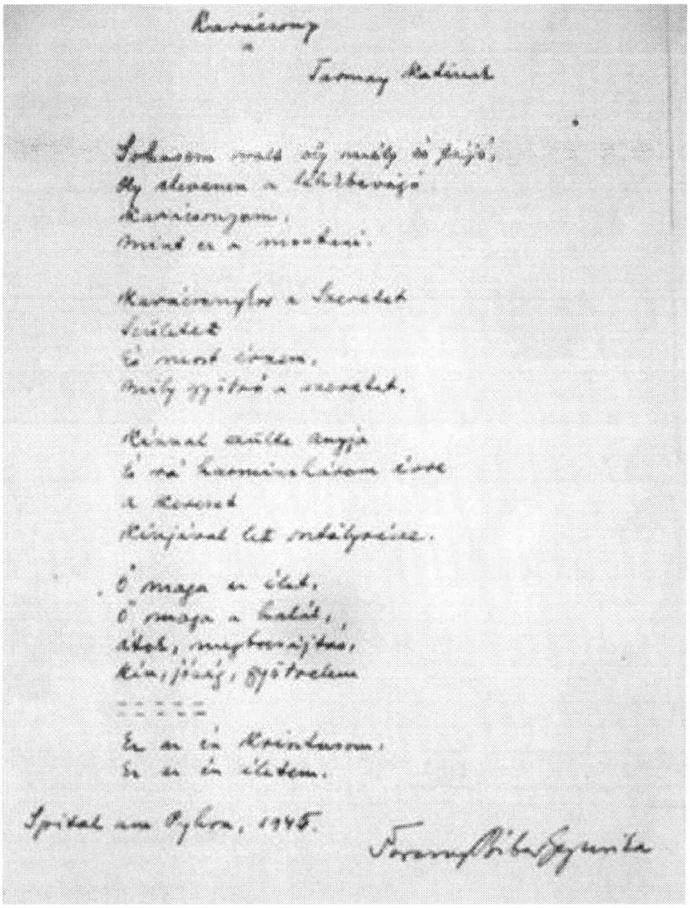

Figure 66: Original poem written by Torzsay-Biber's wife to our mother on Christmas 1945.

CHRISTMAS 1945

To Kati Tarnay

Such a deep and sorrowful,
And so intensely spiritual Christmas
I have never had.

Love was born
At Christmas time
And at this time I realize
How painful love is

His Mother bore Him with pain
And thirty-three years later
By the Cross
The pain became His.
You are the Life,
You are the Death,
You are the Forgiveness,
The Agony and the Goodness.
This my Christ,
He is my life.

Spital am Pyhrn, 1945
Torzsay-Biber Gyunika

Figure 67: Hungarian stencils for Christmas decorations made by our mother from honey kalács. The ornaments were hung on the tree.

Figure 68: Additional Stencils

FREDERICK ELMER TARNAY AND KATHERINE TARNAY

CHAPTER 4:
"NOT ONE GRAM OF GOLD WAS MISSING"

In the aftermath of the war, the Bank was in disarray, its leaders changing and fate unclear. Frici Tarnay was a trusted advisor to the Bank's leaders and past leaders and kept in communication with them about these events.

—⁓—

In Frankfort a/m the gold was meticulously checked by American experts by weight, numbers and pieces against our books and also the origin of every gram was painstakingly investigated. It was a great satisfaction for us to learn that not one gram of gold was missing when this big gamble was over. The deposits and other assets of the Bank including the banknotes and the treasures of the museums stayed in Spital a/P safeguarded by the Bank's employees and the gendarmes under the supervision of the US Military Government. Except some foreign owned assets and the banknotes, subsequently everything was returned to Hungary. Since a new currency, the Forint 2 was issued in Hungary in 1946, the pengő notes stored in Spital a/P became worthless and there was no use returning them to Hungary. With a face value of about 700 million dollars they were sold to an Austrian paper mill for 400 dollars.

— And the gold? Well, in accordance with the stipulations of the Peace Treaty of Paris it was turned over by the U.S. Government to the Hungarian Government and shipped back to Soviet dominated Hungary.

I frankly admit this was not the end I was dreaming of when the story started. But I have the satisfaction that in a team of fine cooperating colleagues, I did my best. I had my good share in turning over these treasures of my former country into the safe and trusted hands of the U.S.A., hoping that once they would be returned to a real free Hungary. Now, I only have the comfort that I had no part whatsoever in returning them behind the Iron Curtain.

—⁘—

REPORT: THE FATE OF SOPRON, MARCH 31, 1946

In 1946, Frici volunteered to go to Reichenau, a staging point in the MNB evacuation from Sopron to Spital am Pyhrn.

Back in early 1945, the Bank had continued to work from Sopron under the direction of Torszay-Biber after the train had left for Spital am Pyhrn. The sudden bombing and rapid Russian advance at the end of April 1945 created a panicked evacuation of the Bank to Reichenau. Frici was one of the last Bank persons to leave Sopron before the city was overrun by the Russians. The battle was intense. The Hungarian civilians of Sopron suffered bitterly from both the German SS and Russians.

While in Reichenau in 1946, Frici went to discover the fate of the Bank's possessions left behind in Sopron. He wrote this report for MNB Manager, Torzsay-Biber.

—⁘—

Report
By Frederick Tarnay

At the end of April 1945, Sopron's drunken-like evacuation began as the result of the fast pace of the Russian advance and changing situation of the war. Most of the Sopron Bank valuables, documents and personal belongings of bank personnel were left at Reichenau. Since the Bank had not received information from several sources about what happened to the Bank and personal properties, the Bank saw that this issue needed to be handled.

Since a lot of personnel valuables were also left in Reichenau, I asked the Bank Director if I could volunteer to travel there to determine the fate of the Bank's belongings. I started out on March 25th to Reichenau as the Bank's representative.

I arrived on the evening of March 26th at 6 o'clock and went immediately to the pastry shop, where the Bank's valuables and personal belongings were stored at that time. I notice that the truck and the printing press that were left there were nowhere in sight near the pastry shop.

The pastry shop was occupied by the police department and I immediately went to see them. I explained to them what my situation and purpose was and asked them if they knew what happened there. The two young policemen around (ages around 20-22) said they didn't know very much because they hadn't been there very long.

They said they don't know a lot about the events because they had just arrived recently. They heard that there were valuables from the Bank stored there, but didn't know if there was anything left after the war. They mentioned that their police captain would know the most about what happened to all the things from the Bank. The captain came with the Russians to Reichenau from Frieheistskampfer and took over the police duties of the City.

This captain was in Steiermark at that time and it would be a week later before his return. The police suggested that I go see him at his home. He would tell me if the authorities at that time saved any of the Banks belongings. The police thought I was sent by the Austrian authorities and that's why I was interested about the Bank belongings, but the Bank belongings went back to Hungary after they were in Austria.

At the policemen's suggestion, I went to the hotel to find a person named Pongratz. I knocked on the front door, but they did not answer. I went and knocked on the side window and heard a voice that sounded like I scared them and the lady asked me what I wanted. After a long explanation, her husband let me in the back door and after long conversation with cigarettes we were comfortable with each other. They however, did not give me a room.

We talked for a long time and they told me what had happened afterward in Reichenau. The Russians came and occupied the town and the Bank personnel were obliged to leave town. The territory in the local area was "no man's land," because the Germans, mainly the SS, were in charge of the whole Reichenau area.

The adjacent town of Payerbach is where the Russians were and there were skirmishes between the two all the time. The SS told everybody to leave their homes and go into the hills and areas further back. Their homes were completely plundered and everybody was in despair. The SS ruthlessly oppressed all the opposition. A lot of the residents were shot dead and a lot of the victims who were shot then were hanged.

The restaurant owner fled towards the Russians ahead of the SS terror, but the SS caught his wife and put her in the cellar. They threatened to shoot her if she didn't tell where her husband was. She collapsed and that saved her life, since when she fainted the SS didn't care about her anymore.

The Bank and personnel belongings became essentially the plundered possessions of the SS. The bank's books and documents were worthless to them and they gathered them and threw them out on the street. The local people also helped themselves to the thrown away material and a lot of paper money went into the hands of the locals.

The Russians didn't find much left from the Bank's belongings because during the six weeks before they came to occupy the town, the locals had pretty much carried off the valuables. The Russian military and the Austrian authorities required the locals to return all the paper money. The Russians used the money to go shopping around

Hungary afterwards. Later on, the money people had could be exchanged in Austrian financial institutions and they received a voucher. After the Russian occupation, all the Bank's belongings that were considered useless by them were gathered together and burned.

The following day, March 27th, I went to the main town building. I met a man called Graglmayer who I asked if by chance he knew anybody who picked up any of the Bank's belongings and saved them. The town clerk said he didn't have any knowledge about that. Two other female clerks mentioned and confirmed that everything was taken or destroyed during the six week siege by the Russians.

From all the information gathered, it looks like the entire Bank's books, documents, and belongings can be considered lost.

Spital am Pyhrn, 1946, March 31.
Frigyes Tarnay

ADDITIONAL NOTES: [FROM THE GOLD RUSH 1957]

The war was over and I went back to Reichenau, at that time under Russian occupation, to investigate what happened with our valuables and belongings. I learned that everything, the load of currency on the broken truck included, was looted during two weeks of fierce fighting between the Germans and the Russians.

Our truckload of money was gone, of course. The crates had been broken up and millions of dollars in pengő notes were dispersed among soldiers and civilians as well. Bundles of notes were scattered in the streets and nobody wanted to miss the chance to become rich once in his life. You cannot blame them. In that no man's land the arms had the word. Law and justice were silenced. The only things left were our apparently unattractive business records and books.

When the battle was over, they were collected with other rubbish, incinerated and reduced to ashes. When the Russians took the village, they ordered the population to turn in all our notes. Then the Russian soldiers used the money to buy wine and liquor in Hungary. The money was not officially in circulation, but who would have questioned the validity of the money offered by a Russian soldier? The fact that he paid for something was a miracle anyway.

An innkeeper and his wife gave me this account about the fate of our abandoned belongings. I scared them to death when in the evening I knocked on their door and asked for room and some food. This was a very unusual thing that time because all restaurants and hotels were closed and nobody dared to walk in the streets after the sun went down. The town was filled with Russian soldiers who had lots of fun by hunting for souvenirs, preferably for watches and fountain pens, but the top of their pleasure was the riding and, of course, wrecking of bikes, if they could get hold of one.

My innkeeper complained bitterly that one night a bunch of Russian soldiers knocked on his door. After lecturing him about the "Kulturera" (culture) in Russia, they took everything they found and liked in his home. The innkeeper took a 50 pengő note out of his wallet and solemnly handed it over to me as a souvenir and as the only copy "saved" from our lost stock on the broken truck....

APRIL 8, 1946, STATEMENT: FÜR DIE WIRTSCHAFT

In this statement, Frici reaffirms Leopold Scheffler's position with the MNB. Scheffler was directed and commissioned by the German Reich in March 19, 1944 to be in charge of managing the MNB. Scheffler kept his commission and skillfully manipulated his superiors in keeping the personnel and gold together during the evacuation to Austria. He accomplished this with the collaboration of Frici representing the MNB. He sided with the MNB and successfully thwarted attempts by his German superiors Boden and Schnellner as well Arrow Cross factions of the MNB headed by MNB Nazi President Temesváry.

—⚏—

Statement:
By Frederick E. Tarnay

Following March 1 1944, the German government appointed an economic representative (Für die Wirtschaft) in the person of Dr. Boden to the side of the German procurator and ambassador in Hungary. Scheffler, the Director of the Reichsbank, belonged to this circle. His job included administering the cases dealing with Hungarian-German payments and managing the general tasks of the Hungarian National Bank.

Scheffler was neither a foreign currency expert nor a clearing expert, but was more experienced in the field of issues concerning the working of a Central Bank. This is reinforced by the fact that the Germans put more emphasis on the general functions of the MNB.

Later on, when military action was moving closer to the capital and the Transdanubian Region, Mr. Scheffler's task also included relocating the employees as well as the assets of the MNB. When the Bank moved to Veszprém in the beginning of December 1944, Scheffler left behind his official office and moved to Veszprém with Reichsbankinspektor Stöwer, where he immediately made the preparations to receive the transferred assets. Mr. Scheffler had the full authorization from the German Procurator and Ambassador to complete the assignments related to the transfer of the employees and the assets of the Bank, including issuing the necessary travel documents, delivery notes, etc., as well as the authority to sign all documents .

During the negotiations held with German officials on the transfer of the bank, Director Scheffler introduced himself as "der deutsche Betreuer der Ungarische Nationalbank" [*The German Supervisor of the Hungarian National Bank*].

I must mention that Director Scheffler also could have received orders not only to secure the gold reserves of the Bank, but to also keep safe the national silver reserves which the Ministry of Finance was responsible for, since in Budapest he urged Secretary of State Turvölgyi to relocate the silver reserve from Budapest to the west, and he stuck to this. The Bank brought with it the national silver reserves it held in its storage facility in Veszprém.

In summary, it is obvious that the German government placed the greatest amount of emphasis on relocating the Bank and its assets and put the responsibility of the managing and administration tasks of this job in the hands of Director Scheffler. Scheffler himself stated this fact.

Spital am Pyhrn, April 8, 1946

JULY 24, 1948, "THE HUNGARIAN NATION IS DEEPLY OBLIGED TO HIM"

During the time we were in Innsbruck waiting to relocate as refugees, our parents kept in touch with the Bank personnel. Some of them had already left Spital am Pyhrn to other countries. We collected the wonderful stamps from around the world.

Torzsay-Biber, Manager of the MNB after the war, eventually went to Morocco after being released from the Andrássy 60 prison in Budapest. He wrote this letter to our father just before we left for America.

This document includes 12 official statements by Torzsay-Biber relating to his tenure as manager. He commends Father for his role in saving the gold. He wrote the statements in both Hungarian and English.

Torzsay-Biber attached the letter he received from Frici when came back from Salzburg. The letter had the original signature "as received by Lt. Leonard Cowles U.S. Army, 3r CIC Det."

—ᴍᴠ—

Figure 69: George Torzsay-Biber, Stanford Law School Lecturer from 1961 to 1973 and Emeritus until 1988. He was the last president of the Hungarian National Bank before the Bank returned to Hungary. (From Stanford Law School Archives, Sarah Wilson Reference Librarian & Archivist.)

—ᴍᴠ—

Declaration by Torzsay-Biber

I, the undersigned Dr. George TORZSAY-BIBER declare as follows:

1. I am the last legally designated Manager of the National Bank of Hungary, Doctor of laws and Barrister at law. I led the Judicial Section of the Bank in Budapest until December 1944. In January 1945, all the gold assets as well as the other properties of the Bank were transferred from Hungary to Austria /Spital am Pyhrn, Upper Austria/ and the appointed Arrow Cross management of the Bank followed them to this place. I remained in the Western Part of Hungary until March 1945 and directed all the branches of the Bank which were not yet occupied by the Red Army. A smaller staff collaborated with me there and Mr. Frederick TARNAY belonged to this staff as well. In the last days of March 1945, the Red Army occupied the entire Hungary and we were obliged to leave for Austria, taking along the last possessions of the Bank under our control. We had the greatest difficulties during this transportation effort and we were constantly exposed to danger to our lives.

In this difficult time Mr. Tarnay did his part with the greatest self-sacrifice although he was the father of 3 children. Due to his efforts, he helped save the considerable assets of the Bank.

2. In Austria those who did not belong to the Hungarian Arrow Cross party, like Mr. Tarnay and myself, had the most difficult problems. The Arrow Cross management of the Bank wanted to take the gold assets of the Bank to another place in the western part of Austria accompanied by a small selected staff. Later they had the idea to submerge the gold in a lake in the mountains. We succeeded in preventing these attempts. Later there was imminent danger that the 6th German Army would capture the gold assets and take them to an unknown place. Additionally we were running the risk that the rapidly advancing Red Army would reach us and the gold reserves fall to the Soviets and Hungary would lose them forever.

3. In order to save the assets of the Bank for Hungary I decided on a risky plan with assistance of my collaborators. I would send two couriers in two different directions whose mission was to contact the approaching victorious U.S. Army and request protection of the gold assets and possessions of the Bank.

4. The situation was very critical. The courier had to reach the U.S. troops through the lines of the withdrawing, but still fighting SS-formations, while the Red army was moving forward from the other direction and was only 3 miles from the village where the Bank was located.

This plan was extremely dangerous because if the SS-troops captured the courier and found the letter addressed to the U.S. Army, he would be killed on the spot as well as myself who signed the letter.

5. Mr. Tarnay volunteered to carry out the self-sacrificing mission as one of the couriers. After encountering great danger and the greatest of difficulties he arrived on May 4th, 1945 in Salzburg just as the U.S. Army was occupying the town. On the next day, he handed over the letter to Lt. Leonard R. Cowles /3rd CIC Det./ who immediately wired it to the appropriate command./See enclosure./

6. Mr. Tarnay's efforts were completely successful. The U.S. troops left Linz, the capital of Upper Austria and entered Spital am Pyhrn on May 7th, 1945. As a consequence the entire gold assets and possessions of the Bank were saved from being captured by the Germans or looted by the Red Army. I must add that the other courier did not reach the U.S. Army in Linz and turned back without completing the mission.

7. The U.S.A. Authorities accepted my legal case based on international law and did not consider the assets of the Bank as a war-prize. It was therefore possible to save the gold reserves of 32 million dollars and the other assets /bonds, notes, bank deposits, the treasures of the museums etc. / representing a total of about 220 million dollars.

Mr. Tarnay had a most significant part in the success of this effort and not only the Bank but also the Hungarian Nation is deeply obliged to him. Unfortunately this gratitude could not be expressed under the then actual political situation as Hungary had lost her freedom and was under Soviet oppression.

8. This action of the Hungarian National Bank won the full recognition of the U.S. Army authorities, since this proved that the Hungarian National Bank upheld its noble Western traditions and the trust that had always bound it to the Western powers, even under the most difficult circumstances.

9. I was grateful again to accept the excellent services of Mr. Tarnay when the U.S. Army took the gold assets of the Bank to the Headquarters in Frankfurt. It was necessary to assign certain Bank experts to the U.S. Headquarters. Mr. Tarnay was ready again to voluntarily assume this mission and he worked for 6 months in the Headquarters of the U.S. Army furnishing all the information the Headquarters needed.

10. After such activities, it is evident that Mr. Tarnay as well as myself lost our posts with National Bank of Hungary. We could not expect any kind of favorable treatment from the Bank under communist control. Both myself and Mr. Tarnay could not return to Hungary where prosecution and prison would be our fate. We are compelled therefore to live as displaced persons in the worst conditions far from our homeland and facing an uncertain future.

11. I, as manager, am witness to Mr. Tarnay's excellent services, take full responsibility for his loyalty, reliability and honesty and esteem him worthy of the greatest support. I should be glad to know that he succeeded in entering the free soil of the U.S.A. where as free man he could begin a new life with his family.

12. I give this declaration according to my best knowledge, being conscious of my full responsibility and I am ready to affirm it under oath as necessary.

Tangier /Morocco/July 24th 1948. Dr. George Torzsay-Biber
Manager of the National Bank of Hungary

JUNE 12, 1949, TO THE GERMAN COMMISSIONER, LEOPOLD SCHEFFLER

The time was getting close to our leaving Innsbruck for America in June 1949. Our father wrote several letters to acquaintances and people at the Reichsbank. It was through these letters that he found the German Commissioner Leopold Scheffler. He wrote him a summary of events of the gold journey. Our father was dismissed from the MNB because of his collaboration with Scheffler.

—⚹—

[Note: This is placed here due to the proximity of the events described above. Ed.]

[Translated from German]

Igls, 12 June 1949.

Dear Mr. Director:

I have your address and received the good news that you and your family are well. You cannot believe with what great pleasure we heard this message, because we have thought a lot about you and we often wondered what may have happened to you. We were very concerned in the difficult times after the collapse particularly health-wise who survived. I have also inquired about the fate of several acquaintances who have other friends who made inquiries, but always in vain. Every trace of you was gone. So much the better was our pleasure that we have rediscovered you.

I do not know if since then you ever heard from someone from the National Bank and whether you were informed about our fate, but I assume that you are interested in what happened with us after you left us.

I will now briefly tell about the events that we have experienced. Perhaps they are unique in the history of the bank and are recorded here.

I will start with the day / 5.5.1945. / when I left them in Spital a/p in the direction of Vöcklamarkt enroute to Salzburg.

They knew that I had the official MNB letter to Salzburg cleverly hidden to deliver to the U.S. Army there to request protection for our treasury and for the staff. With the help of the papers I received from you, I reached my goal. But we could not enter further into the city of Salzburg because it was on that day the Americans had entered. The city was transferred from the German police and cordoned off.

I therefore, waited on the outskirts in a farmhouse until the first tank appeared. After an attempt to contact the military authorities (which was inconclusive because the senior officers wanted to see the gold and each lost interest after learning that it was not possible), I was able to contact a CIC (Counter Intelligence Corps) officer who understood and realized the importance of the matter from the letter handed him. He immediately got into a Jeep and quickly took it away.

On the next day, he informed me that the letter was sent by wire to the proper command authority and the treasure would be taken care of as soon as possible. At my request, he signed my copy of the letter. — My mission was finished and after a 2 week stay in Salzburg the Bank sent a car for me.

During my absence, the situation in Spital a/p was very tense. A delegate of the German army operations there (or as he was portrayed) had twice tried to "secure" the gold. It was through the strong opposition of the Bank that these attempts were repulsed. We called and asked that, with the high value of the goods under our care, we wanted to be under the protection of the Americans. They sent us a train with Military Police with an armed officer to take over the security and the control was handed over exclusively to the Americans.

This happened on May 7th. In the next few days, an American Commission appeared and gave us a written warrant transferring the gold to them. It was loaded into trucks and accompanied by 2 tanks to Frankfurt/Main. Even General Patton, along with Bank representatives, came to see it.

The Americans replaced the Bank leadership with Dr. Torzsay-Biber as the acknowledged head of the bank. Several persons were interrogated by the CIC, but only Temesváry and Fazekas were arrested. Temesváry was later extradited and sentenced to life imprisonment. Fazekas sat 2 years in a prison, now he is free to continue to dream his dreams.

The leadership of the bank was divided into two camps. One wanted to go home, the other not. Torzsay-Biber set all our hopes with the Americans to stop the repatriation of the treasury (into Communist or Nazi hands). Jánkovics was his opponent and using a delegate from Hungary, he had Torzsay arrested by the Americans in September 1945 and delivered to Hungary "along with the most serious war criminals."

That this was an unfounded arrest was shown by the fact that Torzsay was acquitted by the Hungarian People's Court in May 1946. Meanwhile, he had to endure the infamous torture dungeon of 60 Andrássy Street in Budapest. Following his release, he again fled from Hungary and after a few months stay in Austria, went to France.

In June 1945, I drove with an American official to Frankfurt/M and worked at the headquarters there for 6 months. On my return I found the situation in Spital a/P very sad. After Torzsay was arrested, the Bank was led by a committee. Then Quandt emerged from a camp and took over the organization. It aligned itself with the new Hungarian (Communist) regime and did not have the courage to continue the work which Torzsay began against the repatriation of the treasury.

I was told by the new regime that my cooperation was not desired because of my collaboration with Director Scheffler. Since I had found a place for us in the French zone, I left Spital and so we lived here since August 1946.

After the removal of Torzsay-Biber, I had no contact with Budapest. Long reports were sent to Budapest. The fault was slid as much as possible into your shoes for the shift to clear them and be taken back. You had expelled us by force and taken up etc. even armed forces in Veszprém to this end; etc.

I had the courage to refute some entirely false statements that were written in these reports about you, although it was clear to me that it was absolutely useless.

I just hope that there is still time on the earth where one can say openly that we also owe something to you because without your assistance we would not have been able to complete the plan so well.

I can state with calm conscience the fact that our plan was best organized and there you have helped us. From our collaboration, I will always preserve the impression that you have acted not only as official representatives of a foreign power, but also as a colleague of issuing bank to issuing bank.

That is all very nice, but even sadder is the fact that all efforts were in vain. In fact, the treasury was returned to Hungary and thus it is now all in the hands of the Russians. A completely small group still "manipulates" the securities in Spital/P. Quandt went some months ago to New York where he leads the branch of an English company.

The remaining employees are very scattered; many have gone to Germany, many to England as household employees, some in Argentina. Cottely is with the Argentine Notenbank.

We have both started a job with the French military government of Morocco which we both like better, but the U.S.A. plan is already concrete and due in a few weeks. This is also one reason why I write to you now, in the hope that we will still hear from you in Europe as to how you and your family are doing now, etc.

My sons are growing up like mushrooms and hence my concern. The small Fritz goes to the French Lycee and István and Hapsi to the local Hungarian school because they must learn their mother language again. They spent 2 years in Austrian children's homes and entirely forgot the Hungarian language.

István is still the straight character, diligent and honest. Hapsi, the humorist of the family, is as droll as ever. My in-laws and my sister-in-law have returned to Hungary and live a difficult life in the small vineyard at Lake Balaton. We regularly receive letters from them, but of course they cannot write about the real situation.

My address is otherwise: F. Tarnay, Igls 5th Tyrol – Austria.

With the warmest greetings from us both to you and to your dear family, I am

Yours
Fred E. Tarnay

—⁂—

This verse and our book title show what drove Frici to accomplish his missions. His love for his family was deep, but his yearning for freedom was even stronger and surely very difficult for him to bear.

—⁂—

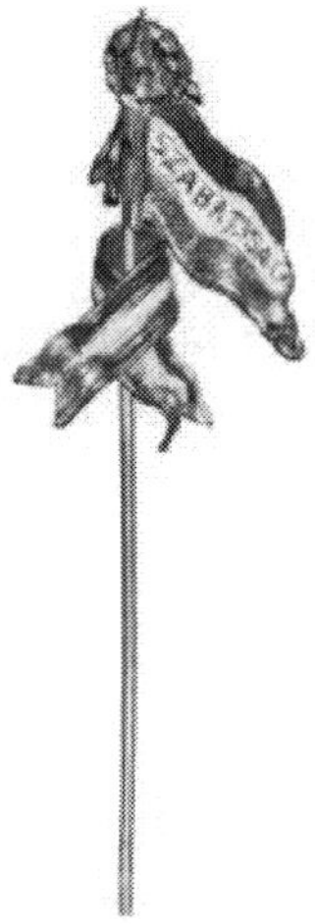

Freedom, Love!

These two I need

For my love I sacrifice life

For freedom I sacrifice my love

Sándor Petöfi, 1847

Figure 70: Petőfi, Sándor (1823-1849) was a Hungarian poet and patriot who died in the 1848 Hungarian Revolution. The pin is a 1948 Revolution flag pin from Iren Tarnay. The word "Szabadsag" means "Freedom."

CHAPTER 5:
DISPLACED, BUT NO MORE BUGS

Innsbruck, Austria
1946 to 1949

It was the post-WWII era between 1946 and 1949. The Iron Curtain was established and Hungary became a Russian Communist satellite country.

Our family found ourselves as refugees stranded in the chaos after war. We became DP's, Displaced Persons. From this "homeless" situation we began our freedom journey.

—⁓—

IT WAS TIME, 1946 TO 1949, BY FRED B. TARNAY

The reasons and the move from Spital to Innsbruck are still somewhat cloudy, but one thing sure, we had to move. The Austrian stay requirement was closing in and the MNB was dispersed. Other forces or opportunities may have had a hand.

My mother once said our final goal was always to move towards Switzerland a neutral nation and Innsbruck was on the way there. Switzerland was also the seat of many banks and my father would have had a better chance of continuing his career there. Innsbruck was also in the French occupational sector and more tolerant of refugees.

My mother spoke fluent French and had a French teaching credential, so that may have had some influence in the decision.

The Catholic Church was heavily involved in helping the flood of refugees fleeing from the Communist takeover. One such organization was the NCWC, National Catholic Welfare Council (today the Council of Bishops) that had arms extending into many countries that were giving sanctuary to fleeing refugees from Nazism and Communism.

The family left Spital am Pyhrn in early 1946 and temporarily settled in Igls, Austria, a village above Innsbruck. We had a room in the Hotel Stern, a converted hospital for refugees. We lived on the second floor in a room no bigger than the one we had in Spital. There was a central bathroom on each floor. Our room had a large enough sink that we kids could take a bath in it.

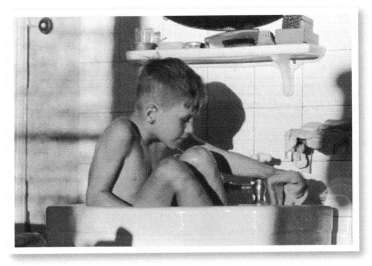

Figure 71: 1948, Steve bathing in our one-room apartment, Igls, Austria.

Steve caught spinal meningitis and almost died. Steve had been bedridden for over a week and was getting worse by the day. He was near non-responsive. The doctor came in, took one look at him and immediately gave him a spinal tap to relieve the pressure from the fluid on his spinal cord. No anesthetics. My mother was beside herself but never showed except in the grave concern on her face. Steve remembers having to learn how to walk again. I came down with pneumonia and the only treatment was warm chamomile poultices around the chest. Somehow we survived.

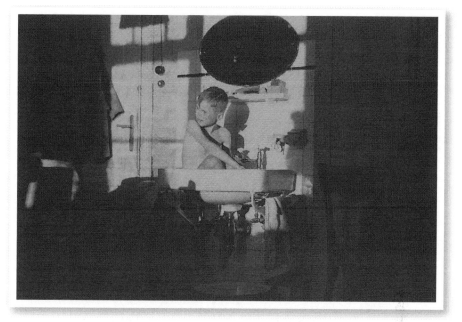

Figure 72: 1948, Steven and cramped quarters. Igls, Austria.

We ate in the restaurant on the bottom floor. I don't know how we paid for all this, but my mother ended up working for the French Occupational forces office in downtown Innsbruck and my father was involved with the Catholic Refugee organization. We were there for almost 4 years.

My mother had a very good job as she spoke both fluent German and French. She became the personal assistant to the French General as a translator in his duties as manager of the region. According to her, she was liked by the entire French staff. This was apparently true because when the commanding general was due to be transferred, he asked my parents and family to accompany him and be part of his permanent staff. The destination was Casablanca where he was to take control of the French forces there. We would have a good salary and permanent jobs with the French government.

This must have been a difficult situation as one of the MNB managers that my father knew well and trusted was also in Casablanca at the time. I don't think we can ever completely unravel or understand the complexity and confusion after the war.

We had to continue our education and I was admitted to the French school in Fulpmes, a nearby town further up the mountain where the French military children were being educated. My brothers went to a German run Kindergarten in Innsbruck.

When we were home together, we could not understand each other as we all had begun to speak different languages. My mother was the translator and made sure we all spoke our native Hungarian at home. There were other Hungarian families scattered in the region and perhaps that was part of the answer to our moving here in some way....

My father was working for the Catholic charity Caritas distributing food and clothing to the refugee community. I remember helping him and he was very fair and made it a point to know each person's true needs. He didn't like dishonest people, but never showed it except in directing how the goods were distributed. He knew who needed the most and who didn't and why. Donations of food and clothing from the U.S. came in through both Caritas and 'The Pope's Children' program. They were kept in a small apartment in Innsbruck which my father managed along with several priests.

We attended the small church in Igls with the classic Austrian steeple and rough wooden pews. The collection during Mass was done with a small velvet pouch at the end of a long pole. That was passed by the usher in front of everyone in the pew and if you didn't put something in it, he would shake the pouch. A small bell attached to the bottom would ring and tell everyone around what a skinflint you were....

Figure 73: Little Fred's First Communion in Innsbruck, Austria.

It was during this time through many correspondences that the real story started to come out as to what happened during the time the MNB was in Spital am Pyhrn.

It was during this time that we were able to function as a family, even if it was only for a few years and even if it was as Displaced Persons (DP's).

It was a time to reflect who we were, where we came from, and where we might be going.

It was a time for a daughter, our mother, to connect with her mother in long letters, to bond with each other, to learn about life, and to love one another.

It was a time to find out what freedom means and to enjoy its privileges.

Figure 74: In 1947, the Tarnay Family in Innsbruck, Austria. Fred and Katherine, children Steven, Fred and Géza (Matt/Hapsi). Mother made most of our clothes and we were always in "uniform".

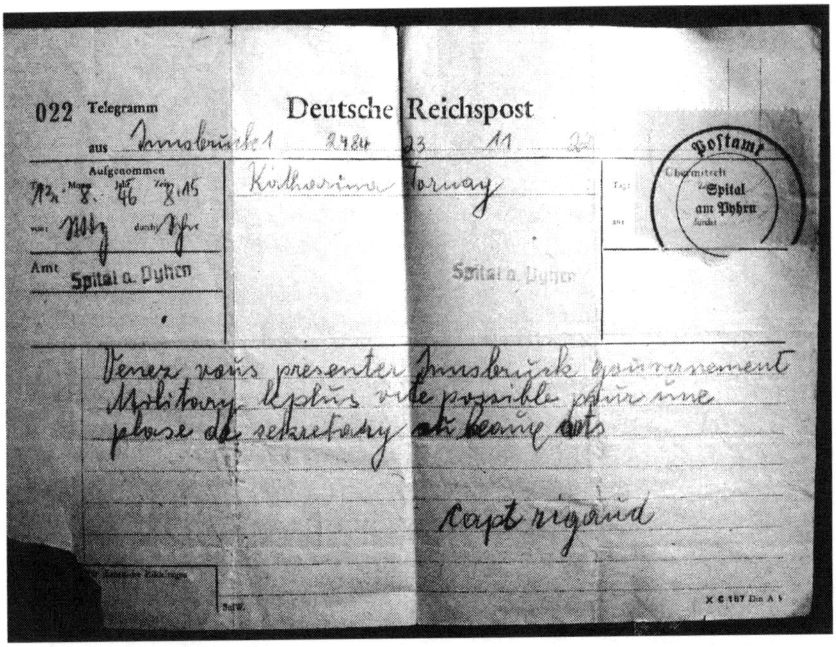
022 Telegramm

Deutsche Reichspost

aus Innsbruck 1 2484 23 11 22

Aufgenommen

Katherine Tarnay

Amt Spital a. Pyhrn

Postamt Spital am Pyhrn

Spital a. Pyhrn

Venez vous presenter Innsbruck gouvernement Military leplus vite possible pour une plase de sekretary au beaux arts

capt rigaud

Figure 75: August 8, 1946, telegram from the French Consulate offering our mother a job in Innsbruck, Austria.

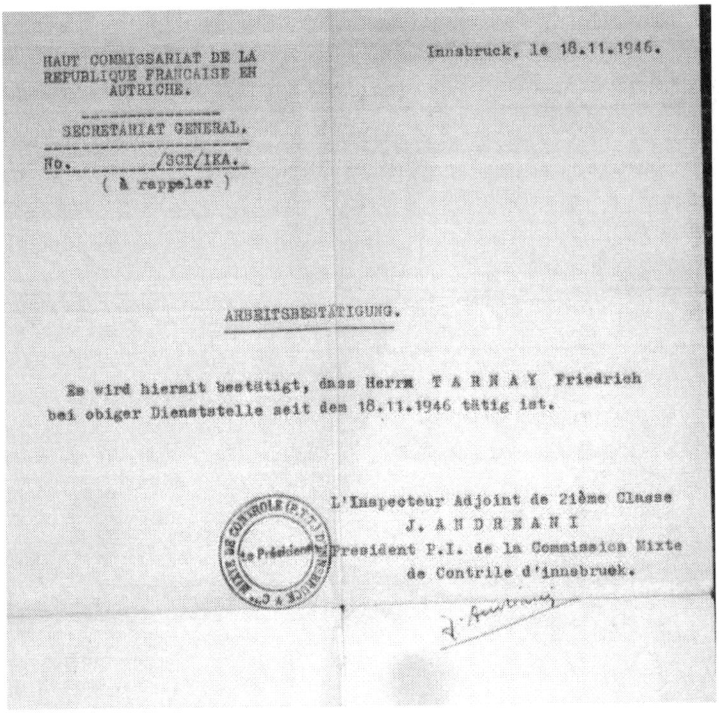
HAUT COMMISSARIAT DE LA
REPUBLIQUE FRANCAISE EN
AUTRICHE.

SECRETARIAT GENERAL.

No. .... /SCT/IKA.
(à rappeler)

Innsbruck, le 18.11.1946.

ARBEITSBESTÄTIGUNG.

Es wird hiermit bestätigt, dass Herrn T A R N A Y Friedrich bei obiger Dienststelle seit dem 18.11.1946 tätig ist.

L'Inspecteur Adjoint de 2ième Classe
J. A N D R E A N I
President P.I. de la Commission Mixte
de Contrile d'innsbruck.

Figure 76: A letter from the French Embassy affirming Frici's employment starting on November 18th, 1946.

Figure 77: Displaced Persons Refugee Camp at Regau. Little girl looking out at chickens cleaning bugs from shoes.

Figure 78: Women "shopping" for donated shoes at a Displaced Persons camp. Also shown are stacks of food from U.S.A., including "Clapp's Instant Oatmeal"

1947, LIFE UNDER THE RUSSIAN "LIBERATION": "GOD...GIVE YOU A CALMER LIFE THAN THIS."

This letter is from our grandmother to our mother during the Russian occupation of Hungary. Many things were expressed in hidden words because of censorship of the mail.

—⚞—

1947

My Dearest Daughter,

We were happy to read in your letter that, thank God, you feel better. Thank you for the new battery, I missed it very much. As for painting, I'll give it a try. I hope I'll succeed.

I also hope that you will get the parcel by Tuesday and will have time to eat its contents. I transformed the birthday cake, with moderate success, since I flavored it with coffee beans. It still didn't come out well, but it is edible. As for the faultless packaging, it is your father who deserves credit for that. Enclosed are also our best wishes and warm love. God keep you in good health, help you in your work and give you a calmer life than this.

We are alive, in our changing physical condition, but we find the winter days beautiful.

Two days ago your father was busy planting on the veranda, but today it's snowing again. The tailor from Kővágóörs has agreed to repair the grey slacks for your father, by extending some of the lighter material from below. He asks 30 forints for them and they'll be ready by next week.

I am not all that well. I lose my breath quite often and then, if I take too much medicine, work does not go well. Your father, thank God, feels much stronger.

JUNE 6, 1948, FROM DAUGHTER TO MOTHER, "WE SLEEP PEACEFULLY"

Our grandparents were in Hungary while we were in Innsbruck. Our mother wrote to our grandparents in Hungary when she was not busy at work at the French Consulate. Our mother spoke fluent French and made more money than our father. As in her position as Secretary to the MNB President, she had a very important position as Secretary for the French Consulate. With her working there, she was able to send little Frici to French school for free.

—⚏—

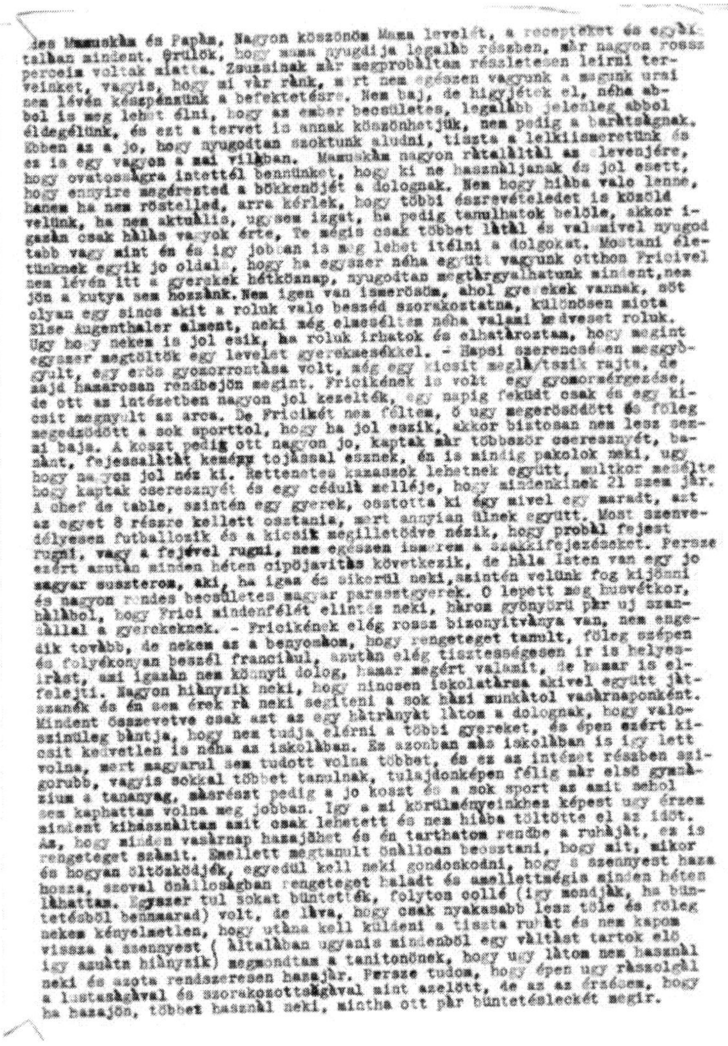
des Mamuskàm és Papàm, Nagyon köszönöm Mama levelét, a recepteket és egyàl-
talàn mindent. Örülök, hogy mama nyugdija legalàbb részben, màr nagyon rossz
percein voltak miatta. Zsuzsinak màr megprobàltam részletesen leirni ter-
veinket, vagyis, hogy mi vàr rànk, mert nem egészen vagyunk a magunk urai
nem lévén készpénzünk a befektetésre. Nem baj, de higyjétek el, néha abbol is meg lehet élni, hogy az ember becsületes, legalàbb jelenleg abbol
éldegélünk, és ezt a tervet is annak köszönhetjük, nem pedig a baràtsàgnak.
Ebben az a jo, hogy nyugodtan szoktunk aludni, tiszta a lelkiismeretünk és
ez is egy vagyon a mai vilàgban. Mamuskàm nagyon ràtalàltàl az elevenjére,
hogy ovatossàgra intettél bennünket, hogy ki ne hasznàljanak és jol esett,
hogy ennyire megérezted a bökkenöjét a dolognak. Nem hogy hiàba valo lenne,
hanem ha nem röstelled, arra kérlek, hogy többi észrevételedet is közöld
velünk, ha nem aktuàlis, ugysem izgat, ha pedig tanulhatok belöle, akkor i-
gazàn csak hàlàs vagyok érte, Te mégis csak többet làtàl és valamivel nyugod
tabb vagy mint én és igy jobban is meg lehet itélni a dolgokat. Mostani éle-
tünknek egyik jo oldala, hogy ha egyszer néha együtt vagyunk otthon Fricivel
nem lévén itt a gyerekek hétköznap, nyugodtan megtàrgyalhatunk mindent, nem
jön a kutya sem hozzànk. Nem igen van ismerösöm, ahol gyerekek vannak, söt
olyan egy sincs akit a roluk valo beszéd szorakoztatna, különösen miota
Else Augenthaler elment, neki még elmeséltem néha valami kedveset roluk.
Ugy hogy nekem is jol esik, ha roluk irhatok és elhatàroztam, hogy megint
egyszer megtöltök egy levelet gyerekmesékkel. - Hapsi szerencsésen meggyö-
gyult, egy erös gyomorrontàsa volt, még egy kicsit meglàtszik rajta, de
majd hamarosan rendbejön megint. Fricikének is volt egy gyomorsérgezése,
de ott az intézetben nagyon jol kezelték, egy napig feküdt csak és egy kicsit megnyult az arca. De Fricikét nem féltem, ö ugy megerösödött és föleg
megedzödött a sok sporttol, hogy ha jol eszik, akkor biztosan nem lesz sem-
mi baja. A koszt pedig ott nagyon jo, kaptak màr többször cseresznyét, ba-
nànt, fejessalàtàt keménytojàssal esznek, én is mindig pakolok neki, ugy
hogy nagyon jol néz ki. Rettenetes kamaszok lehetnek együtt, multkor mesélte
hogy kaptak cseresznyét és egy céduli mellé je, hogy mindenkinek 21 szem jàr.
A chef de table, szintén egy gyerek, osztotta ki ügy mivel egy maradt, azt
az egyet 8 részre kellett osztania, mert annyian ülnek együtt. Most szenve-
délyesen futballozik és a kicsik megilletödve nézik, hogy probàl fejest
rugni, vagy a fejével rugni, nem egészen ismerem a szakkifejezéseket. Persze
ezért azutàn minden héten cipöjavitàs következik, de hàla Isten van egy jo
magyar susztersom, aki, ha igaz és sikerül neki, szintén velünk fog kijönni
és nagyon rendes becsületes magyar parasztgyerek. O lepett meg husvétkor,
hàlàbol, hogy Frici mindenfélét elintéz neki, hàrom gyönyörü pàr uj szan-
dàllal a gyerekeknek. - Fricikének elég rossz bizonyitvànya van, nem enge-
dik tovàbb, de nekem az a benyomàsom, hogy rengeteget tanult, föleg szépen
és folyékonyan beszél franciàul, azutàn elég tisztességesen ir is helyes-
iràst, ami igazàn nem könnyü dolog, hamar megért valamit, de hamar is el-
felejti. Nagyon hiànyzik neki, hogy nincsen iskolatàrsa akivel együtt jàt-
szanék és én sem érek rà neki segiteni a sok hàzi munkàtol vasàrnaponként.
Mindent összevetve csak azt az egy hàtrànyàt làtom a dolognak, hogy valo-
szinüleg bàntja, hogy nem tudja elérni a többi gyereket, és épen ezért kicsit kedvetlen is néha az iskolàban. Ez azonban màs iskolàban is igy lett
volna, mert magyarul sem tudott volna többet, és ez az intézet részben szi-
gorubb, vagyis sokkal többet tanulnak, tulajdonképen félig màr elsö gymnà-
zium a tananyag, màsrészt pedig a jo koszt és a sok sport az amit sehol
sem kaphattam volna meg jobban. Igy a mi körülményeinkhez képest ugy érzem
mindent kihasznàltam amit csak lehetett és nem hiàba töltötte el az idöt.
Az, hogy minden vasàrnap hazajöhet és én tarthatom rendbe a ruhàjàt, ez is
rengeteget szàmit. Emellett megtanult önàlloan beosztani, hogy mit, mikor
és hogyan öltözködjék, egyedül kell neki gondoskodni, hogy a szennyest haza
hozza, szoval önàllosàgban rengeteget haladt és amellettmégis minden héten
làthattam. Egyszer tul sokat büntették, folyton collé (igy mondjàk, ha bün-
tetésböl bennmarad) volt, de làva, hogy csak nyakasabb lesz töle és föleg
nekem kényelmetlen, hogy utàna kell küldeni a tiszta ruhàt és nem kapom
vissza a szennyest (àltalàban ugyanis mindenböl egy vàltàst tartok elö
igy azutàn hiànyzik) megmondtam a tanitonönek, hogy ugy làtom nem hasznàl
neki és azota rendszeresen hazajàr. Persze tudom, hogy épen ugy ràszolgàl
a lustasàgàval és szorakozottsàgàval mint azelött, de az az érzésem, hogy
ha hazajön, többet hasznàl neki, mintha ott pàr büntetésleckét megir.

Figure 79: June 6, 1948, the first page of the original letter

Dear Sweet Mother and Father,

Thank you for your letter and the receipts and also just everything. I am glad Mama received part of her pension. I worried about that. I already tried to write Zsuzsa about our plan about what is ahead of us. We don't really know about our budget.

But it doesn't matter, believe me, a person can make a living by being honest. We live that way and we sleep peacefully. Our conscience is clear and this is a wealth in today's world.

My Dear Mother, you very much realize our situation and you have given us wise advice to be careful about people using us. It feels good that you are so aware of our difficulties. I am always very grateful for your advice, even if I don't agree. It doesn't bother me. I can learn from it. You have seen so much more than I have and you can more peacefully and wisely take care of things.

There is a good side of our present situation. Sometimes I can be alone with Frici during the weekday when the kids are at school and we can talk and work out everything peacefully. Nobody comes by, not even the dogs. We don't know anybody at the school where the kids are; in fact we don't have anybody close that we can talk to about the kids, especially since Else Augenthaler left. I used to tell her some nice stories about the kids. It is a good feeling to sit down and fill out a long letter to you about the kids and I will do it again in the future.

Hapsi luckily is getting over a severe stomach problem. He still looks a little pale, but he soon will be all right. Little Frici also had the same problem, but he was well taken care of in the French boarding school. He only stayed in bed for a day, but he still looks a little pale. I don't worry as much about Little Frici because he has become very strong and hardy from all the sports at the French school. As long as he eats well, he will be all right. The food is very good there. They often get cherries, bananas and salad with hard-boiled eggs. I also always pack him some food and he looks very good.

They are typical teenagers. The other day he told me the story when they got some cherries with a note beside it that everybody has to share 25 cherries. There were 8 kids at the table and one was assigned to divide up all the cherries. After dividing them up, there was one left. He had to cut the one cherry into eight pieces so everyone at the table can get an equal share. Now he is playing football (soccer) and he wonders a little when he comes home about the use of his head in hitting the ball. Of course, every weekend when he comes home there is shoe repair work. Luckily, there is a young honest Hungarian shoe repairman who always fixes his shoes. If it is possible, he will come with us when we leave. Frici always made sure he was taken care of and for this on Easter, he surprised us with three beautiful leather sandals for the kids.

One time he (*young Fred*) was punished, "colle" (this is how they called it) for something and he could not come home on Sunday. This didn't help him. It just made him more stubborn and it was very inconvenient for me to have to send over the clean clothes and not get the dirty clothes back. It was set up so there was a change of clothes of everything. I told the teacher that it was not helping to keep him from coming home and afterwards he always came home every weekend. It helps much more if he comes home every weekend and writes some punishment lessons in school.

I think there are a lot of things that happen at school that he doesn't tell me when he comes home. I think it is because he doesn't have that much time and it is good to just be home in a safe and peaceful place. There will be a time when he will tell the stories. I notice that when it is time to leave back to school on Sundays, he is not sure he wants to go, but he very nicely holds his emotions back. This will not hurt him, just so he doesn't become indifferent about it and he may be susceptible to it.

Now I feel with little Frici and that we should be closer together. I hope this will somehow happen. Of course I would have to quit my job. I always felt that we are good friends. He has such a great awareness of everything around him, especially when we are preparing for Christmas and for surprises for the little ones. Little Frici often suggests what we should do for the little ones and acts a lot older than just the oldest brother. But he also becomes a little boy and can become a very big donkey, or a wild teenager. But I enjoy this also, and I never say no or scold him.

He has such good movement because of the sports. This Sunday he said that he can leap one meter high already. He will be swimming now, of course he already knows how, but I think that it has been so long since he's been in the water that he will be a little reluctant to start. There is a swimming place there and a physical education instructor who watches them. Of course there is a lot of splashing around.

Just think how happy I am that he is able to swim in May outdoors. No Austrian school can give him that. It was very unusual, two weeks ago they were swimming and all of a sudden it got so cold that a half meter of snow fell and then they were skiing.

Now it has started to get warm again, especially during the day. Around 2 o'clock, it is hot near the mountains. Now that the weather is nice, we are getting together with other people. On Sunday I took them to a family that lived in a nice villa. They were Hungarians. The kids were smart and well behaved. I liked them and I think they will be good for my kids to get acquainted with them. Now they are also starting to learn how to greet and not to just wildly run everywhere.

The kids remember their grandparents very well, especially the two older ones. My Dear Mother, believe it or not, Hapsi also remembers some things here and there. István also had a good memory when he was smaller. Frici remembers all the different things on Nagypapa's desk and what he promised to give him. I told him to write to Nagypapa and I'm sure he will send it to you.

The letter writing is in fashion now. Every Sunday after lunch, they sit down and write a letter. Even Hapsi asked me to help him write a letter because he cannot yet do it by himself. Of course, one letter usually takes two Sundays because they take a break to go down to the yard to play.

I just realized that I have been just writing about little Frici, but there is lots to write about István also. He does only those things that you would expect of his age. He is totally involved with school and speaks Hungarian very fluently. He knows the Our Father and Hail Mary. The catechism teacher is very nice and doesn't mind repeating with the kids their catechism. He is now started writing a little. He has been learning this for the last two months, but he is still a little behind the others in the class. I was very happy when on Sunday he asked me to write a page in his workbook and then he asked me to write a second page.

He collects everything, pencils erasers, and of course money and he seriously guards them. He thinks of what kind of things he can buy, but I can see that he will not let go even a cent. When he comes home, the first thing he does is count his money to make sure it is still there. He is so involved with the money that he was upset when I only gave him 30 garast out of the change from the milk run he does.

We and the kids got a wonderful laugh out of this. He gets furious, but you can't pry any amount of money from him. Frici will spend his money on marbles, comics, and things like that and he buys them for his brothers too. István has a very angry disposition. He is jealous of Hapsi. He wants to be the one to follow Frici. If all three of them are together, the two small ones always fight. But in the school, they understand each other very well. Hapsi is like his mother. He knows how to tease István and it is fun watching them.

Now I started an idea. When István is pouting, he has to give me 10 cents. Imagine what kind of face he has. But when I ask for the 10 cents, he immediately starts to smile, so he doesn't have to pay the 10 cents. And everybody laughs with him. We are amused by him, but he isn't aware of that. István looks the best right now. He does everything slowly, but efficiently.

Hapsi is at a stage where the school kids are becoming strong. He suddenly gained weight in the last two weeks. He became a very strong child with muscles and so much that Hapsi went ahead of his two older brothers.

István is very stubborn. If he wants something, he will not stop and he doesn't do this very slowly like the little one. If once he starts writing, he doesn't stop till it is finished, no matter how hard it is. Even if the others are playing around him. He writes with his right hand and left hand just as nicely. He just sometimes gets confused and starts reading from the left. It is just with this strong will that he is able to write. He eats very well with his right hand, but he so much stronger with his left hand. I see how hard it is for him. Even now, he will switch to his left hand when he wants to do something in a hurry, or draw something. It is probably because of this that he has such a good sense of balance. His teeth are now coming out very slowly and not easily. The new teeth are coming out, but his old ones still are there. We had to already twice pull his teeth so they would come out straight. I think he has very strong bones even though he is very skinny. He started to like learning and he wants to know everything. His [mind] is very good. He doesn't have any trouble adding and subtracting. I enjoy how he can concentrate with his little head. We laugh about him many times because he wisely puts something together in a different way.

Hapsi is very social. His jokes are very grown up and socially appropriate. It is boring when he is not home. He always figures out something to play with and he laughs with such feeling like an old man. It has been a long time since I enjoyed myself as much as when he starts making jokes. I think in time when he is more comfortable around us, he will not be able to resist to let go with a flurry of his good humor jokes.

He respects Papa and likes him very much. Unfortunately, they don't get a chance to be together very often, because he is away so much. He is careful about his jokes and sometimes before he does something funny, he will ask what I think of it. He hasn't found out yet that he can do whatever he wants with his father. Whatever he does, his father enjoys.

He likes the little one very much. Little Frici is a lot like him. When something bad happens, Little Frici can pull himself together. Even though he is so young, he can hold back his tears like a grown up. Not like István who starts crying right away when we leave him. Hapsi sees that he can't do anything about it and he quickly tries to find something else to do. He is the one I would like most to bring home (to Hungary) because he really wasn't there much, but at this point it is not in the cards.

They are very sweet when they come home here. They are all different. A little bunch of kids that have come of age. Now the kids are the most enjoyable. They behave very well when they are home together for one or two days, but if they are home longer, of course I have to be with them more to keep order. This is probably because we are so crowded in the one room and it is hard not to be on top of each other sometimes.

You can laugh at this, but Sunday morning someone crawls out of every corner of the room and everybody tries to get dressed and have breakfast between pillows and down covers. One can easily get mad about it, but we laugh a lot with Frici and give a big sigh when we finally start out to go to Mass. It gives the room lady time to clean and put the room back in order while we are gone.

Figure 80: In 1948, our parents in Innsbruck, Austria, on the way to Mass

We finally threw away the beds. Now we sleep on our own mattresses and there are no more bugs.

It doesn't look nice, but we can sleep peacefully. We are in very good condition. I'm sending you these pictures you asked for. If only my father could see me now. I am just like a kid running around like he remembers me. I talk just as much, except I talk with a little more confidence. And of course I can organize my time much better. I can thank my troubles for not looking as old as I am.

A few times, I was asked out by 20-25 year old young men who thought I was their age and didn't believe how old I was. I decided that to them I am "Kati neni"(Mrs. Kati) and I put it in front of their noses – making it very clear to them!

My children don't respect me sometimes, but I bear that and know they love me very much.

The picture was ready on Pentecost. Once in a while, I manage to get ahead of my work so that Sunday can be spent more peacefully. Don't you think we look somewhat distinguished in the picture? Frici's picture was developed while he was working. His job is to package gifts and distribute them. He has a lot of lifting and sorting to do and makes a lot of packages.

They also had to move the things from the storage and the people from the Lager storage were able to help. I surprised them one day when I went to visit them unexpectedly and we had a very good time. The salaries are up to Kutko's discretion, but of course, Frici doesn't take advantage of the situation. This way there is big trust and if we really need something we will receive it without question. We don't have to go to the black market because things like shortening, flour, sugar, chocolate, etc. are available. And if I get into a jam during the week, we can eat from canned food, which saves a lot of time.

The way Frici wants is, "We do not want to load up our bill." But he shouldn't worry about this. Another reason we don't want to exploit the situation is so we are not tied down to anybody. This way it is also good for us and I can make something from anything. Sometimes I think of what I can do for meals all day at the office and I am very nervous when I get home to have enough time to put everything together.

Frici also handles Kutko's money accounting (this he does for free). This way, everything we claim for the help is honestly claimed. He also gets extra portions for the kids, which really helps because it covers all three of them very well. This just happened in the last two months, but it is a big burden off our shoulders. He also handles the money account for other people like the Apartments, upkeep, and supply needs. He gets paid for this also. With his two jobs and my job we can get by comfortably.

Of course, none of our jobs are secure and it is not a normal lifestyle. We are happy to have this situation at this time. My job in the office is very good now. I have very little to do and that is why I have time to write these long letters, which would have taken a whole evening to write at home. I'm a little tired of the job because there is no time for the family.

I gave up a whole lot of what I pictured our family life to be. Nevertheless, Mother, I'm not about to stay up all night waiting for something to happen the way I would like.

The office situation is such that I don't know when they will close up. I am doing well with my colleagues here at work, but I can picture even a better situation then this; like finding the Director a 23-year-old, somewhat simple secretary who has a lot of energy.

Fortunately I'm not working next to the director now, so it is not as uncomfortable. They just send me the work and if they don't send any work, that is okay, too. There is a different feeling when someone is always looking at you. I do have a telephone, a good typewriter, and I am not closed off from the world like if I was doing housework at home.

This way, I can give the kids more and they are with kids their own age all day and they learn to get along with each other. But now it is time for us to get together as a family and hopefully we can do that.

I haven't added to this letter in a couple of days because I had a lot of work to do. This took a lot of energy out of me, because it was mentally very tiring work, but I finished today and now I'm free. I'm now just coming from the school where István is. Sometimes I go early to the school and sit with him at the bench and we practice some lessons together. Surprisingly, he remembers a lot about what we read and he writes very nicely. He now enjoys being able to read sentences and he understand and he can speak fluently in Hungarian. Next time I will try to dictate to him. Now they are learning the letters and sounds of the combinations and after that the capital letters. I hope by the end of the year he will know his ABC's.

Just now, I am having a terrible soul-searching moment. We Hungarians with a little selfishness for ourselves, how good and beautifully we like to live our cultured lives. It is hard to get used to other customs. I have a hard time. This happens to me once in a while.

The package with the little watch and the books that Zsuzsi wrote about hasn't arrived yet. If you sent the package, we should have received it by now and I think it won't come. We will send a package soon to Gonga's address. Inside we tagged the items for her. You can arrange whatever else she needs from there. We will send another one also and maybe more, but right now we don't have anything more to send.

It is too bad they don't allow sending food (coffee and the like) because the permit cost excludes those items. Now the living conditions here are better. Today I bought some lemons. Yesterday I bought some oranges and chocolate and brought them to the kids at school. You can be sure that we will get whatever we can find for the kids and they won't go without anything. We have so much milk that we can give some away, which helps Frici a lot. We can get 2 liters if we need it.

Today, the problem is we have to budget the money ahead of time for everything, but as of now we are doing all right. Next week, I would like to take off from work. I hope they give it to me. Afterwards, I will be a little more peaceful after catching up with my things at home and getting ahead of the work.

Now I will say good-bye because I never know when the postman comes and I want to be prepared for him. Papa, Mama, good-bye with lots of love.

Kati

Figure 81: Family Christmas, Innsbruckk

NOVEMBER 13, 1948, SPONSORSHIP LETTER FROM THE U.S.A., "I CAN GUARANTEE THAT NONE OF THIS FAMILY WILL EVER BECOME A PUBLIC BURDEN."

This "dream come true" sponsorship letter was accepted by our parents and we planned for the journey to the U.S.A. Our parents also had a chance to go to Morocco with a job offer from the French Embassy; however, they had already made the commitment to go the U.S.A.

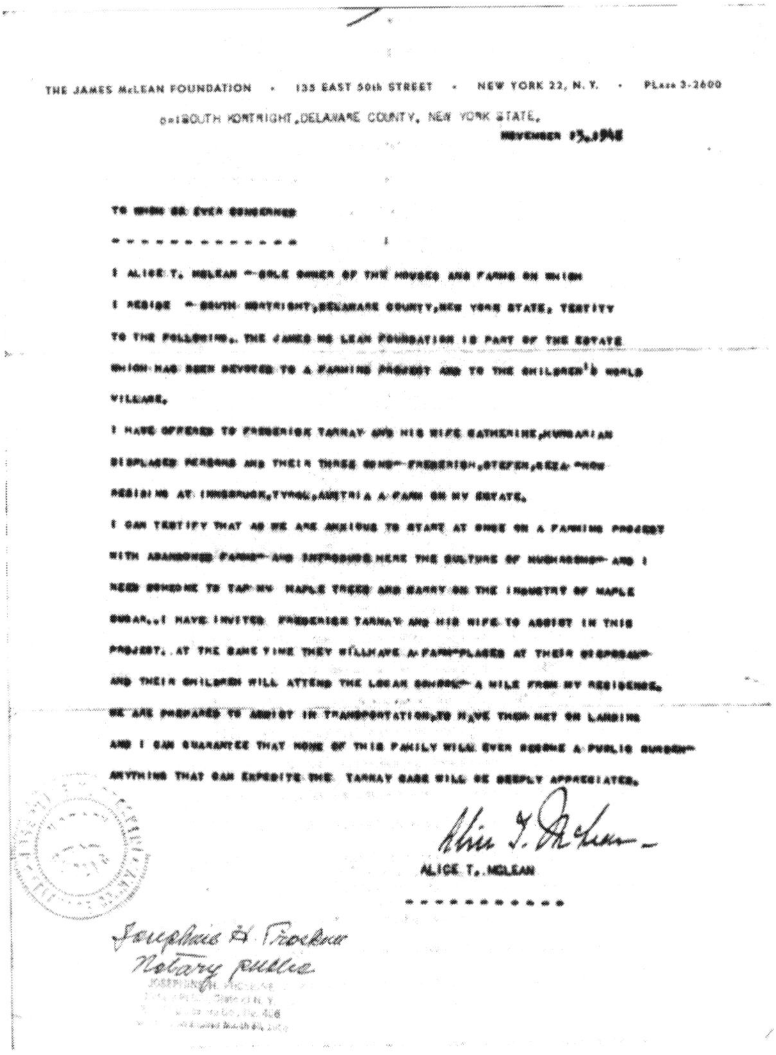

Figure 82: The original sponsorship letter

James McLean Foundation 135 East 50th Street, New York 22, N.Y.
Or: South Kortright, Delaware County. New York State.
November 13, 1948

To Whom So Ever Concerned

I, Alice t. McLean, sole owner of the house and farms on which I reside, South Kortright, Delaware County, New York State, testify to the following. The James McLean Foundation is part of the estate which has been devoted to a farming project and to the Children's World Village.

I have offered to Frederick Tarnay and his wife Catherine, Hungarian displaced persons and their three sons, Frederick, Stefan, Geza, now residing at Innsbruck, Tyrol, Austria, a farm on my estate.

I can testify that as we are anxious to start at once on the farming project with abandoned farms and introduce here the culture of Hungarians and I need someone to tap my maple trees and carry on the industry of maple sugar. I have invited Frederick Tarnay and his wife to assist in this project. At the same time they will have a farm placed at their disposal and their children will attend the locan [sic] school a mile from my residence. We are prepared to assist in the transportation, to have them met on landing and I can guarantee that none of this family will ever become a public burden. Anything that can expedite the Tarnay case will be deeply appreciated.

Alice T McLean

Notarized
Josephine H. Proskine

FREDERICK ELMER TARNAY AND KATHERINE TARNAY

CHAPTER 6:
"YOU CANNOT FAIL IN THIS WONDERFUL COUNTRY"

Innsbruck to the U.S.A.
1949 to 1956

Our determination, faith, and love persevered as our journey was fraught with difficult times.

───※───

When the war was over, we stayed in Austria as refugees for 4 years until the Displaced Persons Act opened the gates and we were admitted to this country in 1949. It was hard to start a new life in an entirely new world with three little kids, but if you work hard and have endurance you cannot fail in this wonderful country. Now we are citizens, we have a steady job, have our own home, a good car, in other words we are a happy American family.

JULY 15, 1949, THE JOURNEY, A DIARY BY TRAIN AND TROOP SHIP

Frici wrote a diary of our journey from Innsbruck, Austria to America. He started on July 15, 1949 and ended when we arrived in New York on August 12, 1949.

Leopold Scheffler and Father made special arrangements to be able to meet just before we left on the ship to the U.S.A. They met on July 26th. They knew that it would be the last time they would see each other. They met for 3 hours before Scheffler's train had to leave. They had many stories to tell.

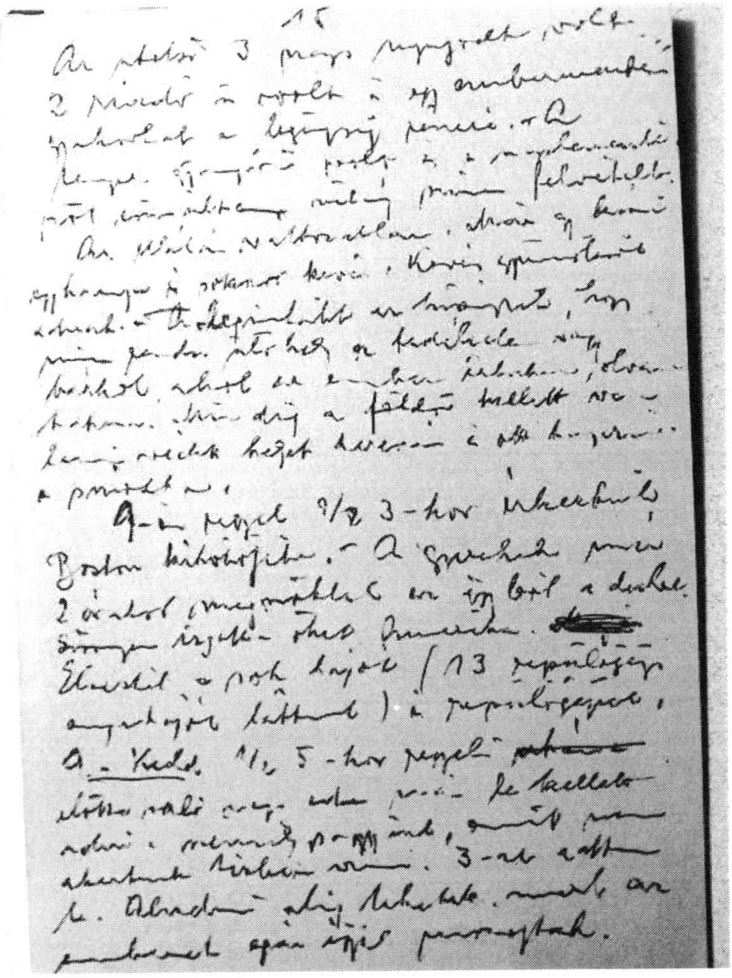

—⁓—

Figure 83: A page from our father's diary

JULY 15, 1949

The IRO (International Refugee Organization) orders at 5 p.m. came to gather in the main square for everybody to start packing up. The packing started at 3 a.m. Everybody had to think about how to pack his or her belongings and the IRO official oversaw the packing. 61 pieces had to be put into 3. We got a Pullman sleeping car and one place was enough for us. The train left (Innsbruck) very quickly. The IRO officer in charge gave me the position to take care of things on the train until we reach Salzburg, 5 a.m.

Figure 84: Our mother watching a little girl while waiting for the train. At the station the Schmidts, Daunek, Ejarek, Denes Feri, Stomfer Imre, Jesl–, Ricker Waktraund were outside and we said good-bye for the last time.

We arrived in Salzburg at 10:35 that night. Two people from the IRO organization were waiting for us. They transported all of us with three trucks to the Lehener Kaserne. We had made reservations for a room, but they had given it to somebody else. We finally got to bed around 1 a.m. in the morning. The next day we had to find another place to stay. We finally found a room in the Norringer Hotel.

JULY 16TH

The next day we went to IRO office. They were at first very upset at us because we unpacked everything without their permission. However, later we became better acquainted and everything went very smoothly.

Registration for the transportation was made. They gave each of us an identification card so everybody in the Leger group could get bread. The milk we got by some other means. Monday they brought the packages. Saturday afternoon the packing was done.

Figure 85: Our Displaced Persons ID cards. Issued to all refugees, the stamp patch says, "Hungarian Committee Upper Austria." The back says, "Keep this card at all times to assist your safe return home. The registration number and your name identify you and your registration record."July 17th Sunday

After the 9 o'clock Mass, we went to see the Peters Cemetery and also went downtown. I took some colored pictures. We went with the Kutko's to Anifba a Waldbaba which was a ½ km walk. It was allowed to swim there, but there were no cabins. We got a good tan and the water felt very good. The kids had a very good time. At 5 P.M. we came back with the bus and we bought a few small things in town.

Figure 86: A trip to a lake with the kids near Igls, Austria.

Csaszar Imre came at 8 p.m. He connected with the Nouvelle Equipe Vice President, Kozi Harvath. Talking business.

JULY 18TH MONDAY

We were written up in the IRO magazine. We got our number for our packages and pasted these up. They did not weigh the packages, but the official questioned their weight. The official was a Polish Ukrainian. We invited him for a drink of palinka and the question of the weight of the packages was taken care of. He even gave us some paint to specially mark the packages.

We registered at the NCWC (National Catholic Welfare Council). We had to let them know what direction we were going and to whom we were going to. The NCWC said that we were either going to the Benziger's in Los Angeles or to the McLean's in NY, but under the NCWC program we are to go to the McLean's.

Figure 87: Camp Grohn Refugee Center in Bremen

We went to see our Lager accommodations. It is very sad that the IRO is putting refugees in such deplorable places. Men, women and kids together were put in areas where rats and mice were common. The cleaning up was beyond our ability.

Figure 88: Refugees gathering to board a truck to the train station in Salzburg

JULY 19, TUESDAY

Today is medical examinations. We were in line all morning. We finally got examined at 3 in the afternoon. They examined our eyes, our mouths, our hands, and our abdomen. This was all! The doctor declared us fit and we had to take the report to the registration office. There they thanked us and told us that there will be a transport meeting at 4:30 p.m. where we will find out our departure time.

JULY 20, WEDNESDAY

We went for an outing to Hellbrunnba at 10 o'clock. We went to see the fountains and deer. Bad weather came in at lunchtime. It rained and the kids got wet. Hapsi and István caught a cold. I took some color pictures. It was very cloudy and bad weather. We couldn't expect the kids to behave well in this weather. At 14:50 we arrived back in Salzburg and I went with Kutko to the transport meeting at 4:30. They announced that we will start out at 21:00 tomorrow. They divided us into 24 people per group with a leader in each one. They ordered me to help at 8 a.m. tomorrow to pack the luggage from the barracks on to the train cars. The families had to meet at the front of the barracks at 9:30 a.m. That night everybody packed in such a way that in Bremen the men and women were in separate quarters.

JULY 21, THURSDAY

Got up at 7:30 a.m. and at about 9 a.m. the first truck left the barracks with the women to the train station. I went with them. We packed bags till 10:30. Then I went back to the barracks where my family was waiting.

There were 13 in our group. We arrived at the train station about 11 a.m. We were given two sections on the train. The car train porter brought in the handbags. We were all in order at 12:00 noon.

Lunch menu: A good meat and vegetable soup, goulash with potatoes, the kids also got some dessert of cookies.

I had 340 shillings left. I gave 320 shillings to Deak to arrange to send back home 400 forints. The rest of the change I spent. I wrote a page to Jestl, The Kutkos, and Radoek. We got a place to sleep in the hospital car. We were by ourselves with Peter. The kids (István, Hapsi, Peter) slept in one bench and I and little Frici slept in the other. We didn't sleep very well.

The covers were not enough and the bench was very hard.

Figure 89: Kitchen car on the way to Bremen. Our mother is inside helping with the cooking.

JULY 22, FRIDAY

We had breakfast in the morning. The kids had milk and bread and the adults had coffee and bread. There was lunch also, but we did not take it. We had to get ready to get off the train. We arrived at the train station in Bremen-Vegesach around 1 p.m. Here the Lager police surrounded the train and didn't let anybody get off.

Figure 90: Train arriving in Bremen. Children watch each other. Military police guard so no one leaves the train.

About an hour later, a truck came and all the suitcases and packages were loaded as well as all the people in our group. The truck number was #6, which we had to write down for identification. They registered us in the Lager and gave us a place to stay. The Lager was already quite full and we got a very bad place. Especially the women; 100 of them had to share the attic.

We (men) had iron bunk beds with straw sacks. The women had cross-legged narrow (called "goat legged skinny") beds with linen.

They started dinner at 5 p.m. The menu was something on the order of milk and oats or wheat, bread with cottage cheese and black coffee. We had to wait in line with about 300 people before us.

We got blankets, pillows, pillowcases and sheets to make our beds.

JULY 23, SATURDAY

In the morning, for breakfast we had black coffee, kasha, bread with cottage cheese. 15 minutes waiting in line. We found the NCWC (National Catholic Welfare Council) and we just have to be present at the meeting. After that the post office.

I quickly wrote to The Commissioner Leopold Scheffler, that we are here till July 28th and to hurry if they can come. I will wait for them at the train station.

Figure 91: Waiting in line for lunch at Bremen

Lunch is from 12 to 1:30 p.m. There is a waiting line. The meal was soup (meat and vegetables) Potatoes with very little goulash and meat and one slice of bread (not much).

We went into the city with Kutko.

A very sad scene. I have never seen a city so bombed out!

We bought some photo supplies. We took pictures.

We had fish for dinner (1.65 DM marks)

JULY 24, SUNDAY

In the morning, we went to Mass. The sermon was in Polish. Lunch was the same as yesterday. At 2 p.m. we went swimming. We enjoyed it very much. We took pictures. The kids enjoyed watching the many ships, sail boats, the water and the new sound-making toys.

JULY 25TH, MONDAY

Vaccination. They did not vaccinate us because we had our certificate from IRO. The women had to wait in line for shoes, along with 215 others in front of the American Red Cross. We had to come back another day.

In the afternoon, R. Pista took the kids to the water. We went into Bremen with the women. We came back in the evening at 8 o'clock. We ate dinner in the city. The Seelachsot was very good. Took a lot of color picture, mainly of the ruins.

JULY 26, TUESDAY

Breakfast is the same. I met with Kalmann Otto. He will go to Vorkomman tomorrow to meet with General McRae. He met with someone in his office to start work there and we will get better food. Scheffler arrived in the afternoon at 2:18. It is too bad we will only have a very short time together because the train he was planning to take at 9 p.m. is not running. I had to take him to the Lager because the family could not enter the consulate. When we arrived, Kati had news that we are too late to stand in line for a meal and we could be together to talk until 6:00 p.m.

The old man (Scheffler) had a lot of stories and was very dear, nice and sweet.

JULY 27, WEDNESDAY

Finally at noon, we arrived in front of the consulate. They asked the children to say their name. The big x ray machine took a picture of little Frici and it showed that everything is all right.

General Langfitt has already left and tomorrow General Mc Rae will leave also. The Lager is empty. They have also moved Gen. Howze, but it's not for sure.

Lunch and dinner have not changed. The women moved to a smaller place where they are a little more separated. István and Hapsi still have a cold and Kati a little bit.

JULY 28, THURSDAY

8 a.m. We are scheduled to help load the packages and suitcases today. It wasn't hard because they had already done the heavy packages with workers and heavy equipment; we just put the small packages in the cars. At noon we found out we are signed up for the Sunday departure with the ship General Haan. The list was only for those with baggage and is not complete. Rado and Mondol were not on the list yet and not in the evening either.

The next day, we sorted and arranged our baggage in the baggage area. We got a new number and we had to paste the first letter of our name on all the baggage. We piled the lettered baggage. We put three more packages into the pile making a total of 13.

    3 large chests
    2 baskets
    3 bales
    2 traveling suitcases
    2 ship suitcases
    1 traveling sack

We arrived quickly at Vorkomman for a doctor's visit in the afternoon, but it was not successful because the line was too long. We received emblems and signs from NCWC to be put on the baggage. We wrote on the sign our sponsor's name, McLean.

JULY 29, FRIDAY

Rado and Mondol are on the list now. They are in Vorkomman. Kutko and I are designated interpreters and they are designated police. Finally at 6 a.m. we had a doctor's exam, numbers check, in a small sack, shaving things, tooth brush, toothpaste, and letter paper.

I signed a paper that we are no longer in the hands of the IRO.

We brought the women's' baggage with us also. I also carried three suitcases for Kutko. I almost collapsed.

At 6:30 we turned in our bedding.

At 7 we had breakfast.

At 7:30 we are ready for departure.

At 8:00 we started out. We were in Bremen harbor until 10:00 because the lights in the sleeping quarters did not work. We had a very good lunch at noon. In the afternoon we started to work in our assigned positions. I was assigned as the German interpreter. The whole list of German speaking people on the ship was assigned to me. I saw that that all three kids were assigned to me. I tried to ask the officer in charge that at least let Hapsi stay with his mother, but he said to talk to the chief about that. I talked to the chief and he said to come and see him tomorrow. I went to the work supervisor and told him that my three kids were assigned to me and we figured out that maybe I can be assigned to be a medic. I recommended Kutko instead of me for the position and he agreed.

JULY 31, SUNDAY

A wonderful breakfast, grapefruit, porridge, jam, kalacs, coffee. Afterwards the assigned work. At noon the family arrived. At two o'clock they came up on the ship and we left.

We left behind the shores of Europe.

I announced that everybody should find their place on the ship. Later the families came up top on the ship.

Kati emotionally fell apart. (I think she realized that the hope of returning to Hungary was gone. That walk across the Chain Bridge to work became just a dream.)

Hapsi was very upset and shouted he didn't like the ship.

The lunch was terrific. The dinner was filling, but not as good, with beef stew, salad, potatoes, jam, kalács, coffee, and green beans.

Figure 92: Our mother gazing back at the shores of Europe. She is leaving behind that beautiful walk across the Chain Bridge in Budapest, her way to work with our father. She is looking ahead to the unknown, knowing she may never see her beloved homeland again.

The ocean's wave became stronger towards evening. People started to get sick. I didn't feel anything. The kids also did well, but Kati complained the day after that she was not feeling well. I was able to find a good place for her and I was able to arrange so that Hapsi will be with his mother.

The chief was very lazy and avoided anything that was work. I saw him in Frankfurt where I got a travel permit from him. Kati was with Radon and his family. The little ones fell asleep around 10 p.m. in the best beds.

I didn't sleep very well, even though the ocean was quiet, probably because I had a runny nose so that I always had to use a handkerchief.

The inside of the ship was very warm, people were sweating and the wind always blew on deck. It was easy to catch a cold.

(From Bremen I wrote Mrs. Teri and Eva and Kati wrote to her parents in Révfül-öp.)

—⚬—

I thought I would have lots of time on the ship. But I didn't even have time to write into my diary the occurrences of every day.

Exactly a week past since we boarded the ship. So far there hasn't been too much I had to do as interpreter, but a lot of time is spent keeping track of the kids and giving them direction. I gave the officer on duty position to Kutko Ronay because it would have tied me down too much. Everything went very smoothly the first few days, but afterwards the weather became very bad and the ocean was very stormy. Everybody felt sea sick.

The kids were okay the first day, but on the second day they were tired out and threw up their breakfast. They got some seasick medicine. István was much better by the afternoon and afterward the most severe weather did not bother him. Little Frici was more sensitive to the seasickness, but wasn't too bad. Kati was sick for two days and Hapsi not as much.

Figure 93: Steven and Little Frici in ship training exercises for shipwreck

The last 3 days were quiet. There were two alarm training exercises and one medical emergency exercise. The ocean was beautiful; I took some colored pictures of the sunset. The everyday life is the same. A little change is very rare. There was very little fruit. What is most missing are decent places to sit on deck or anyplace where one can write or read. I always have to sit on the floor and to find a safe place to put my papers.

We arrived in Boston at 9 in the morning and tied up at 2:30 in the afternoon. The kids already got up at 2 a.m. from bed and went up to the deck. They were very excited about America. They enjoyed the many ships (we saw 13 aircraft carriers) and planes.

AUGUST 9, TUESDAY

At 4:30 in the morning. The day before we had to check in the baggage that we did not want to carry with us. I checked in 3 pieces. We could hardly sleep at night because everybody was moving around.

Figure 94: (Photo taken on the Bremen train) We are wearing identical green checkered shirts made by our mother to make us look presentable as we traveled toward our new country. *From right to left:* Fred, Steve and Matt Tarnay and Peter and Edith Ronay.

At 8 o'clock in the morning, American officials and doctors boarded the ship. We were immediately asked to be interpreters for the officials. But later they saw my large family and said it is all right to remain with the family. We went up to the B deck and waited. There was lots of commotion.

A reporter walked among the passengers to get a story. The reporter found our five kids dressed in checkered green shirts on deck A and he asked if he can interview them.

We went up to Deck B were he took 3 pictures of them. I had to write their names down for him and who made the shirts. I also remembered and told him that the material the shirts were made from came from America as a gift to refugees. We had to wait until they took the baggage from the ship so that the handling of the baggage is made easier for passengers.

We stepped onto the dock at 11:30. It was very hot at the baggage area. We had to wait an hour because it was lunchtime. The kids were given toys, ABC milk, orange juice, and baked cookies. The families with kids were put in front of the line. Everybody had to get their papers together. A person came and escorted them to the baggage area where all the bags were in alphabetical order. There we had to find our own baggage. They only opened one chest and a suitcase. The others they just looked at and those that had iron fasteners they took off. After customs were through, the bags were taken to the baggage area.

We signed in at the NCWC, where they were waiting for the DP's.

A woman guarded us constantly. They registered us. We received our train tickets to Oneo and $4.00. The baggage was a problem because the Special train to New York carried the luggage and they only carried them free to that point. The NCWC officer promised that he would arrange it so the bags will be delivered to Oneo, "cash on delivery." The baggage will arrive a day later and we didn't mind the transfer.

The special train started out at 6:00 p.m. We were in NY at 11 p.m. There, a NCWC representative took us to the main train station in a taxi. We traveled in a first class train with air conditioning. I bought a sandwich for Kati because she became ill from the heat and humidity. From Binghamm, we went to Lackawanna with a car. There we have to change at 6 in the morning to go to Oneonta.

AUGUST 10

8:44 a.m. was the official time. We arrived in Oneonta at 9:44 a.m. Nobody was waiting. We waited a while until a small man arrived with a big car. It turned out that they got the message just this morning and they couldn't figure out which train we were arriving at from Boston. They were looking for us at another train station.

We were 25 miles from the McLean's home. We were put up in a Pension until the McLeans were able to arrange the place where we will be staying. They called the place Asher Edge Tavern. The McLeans and the Center painter group eat here. We had a wonderful lunch after which we laid down.

In the evening we went to see the parish priest who also was looking for us. We found him in the field cutting hay. He was very kind and "was glad to see us." We got a wonderful dinner after which we went back to see the priest to tell him we will come to the 8 o'clock Mass tomorrow.

McLean's friends, Mrs. Smith and Mrs. Breckenridge gave us a place to stay. They brought an Austrian paper for us to translate because they thought we were Austrian. We said we don't need to translate and we can communicate in English.

THE NEXT DAY, AUG 12, THURSDAY

We went to Mass today. We were the only ones there. Afterwards, Mrs. Breckenridge showed us the stables, the car and the rest of farm.

—w—

DECEMBER 2, 1949, "GREAT ZEAL, MARKED CONSCIENTIOUSNESS...AND ABSOLUTELY RELIABLE AND TRUSTWORTHY"

This certificate was given to our father by the former MNB bank administrator Richard Quandt. Frici used it as a reference in his job applications. Our father kept in touch with Quandt who also left Spital am Pyhrn after he completed his assignment as MNB General Manager in early 1946. He was in New York at the time he wrote this certification to Frici.

Quant was placed by the U.S. Military to head the MNB in Austria around November 1945. This happened after Torzsay-Biber, the last manager of the MNB, was put in jail by one of his former colleagues. After a committee was appointed to run the Bank, but failed, Quandt was placed as head of the MNB by the U.S. Military. Quandt, under pressure from U.S. Military and Austrian civilian authorities, ordered all the Bank papers and belongings to be returned to Hungary. He then dismissed most of the personnel stationed in Austria. These events created an upheaval with those who were hoping to go back to Hungary with the Bank.

Quandt quit after he arranged and settled the return of the MNB to Hungary. He later worked with foreign business trade as Vice President of the Near and Far East Trading Co after he left Austria.

—w—

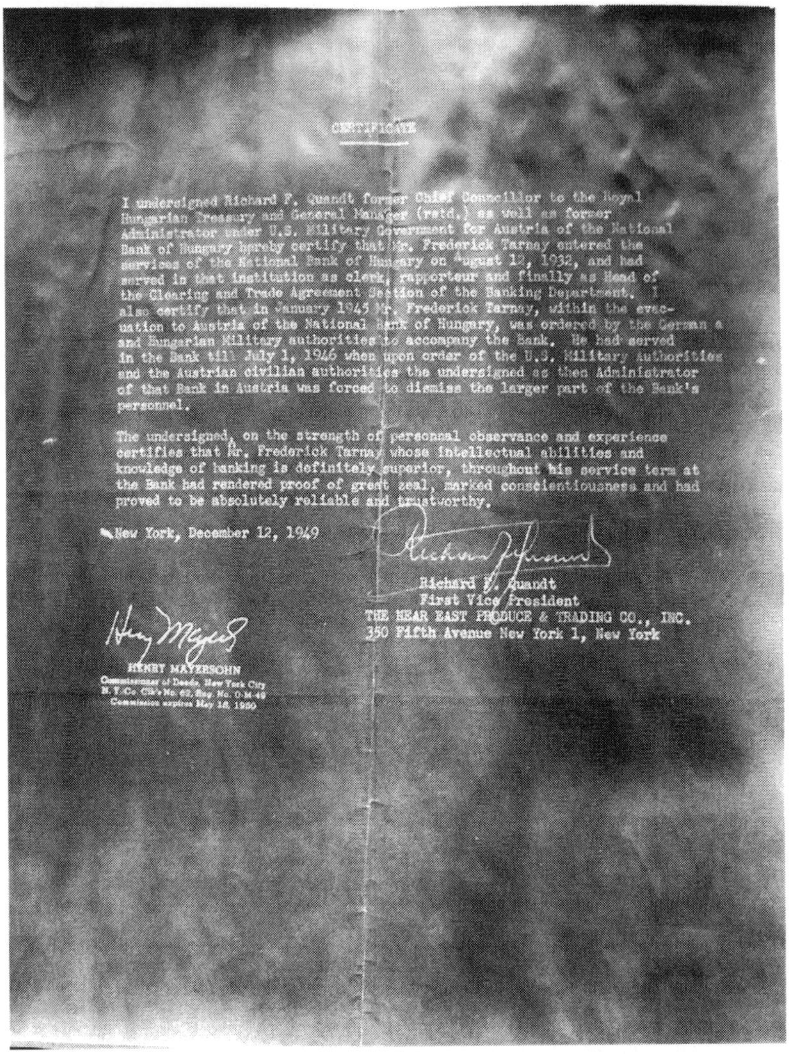

Figure 95: Certificate from Richard F Quandt, December 12, 1949.

CERTIFICATE

I undersigned Richard F. Quandt former Chief Councillor to the Royal Hungarian Treasury and General Manager (retd.) as well as former Administrator under U.S. Military Government for Austria of the National Bank of Hungary hereby certify that Mr. Frederick Tarnay entered the services of the National Bank of Hungary on August 12, 1932, and had served in that institution as clerk, rapporteur and finally as Head of the Clearing and Trade Agreement Section of the Banking Department. I also certify that in January 1945 Mr. Frederick Tarnay, within the evacuation to

Austria of the National Bank of Hungary, was ordered by the German and Hungarian Military authorities to accompany the Bank. He had served in the Bank till July 1, 1946 when upon order of the U.S. Military Authorities and the Austrian civilian authorities, the undersigned as then Administrator for that Bank in Austria was forced to dismiss the larger part of the Bank's personnel.

The undersigned, on the strength of personnal [sic] observance and experience certifies that Mr. Frederick Tarnay whose intellectual abilities and knowledge of banking is definitely superior, throughout his service term at the Bank had rendered proof of great zeal, marked conscientiousness and had proved to be absolutely reliable and trustworthy.

New York, December 12, 1949

(signed)
Richard F. Quandt
First Vice President
THE NEAR EAST PRODUCE & TRADING CO. INC.
350 Fifth Avenue New York 1, New York

(signed)
HENRY MAYERSOHN
Commissioner of Deeds, New York City
N.Y. Co. Clk's No. 62 Reg. No. O-M-49
Commission expires May 18, 1950

FEBRUARY 10, 1950, "IN THE MIDST OF CHAOS, A RED ROSE"

Our father was in New York when he wrote this letter to our mother in California. They were torn apart 3,000 miles away from each other by our sponsors. Here they reaffirmed their love for each other on their twelfth wedding anniversary.

—⁓—

Figure 96: February 13, 1938, our parents' wedding in the Árpád Alsóvízivárosi St. Elizabeth Parish, in Budapest. Founded in 1687.

—⁓—

Febr.10: In three days we will celebrate our 12th wedding anniversary. After the first few beautiful years, came the danger fraught hard times. As if the good Lord wanted to put our love for each other to the test. We passed the test, isn't that true, my dear Kati? I love you even more now and more deeply than I did 12 years ago when we stepped in front of the altar. I would like to hold you close to me and never and never let you go!

Your Fricid

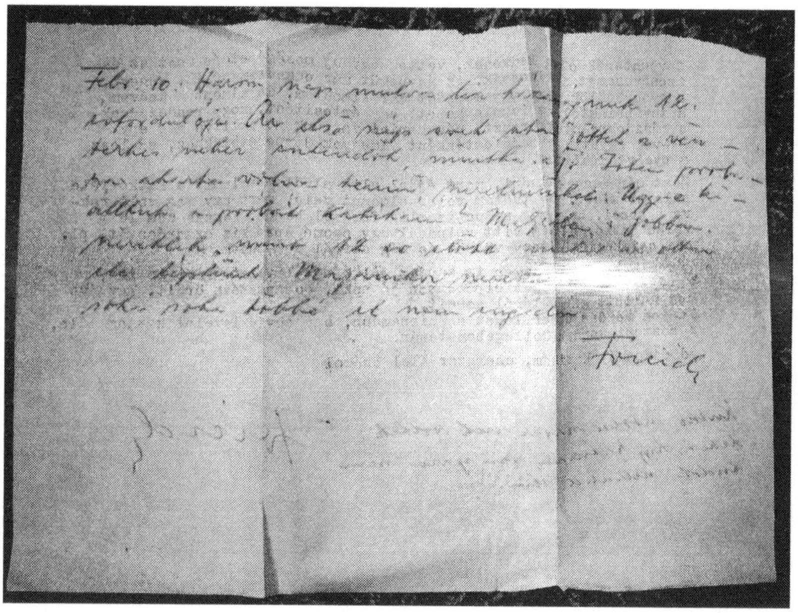

Figure 97: February 10, 1950. The wedding anniversary "Red Rose" note
on the back of a typed letter

WEDDING ANNIVERSARY
Feb. 10, 1950

In three days we will celebrate our 12th Wedding Anniversary.

After the first few beautiful years came the
danger-frought hard times,

–As if the good Lord wanted to put
our love for each other to the test.

We passed the test, isn't that true my dear Kati?

I love you even more now and more deeply than I did 12 years ago
– when we stepped in front of the altar.

I would like to hold you close to me –
and never, and never let you go!

Your Fred

Figure 98: Set to Verse by Steven Tarnay

OCTOBER 3, 1950, LETTER TO MY SISTER, "IF THE LORD EVER GIVES US THE CHANCE TO BE ON OUR FEET"

The love expressed in these letters carried our parents through the many trials that life presented. The struggle continued after their arrival in the U.S.A. and they endured by the love of family and friends.

—⁊⁊—

My Dear Sister,

I think you are next in line for a letter. It has been very long since I received a letter from you and I'm running out of patience. I usually get a letter very fast, within 5 days.

I sometimes get bored with cooking and other times I'm full of ideas what to cook. It changes about every two weeks. Now it is again the boring time, but it helps knowing that it is a way of making a living, even if it is not something that shines. It still keeps up my interest. Frici is the one that criticizes and he is the one that keeps up the cleaning of the house, you know the way he always does everything so thoroughly. He knows just about where everything is and he tells me where things are.

If the Lord ever gives us the chance to be on our feet, I wonder how much would remain. He is not threatened by danger.

Now we pull ourselves together a little more if we can, because with Frici going to night school and with the kids in boarding school, we bought a used car. Before, we didn't go to the movies because we never had time. Now with the car we have time, but now we have to save. Oh well. One thing, it makes it easy for Frici to run to school every night and also it is easier to bring Hapsi home from the boarding school. He was here this Sunday and we hurriedly drove to the older ones boarding school with him.

MAY 3, 1953, "WHILE THE KALÁCS IS RISING I WILL SIT DOWN AND WRITE YOU"

This letter was written just after we moved in to the 11th Avenue house in Inglewood, Los Angeles. It shows the happy times when our family finally was together and could feel at home with our Hungarian culture. Kalács is a Hungarian sweet bread, like brioche, often made for Easter.

—⁊⁊—

MAY 3, 1953

My Dear Mother,

It hasn't been so long ago that I wrote you, but it was in haste and I'm ashamed of myself for that. Today I received your latest letter and now that it is Friday the weekend, I put aside the entire world. While the kalács is rising, I will sit down and write you.

Now we are all sitting at the large table where we all comfortably fit. Yes, we are very happy now. The weekdays are all filled with work and I don't have time to enjoy anything. We wait for the weekend when we are all at home. I go to work every Saturday so we can have a nice Christmas. I fell behind in my work and this hurts very much. It is probably my fault because I was so nervous and tired from all the moving and packing. I think this did it, but the main reason is that the boss doesn't help as much with foreigners. They are very satisfied about all the overtime I'm working. I can work as much as I want.

The house is good, almost perfect. We could not have got a better place considering our circumstances. I think we will buy it when the time comes. Right now I don't have the energy for all the running around and finishing up everything which we need to do until fall. There are a lot of laborers living in the area and we are in very good respectful terms with them. Some of our neighbors are an old couple. The lady is a large Austrian and is really sweet. She brings a lot and feeds the children and has a good humor. She understands a good joke and is a good friend with me.

I would like to stay here. There is only the job and the kids to worry about. The kids are all doing well. Hapsi was so sweet the other day. We broke the wishbone and I won. He was sad and said that we should buy the house. Of course we also secretly feel that way.

I'm always thinking about how to get ahead, get to know people, and moving in a little more, because we are still not settled in yet. I have thousands of ideas about the house, but very little time for work on them. Frici is not the type that can organize the family and that part remains in my hands. The only way I could really save is with the food. I use all the tricks and what I remember from you, which is fast, cheap, and nutritious to prepare the food. I prepare liver pâté for a whole week and make sandwiches for 5 days. This way the meat for dinner is not as important. Tomorrow, we will have cottage cheese palacsinta which István made for me. Can you imagine that the kids are so good at housekeeping?

(The rest of the letter is missing.)

—⚉—

JANUARY, 1954, "THE LAST THREE MUSKETEERS" A LETTER FROM OUR FATHER TO LEOPOLD SCHEFFLER

The correspondence between our father and Leopold Scheffler gave a clearer picture of what actually happened during their partnership and after Scheffler left Spital. This is a portion of a letter written around January 1954 by Frici in response.

—ɯ—

Spital am Pyhrn ist völlig aufgelöst, die drei letzten Musketiere,
die noch einige Depositen bewacht haben, sind auch schon herüberge-
wandert. Von unseren gemeinsamen Bekannten ist Cottely bei der
Argentinischen Nationalbank angestellt, Jankovics in Brasilien,
wie es ihm geht weiss ich nicht, Kartal wurde von der Österreichische
Nationalbank als Oberinspektor übernommen, Temesvary ist in Ungarn
eingesperrt, Torzsay-Biber ist in Canada. Ich habe einen Artikel
über seinen Vortrag unter dem Titel"Was geschah mit dem Gold der
Ungarischen Nationalbank" gelesen. – Quandt und Baranyai sind
bei der Weltbank angestellt, Baranyai leitet die skandinavische
Abteilung von Europa, Quandt die östliche Division von Südamerika.
/Bxxxxxy;Bxxxiixnx Bevor ich aus Österreich herübergekommen bin
habe ich einige Aufnahmen von Spital am Pyhrn gemacht. Habe ich
Ihnen davon Fotos geschickt ?

Figure 99: Portion of the letter from our father to Leopold Scheffler.

—Spital am Pyhrn (Austria) is totally dissolved, the last three Musketeers who were still guarding their last few deposits have all made their way out here. Of our common acquaintances, Cottely is employed at the Argentina National Bank, Jánkovics is in Brazil. Not sure how he's doing. Kartal was named as Managing Inspector at the Austrian National Bank, Temesváry is in prison in Hungary, and Torzsay-Biber is in Canada. I read an article he wrote entitled "What Happened to the Gold in the Hungarian National Bank?" Quandt and Baranyai are employed by the World Bank. Baranyai leads the Scandinavian division and Quandt heads the eastern division of South America. Before I came out from Austria, I took some pictures of Spital am Pyhrn. Did I send you any of those photos?

DECEMBER 9, 1954, FROM LEOPOLD SCHEFFLER, "NOSTALGIC FOR THE BEAUTIFUL BUDAPEST"

Liebe Familie Tarnay !

Jetzt ist schon wider ein jahr vergangen und derWeinachtsfest nacht. Da denken wir immer besonders an Sie, schon weil wir das Schreiben nicht vergessen dürfen. Diesmal greife ichzur Maschine, denn ich weiss nicht, ob Sie meinegotezéhen Buchstaben noch lesen können. Sie sind ja nan ganz international und die Kindersienen sehen richtige Amerikaner, die keine Vorstellung von der Alten Welt mehr besitzen.

Wir hören und sehen viel nor drüben. Ob wir unsaber eine richtige Vorstellung machen können,ist nichts ganz sicher. Es ist doch vieles soAnders. Schon 'der Charakter und die Lebenswieseder Menschen. Ich glaube, wir waren schon zu alt zum Auswandern. Und auch Sie werdensicher oft Sehnsucht nach dem wunderschönen Budapest, dieser unvergesslichen Stadt, demPlattensee und dem kleinen Weinberg Ihrer Elternhaben. Ich denke noch so oft an die Tage, die ich dort verbringen durfte, selbst als der Krieg schon dort war. Was machen Ihre Augehönigen und usere gemeinsames Bekannten? Leben die Eltern noch?

(*Translation*)

Dear Family Tarnay!

Already a year has passed and another Christmas season. We are always thinking about you because we have these many letters that remind us of you. This time, I'm using the typewriter because I'm not sure you can read my writing.

The children must be must be adjusted to a new different world as Americans and have a different view than the old world they came from. Life is much more normal here now. Things have changed these days from the quiet prairie character life of the people. I think we are too old to change.

And you are, of course, nostalgic for the beautiful Budapest; this unforgettable city, the Lake Balaton and the small vineyard of your parents. I still think so often of the days I spent there, even though the war was already there.

Do you still keep in touch with your friends? Are your parents still living?

Leopold Scheffler

NOVEMBER 4, 1956, DURING THE HUNGARIAN REVOLUTION "2000 RUSSIAN TANKS"

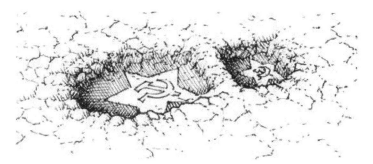

In 1956, our father had time to reflect. He collected all the documents, letters and pictures taken during the war and afterwards. He had preserved all these things, knowing that we were making history at the time. He felt it was time tell the story and that it was urgent to do so, almost as if he had a premonition as to what was to come very soon. He worked many nights at his desk and typewriter writing. He wanted the world to know the real story.

At the time, both our parents worked and we were going to Loyola High school. By the end of 1956 our father had completed his story he called "The Gold Rush from Hungary." And then came the Hungarian Revolution on October 23rd. On November 4, 1956, the tanks rolled in.

Our parents were very concerned. There were rallies staged everywhere in the U.S. by Hungarians and there were plans to go back to Hungary to help support and fight in the Revolution.

When the Russians mentioned "… A state of chaos prevails in Hungary with economic and cultural life paralyzed," they felt the Communists hold weakening. They were afraid it would spread to other satellite countries as well as Russia. They were backed and encouraged by China to put down the Revolution. The Russians took advantage of the Suez Crisis that occupied the U.S.A. interest at the time and trounced the Revolution with 2000 tanks.

Our father sent a letter to the President asking for help for the Hungarian Revolution. He received this letter (as an attachment) in a response from UN Ambassador Henry Cabot Lodge Jr. on December 8, 1956.

—〜—

Figure 100: Freedom flag pin, 1948

DECEMBER 8, 1956, RESPONSE TO A LETTER TO THE PRESIDENT OF THE U.S.A.

Following Father's request for help for the Hungarian Revolution.

—ɯ—

Department of State
Washington
December 8, 1956

Dear Mr. Tarnay:

After consideration at the White House, your recent communication to the President, also signed by others, expressing your concern for the Hungarian people, has been sent to this Department so that we might also see your views. We appreciate very much the spirit which prompted your message and have brought your views to the attention of the interested officers of the Department.

As of possible interest, I have enclosed material describing some of the action taken by this country and the free world to assist the Hungarian people.

Sincerely yours,
For the Secretary of State
John P. Meagher
Chief
Public Services Division

Enclosures: Selected material.

Mr. Frederick Tarnay
4431 Eleventh Avenue
Los Angeles, California

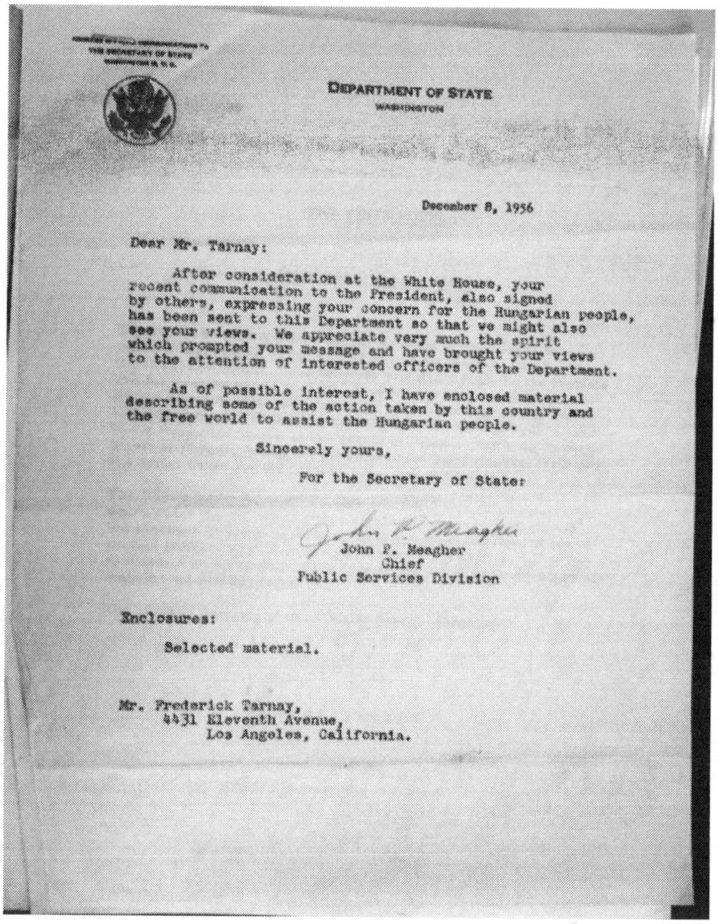

Figure 101: The reply from the U.S. State Department

[Attachment to the letter the above]

UNITED STATES MISSION TO THE UNITED NATIONS
From "News Release" November 4, 1956.
2 Park Avenue New York 16, N.Y.

FOR IMMEDIATE RELEASE

Press Release No. 2500
3:30 a.m., November 4, 1956

Statement by Ambassador Henry Cabot Lodge, Jr., United States Representative, in the Security Council on the situation in Hungary

Mr. President,

If ever there was a time when the action of the United Nations could literally be a matter of life and death for a question which clearly raised a threat to the peace, this is the question.

A few minutes ago we received word of the appeal of the Prime Minister of Hungary for help from the whole world while his city is burning. We learned that Budapest, according to its own radio broadcasts, is at this moment surrounded by a thousand Soviet tanks, which are firing phosphorus shells into the city in order to burn it out. Over Radio Budapest between news bulletins can be heard the Hungarian National Anthem which ends with the words, "Here is where you live and here is where you must die."

Here is what Pravda is quoted as saying in the typical upside-down talk of the Soviet communism: "Imre Nagy turned out to be, objectively speaking, an accomplice of the reactionary forces. Imre Nagy cannot and does not want to fight the dark forces of reaction. The task of barring the way to reaction in Hungary has to be carried out without the slightest delay such as the course dictated by events. It was Nagy who had requested bringing Russian troops into Budapest ", says Pravda, "as it was vital for the interests of the Socialist regime, in other words," says Pravda, "he admitted that there was a danger from counter-revolutionaries, that in fact he turned out to be an accomplice of the reactionary forces. And this in fact aggravated the situation in Budapest and in the whole country. The Soviet government seeing that the presence of Soviet troops in Budapest may lead to further aggravation of the situation ordered that the troops should leave Budapest. But the further course of events has shown that reactionary forces taking advantage of the tolerance shown by the Nagy Cabinet let themselves go even more. The blood terror against the working classes reached an unprecedented scale, the Nagy government in fact fell apart, making way for anti-people's elements. A State of chaos prevails in Hungary with economic and cultural life paralyzed". (MORE)

-2-

A few hours ago in the Security Council in this very chamber the representative of the Soviet Union finally responded to the questioning of his colleagues concerning reported negotiations between the Soviet Union and Hungary for withdrawal of Soviet forces from Hungary. His answer was, "A request has been made to me to comment on the report conferring the continuation of negotiations between Hungary and the Soviet representatives with regard to Soviet troops in Hungary. I can confirm that such negotiations are in progress."

Mr. President, in the light of what we now know is going on at this very moment in Hungary, that statement can scarcely be equaled for its total lack of candor and its indifference to human suffering. It should be matched against the fact that it is the Soviets who all over Asia have been proclaiming their fealty to the so-called "five principles of peaceful co-existence". How far can actions and words be apart one from the other?

Mr. President, shortly after midnight I requested a Sunday meeting of the Security Council to deal with this agony of the Hungarian people. Five minutes later the fact of this request was broadcast to Radio Budapest. This shows how quickly what we say and do here affects the people of Hungary in their struggle.

As I stated in the General Assembly an hour or so ago, we have heard from our legation in Budapest that large scale bombing is taking place on Budapest and that the staff have had to take refuge in the cellar of the legation building.

I have now just been handed the following information, which comes direct from our legation in Budapest: "Cardinal Mindszenty and his secretary presented themselves to the offices of the American Legation and have been given refuge at their request." Now, there is a fact of profound significance.

We can truly say to the Hungarian people: By your heroic sacrifice you have given the United Nations a brief moment in which to mobilize the conscience of the world in your behalf. We are seizing that moment and we will not fail you.

I have presented a revised draft of our resolution on the situation in Hungary and hope that it will be adopted.

—⁊⁊⁊—

In connection with the Soviet representative's attacks on United States activities regarding Hungary, I will merely say this. He would apparently have us believe that our

American program, which aims to fill the people's stomach with food, is somehow inferior to a Soviet program which fill their stomachs with lead, as this night's tragic dispatches all too plainly and poignantly attest.

As far as amendments are concerned, let me say this. I fully appreciate the fine motives which animated the representative of China in offering his amendment and the cogent arguments which he advanced. I do not claim that our draft resolution is perfect, because no human document is perfect, but I do submit that it is adequate, that it meets the issues, and that if we start changing it now we will cause dangerous delay.

I therefore feel constrained to oppose all amendments, much as I dislike not to accede [sic] to the proposal of my eminent friend from China, and in all sincerity and courtesy I ask him not to press his amendment.

UNITED STATES MISSION TO THE UNITED NATIONS

2 PARK AVENUE
NEW YORK 16. N. Y.

MURRAY HILL 3-8810

FOR IMMEDIATE RELEASE

Press Release No.2500
3:30 a.m., November 4, 1956

Statements by Ambassador Henry Cabot Lodge, Jr., United
States Representative, in the Security Council on the
Situation in Hungary

- -

Mr. President,

If ever there was a time when the action of the United
Nations could literally be a matter of life and death for a
whole nation, this is that time. If ever there was a
question which clearly raises a threat to the peace, this is
the question.

A few minutes ago we received word of the appeal of the
Prime Minister of Hungary for help from the whole world while
his city is burning. We learned that Budapest, according to
its own radio broadcasts, is at this moment surrounded by
a thousand Soviet tanks, which are firing phosphorus shells
into the city in order to burn it out. Over Radio Budapest
between news bulletins can be heard the Hungarian National
Anthem which ends with the words, "Here is where you live,
and here is where you must die,"

Here is what Pravda is quoted as saying in the typical
upside-down talk of Soviet communism: "Imre Nagy turned out
to be, objectively speaking, an accomplice of the reactionary
forces. Imre Nagy cannot and does not want to fight the dark
forces of reaction. The task of barring the way to reaction
in Hungary has to be carried out without the slightest delay
such as the course dictated by events. It was Nagy who had
requested bringing Russian troops into Budapest", says Pravda,
"as it was vital for the interests of the Socialist regime.
In other words,"says Pravda, "he admitted that there was a
danger from counter-revolutionaries, that in fact he turned
out to be an accomplice of the reactionary forces. And this
in fact aggravated the situation in Budapest and in the whole
country. The Soviet government seeing that the presence of
Soviet troops in Budapest may lead to further aggravation of
the situation ordered that the troops should leave Budapest.
But the further course of events has shown that reactionary
forces taking advantage of the tolerance shown by the Nagy
Cabinet let themselves go even more. The blood terror against
the working classes reached an unprecedented scale, the Nagy
government in fact fell apart, making way for anti-people's
elements, A State of chaos prevails in Hungary with economic
and cultural life paralyzed".

MORE

Figure 102: Page 1 Press release November 4, 1956, 3:30 AM.

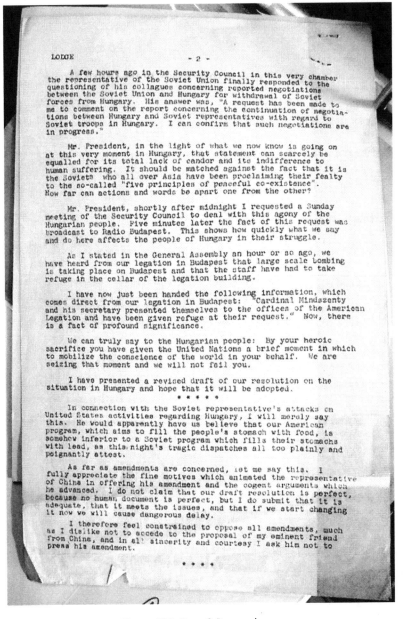

LODGE   - 2 -

A few hours ago in the Security Council in this very chamber
the representative of the Soviet Union finally responded to the
questioning of his colleagues concerning reported negotiations
between the Soviet Union and Hungary for withdrawal of Soviet
forces from Hungary. His answer was, "A request has been made to
me to comment on the report concerning the continuation of negotiations between Hungary and Soviet representatives with regard to
Soviet troops in Hungary. I can confirm that such negotiations are
in progress."

Mr. President, in the light of what we now know is going on
at this very moment in Hungary, that statement can scarcely be
equalled for its total lack of candor and its indifference to
human suffering. It should be matched against the fact that it is
the Soviets who all over Asia have been proclaiming their fealty
to the so-called "five principles of peaceful co-existence".
How far can actions and words be apart one from the other?

Mr. President, shortly after midnight I requested a Sunday
meeting of the Security Council to deal with this agony of the
Hungarian people. Five minutes later the fact of this request was
broadcast to Radio Budapest. This shows how quickly what we say
and do here affects the people of Hungary in their struggle.

As I stated in the General Assembly an hour or so ago, we
have heard from our legation in Budapest that large scale bombing
is taking place on Budapest and that the staff have had to take
refuge in the cellar of the legation building.

I have now just been handed the following information, which
comes direct from our legation in Budapest: "Cardinal Mindszenty
and his secretary presented themselves to the offices of the American
Legation and have been given refuge at their request." Now, there
is a fact of profound significance.

We can truly say to the Hungarian people: By your heroic
sacrifice you have given the United Nations a brief moment in which
to mobilize the conscience of the world in your behalf. We are
seizing that moment and we will not fail you.

I have presented a revised draft of our resolution on the
situation in Hungary and hope that it will be adopted.
                          * * * * *

In connection with the Soviet representative's attacks on
United States activities regarding Hungary, I will merely say
this. He would apparently have us believe that our American
program, which aims to fill the people's stomach with food, is
somehow inferior to a Soviet program which fills their stomachs
with lead, as this night's tragic dispatches all too plainly and
poignantly attest.

As far as amendments are concerned, let me say this. I
fully appreciate the fine motives which animated the representative
of China in offering his amendment and the cogent arguments which
he advanced. I do not claim that our draft resolution is perfect,
because no human document is perfect, but I do submit that it is
adequate, that it meets the issues, and that if we start changing
it now we will cause dangerous delay.

I therefore feel constrained to oppose all amendments, much
as I dislike not to accede to the proposal of my eminent friend
from China, and in all sincerity and courtesy I ask him not to
press his amendment.

                          * * * *

Figure 103: Page 2 Press release

Figure 104: October 1956, a boy holding a Hungarian and American flag. The rally was at the Kossuth Lajos statue in Los Angeles in support of the Hungarian Revolution.

Figure 105: Our family was attending this rally in support of the 1956 Revolution.

Figure 106: Posters say "Hungarians Are Dying To Keep Democracy Alive," "Go Home Russians," "Save Hungary's Children."

CHAPTER 7:
"SUCH TIES BIND EVEN BEYOND THE GRAVE"

Los Angeles
1957 and the Later Years

APRIL 16, 1957, "MY SWEET FRICI – MAY HE REST IN PEACE."

It was a sad period after the failed Hungarian Revolution and it especially affected our father. It was the end of his dream of going back to his beloved Homeland. His health couldn't bear the loss. He passed away on March 18, 1957 at the young age of 51.

Our mother tells Fancsi, a close relative on our father's side, about what happened when our father died. Our mother couldn't bear to tell our grandmother and asked Fancsi to tell her. At times, she seems confused with the time order, probably because she was still in a daze, overwhelmed with what lay ahead of her.

Our father passed away at the height of our family's happiness and fulfillment of the American dream. Another mission accomplished. Our father knew how strong our mother was and believed she would be able to carry on, just like she did when we left Hungary on the train.

—⁓—

My Dear Fancsi!

It was a good feeling to have received your letter. It was a drop of happiness and goodness in an ocean of sadness, because since Frici passed away, we have had just bad luck and trouble. I cannot see through or believe what has happened to us or even imagine seeing through it all. And I cannot see the future.

One morning a week after Frici died, I fainted and a Sister whom I knew well came over. She called a priest and then a doctor, and I went to the hospital. Know that I also received the Last Rites. I was only in the hospital for two days. The kids were taken care of by someone else. Afterwards I had to go home, even though I still needed help. I didn't have insurance to cover the hospital costs. Thank God the doctor said I didn't have any problems with my heart and released me to go home. I took care of myself.

On April 2nd, I let the kids go to school and I prepared myself to find a better paying job to be able to somehow support the kids.

The telephone rang; István had a car accident with his scooter on his way to school. They said they have to take him to another hospital. I was on the telephone three hours trying to find a place that would take him because we had no insurance. I only found out the next day that he didn't break anything, but twisted his knee and ankle. He was in the hospital for two days. He's been resting at home for two weeks now and he should be able to hobble to school after Easter.

Today, 4 weeks after the funeral, little Frici came home the last day before Easter vacation. He was limping with a twisted ankle. My Fancsi, God has taken care of us. Even today the shaking comes back to me. Little Frici was in a lot of pain for ten days and this is what took the strength out of my legs. Also, because of all the care I had to give István, I could not go to work. I'm "on leave" and luckily I get paid. In between all this, I had a couple of days to gather myself together. Fancsi, I don't know where I'm going to get the strength for what lies ahead of me!

I'm going to talk about myself. Believe me; my Frici is always with me. I wait for him to come home. It is a feeling I got used to because I was so much alone and it always comes back. We were married for 19 years, but had only five years together. We worked and worked so that we could give our kids a peaceful happy home.

It is as if the Lord wanted to make us get used to being alone. It has been months that we had very little time to talk. We were just running, working, so maybe sometime we could stop to rest. During the last days, I didn't even dare to speak to him. Just a few words, so not to make him nervous or worry. He got so much morphine that he usually slept all day. The last night, he was not himself. He talked about what worried him most, the kids and his sickness, and then he just closed his eyes and went to sleep.

On Friday March 8th he turned for the worse and I saw that he was worse on Sunday noon. In the afternoon I was in despair and lay down and while praying I fell asleep. I woke up with the thought that I have to call one of the priests that teaches the kids to come see Frici. What made me think of that I don't know. I called the school and the teacher was there. He promised he would come out that evening to visit Frici. This is when Frici received the Rites for the last time. He could not receive Communion because he could not bear to eat anymore. I think later he was able to take Communion. Anyway, I asked the priest at the hospital to see him a couple of times. But I didn't have time to call him up after his visits.

There is about 10 miles of distance for the priest to the hospital. István and little Frici drove him twice a day over to the hospital, which took about one and a half hours.

My Precious Frici. I cannot express the feeling I had when I had to leave him the last minute in the hospital. The visiting time was over. I didn't want the kids to stay there too long. The doctor gave him the strongest medication. It would have been too much for the kids to stay longer. I came home, I prayed, "Maybe, just maybe he will come back." I received a telephone call during the night. He left quietly, modestly, and without complaint. Just like he always was. He kept to himself the last painful moments.

I probably already wrote when I heard the telephone. I was just waking up. Afterwards I waited till 6 o'clock and then started to call all our friends, people at work, the school, the cemetery, and the hospital. Afterwards I went out with little Frici to the hospital to gather his clothes and things and once more to see his father. After this the kids were always with me. Together we picked out the wreaths, the grave and the flowers. The little ones were brave and strong.

The evening before the funeral, the rosary was said for him in the church. The next day was the rosary for Frici. The big church was full. He had lots of friends. Wherever we went, everybody liked him, respected him for spotless honesty and his goodness. Fourteen priests came from the kids school (Loyola High School) including the president of the school (Father Plushkell S.J.). I felt it was a show of their very high respect for Frici. I don't think they ever did this before and we never asked for anything special.

They once again opened up the casket to say our final farewell to him. The burial was on the 21st of March. The grave was in a nice sunny spot with a palm tree next to it which was Frici's favorite. I received a couple of flowers and a piece of the wreath. This showed me all the love and happiness that I received from him.

Figure 107: About 1940, our parents dressed up for an occasion were they received a bouquet of flowers, possibly at an event at Margaret Island, Budapest with the MNB between WWI and WWII.

What else should I say my dear Fancsi? You also knew him as well as I did. If you have time and it is not too much trouble to find, could you send me some pictures of our wedding? The kids want to make an album of their father and we have so few old pictures. A friend of mine is making copies of a good picture of Frici and I will send everyone a copy.

I have to look at the cost of materials now. I get now approximately $235.00 per month salary. Frici got about $100 more. So now I have less than half. I do get some money for the two little ones until they are 18. Frici's life insurance comes out to be about a year's salary. That's how it is now. Just this evening the landlord was here. He was the owner to whom we pay a $100 every month. We have twelve years to go to pay off the house, if we can. I did a lot of counting the money, but on my $320 we can't come out. Even with Frici, we couldn't put money aside. The life insurance is for the kids and I don't want to touch it. I decided to petition some benefit type charitable organizations of which there are a few here. It doesn't matter how hard it is; the kids are the most important. I already filed a petition, but have not received a reply. I just hope and pray for it.

Until then, I told little Frici, we need to show that we are trying to stand on our own two feet. He has to look at his job as being the oldest in the family and, if needed, to help out so that we don't lose what his father has worked for. He had a hard time understanding his position. He is not the most studious student, but he has a good head for it. He is young; this is his nature.

I also have to say I could not have made it through this period without the help of our wonderful old lady neighbor; she was like a mother to me. She brought me to the hospital, fed the kids, and was always there to help. They liked Frici a lot.

I had a guardian established for the kids because we have no relatives here, our friends are all working, and we were by ourselves. I asked the Grey Nun Director who I knew for a long time. I don't know who to thank that she accepted. Of course, we have to be humble and we shouldn't bother her too much. I think she has a lot a lot of work to do, but she is always available when I have an important question to ask. She understands the problem in a Hungarian way. She stood next to me at the burial and was the first one to come to me when Frici died. She dressed up Hapsi in a dark suit, which he was very happy about. The people were very nice at the funeral and a few stayed later which showed they really cared.

The Lord wanted me to stay by myself and why? We can only tell in the end. He wanted to punish me, or he liked me and expected a lot from me. I don't know.

I know it was hard for Frici to leave because he loved his family. Now, if I look at the three beautiful boys, with two of them on crutches, it still hurts my heart that their father doesn't see them.

This I know Fancsi, that my life is that I bring up the three boys to be good people. I ask the Lord to help me do this. All three are good. Little Frici was the most affected by Papa's death. He is the oldest and during the hardest part of his life, he may have to put his ambitions aside. He has a very restless nature.

Papa's favorite was the little one. He shows now what he is. I didn't even know how strong and smart he was. His father always said it. Now that István is sick, all his time is put in doing his chores. He finishes his chores and late at night he does István's chores and then prepares for his tests. He always has a good word for everybody. He is very funny and he still does not let up. He said, "Mama, I don't need money. Just tell me if you need it so I can give it to you." He is very practical and warm-hearted little boy. They like him in school also. Papa was so proud that he did so well in school.

He and István like each other a lot with true brotherly love. István has Papa's disposition. He doesn't talk much, is hard working, and has a prudent nature. His small habits also are like his father's. He was very shaken up the last two weeks after the car accident with his scooter. He gallantly handled the hospital. He was very lucky he didn't get hit. *[István lost control avoiding a car making a left turn and crashed.]* The other driver said that his head was only about a foot from the car when he was down on the pavement and was lucky he didn't get hurt worse. The medics picked him up from the street.

I am writing all this now because I don't know when I can write again. I have to go to work in a couple of days. My main concern is how I come out with the insurance. In this kind of accident there is always some fight over who is at fault and who pays the doctor's fees.

Now during this time, the Lord is thinking about us. Today, the office boss was here with his wife. Since we don't have insurance, he will help negotiate and told me what to do. Tomorrow, I will take István and little Frici to the hospital for some tests. This is the 3rd hospital in 4 weeks and six doctors. Every day, I phone a different place, asking, making appointments, and forever filling out paperwork. There is very little time for keeping up the house and I yearn for some time to remember Papa. March 19th we started St. Joseph Day and asked him to remember us, like Papa asked.

Fancsi, write to us often so we can feel that you are with us. Take care of our sweet Fanni for us. Papa was very close to her as you know very well.

We didn't buy anything for ourselves for Christmas. One evening we bought a bunch of things for you, Pire and Grandmother so we can send it to you. Most of it went by mail, but a few things that were forbidden remained here. The Swiss package arrived on time. Odi received some things from that. Frici didn't send any packages to Odi earlier because he sent some unusual sounding *[censored]* letters.

Fancsi, I'm asking you one more thing. I don't have time or energy to write a long letter like this to Zsuzsa. If you could let her know what's happening? I wrote my mother after the burial. The memories came back again. Maybe the best is they find out slowly how things are here. Ever since April 7, I had nothing but troubles coming up. I could only write Zsuzsa during this time. I received her address in a dried out open letter. The other letters are probably on their way back somewhere. If you can, send the parts of this letter to my mother that you see are readable.

Yes, Fancsi. The Cross, the Easter Passion, now I also walk the road to Calvary. And when I saw Frici silently suffer, I thought how great the suffering of Christ must have also been. Christ changed the world with His final breath, those that saw it. May the Lord give me strength to carry on.

May it be true what one of the teachers of the kids said when he came to see us, "Don't worry. They are their father's kids and they will grow up to be like him."

God bless you, Dear Fancsi. Give Fanni a hug for me. And I will write more often even if it is just a post card about us. With much, much love.

Kati

I just came from the hospital. Little Frici has no real problem just a very hard hit. István will stay home another week. His knee will have to strengthen some more. I received lovely letters from Odi and Piri. I will send them letters. Take care of Fanni my dear Fancsi. This letter waits for you with much love.

Apr. 17, 1957

THE 16TH CENTURY WALDER NEW TESTAMENT, OUR STAR OF BETHLEHEM

Our family's most prized possession, which came with us to the U.S.A., is a rare 16th century New Testament. It was printed in 1531 in Basel, Switzerland by Johann Walder. The New Testament symbolized the faith of our family. It gave us strength and a guiding light for our journey to the New World like the Star of Bethlehem was to the three kings.

Our mother gave it to President Father Plushkell S.J. of Loyola High School. This was in return for his helping put her three sons through Loyola High School after our father died.

Our heritage, culture, and soul are symbolized by this New Testament book safely tucked away and available for viewing now at Loyola Marymount University.

—⁂—

Figure 108: Our Family's New Testament (Pictures by Cynthia Becht,
Loyola Marymount University 2012)

Figure 109: Interior (Pictures by Cynthia Becht, Loyola Marymount University 2012.)

1958, "TWENTY CHRISTMASES AGO, I PUT LITTLE FRED UNDER THE CHRISTMAS TREE"

In this is a short hand-written letter, our mother summarizes our life from the beginning of our family. Our mother uses the many Christmases to describe our story in Hungary.

—m—

Twenty Christmases

For it is the story of your life. In 1938, our first home was a small apartment on the 3rd floor of a new house. Inside, everything was new.

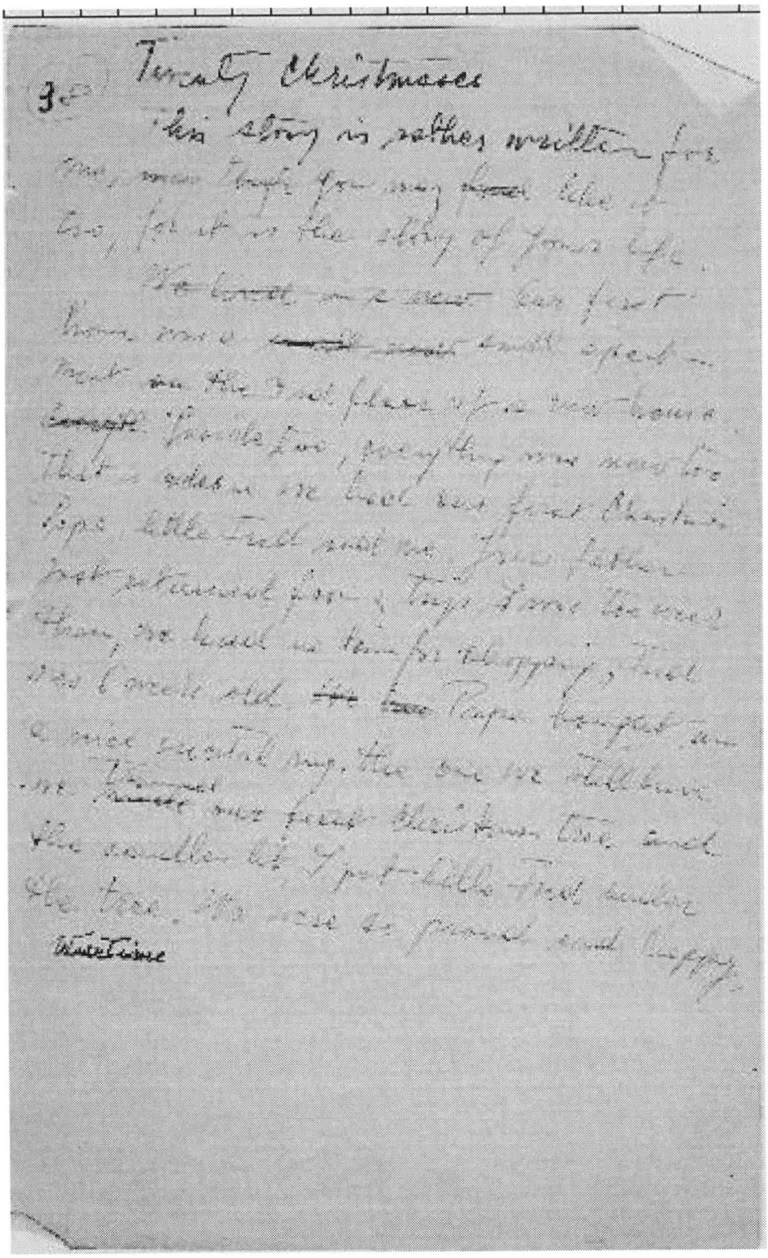
3. Twenty Christmases

This story is rather written for

Figure 110: 1958, first page of the original Christmas story by our mother

This is where we had our first Christmas. Papa, Little Fred, and me. Your father just returned from a trip. I was too weak then; we had no time for shopping. Fred was 6 weeks old. Papa bought me a nice oriental rug, the one we still have. We trimmed our first Christmas tree and lit the candles. I put little Fred under the tree. We were so proud and happy.

We still lived in the same place for a couple of years. Our home looked more cozy and warm after living in it. The little bed replaced the baby basket and the little boy was roaming around. We baked the usual fancy cookies for the Christmas tree and filled it around with toys. A little toy pulled on the string, colored blocks for building, and windup toys, as I remember.

Nagypapa and Nagymama were there as always for Christmas. We were watching Fred pulling candies from the tree and feeling lost among the toys and the eagerly marveling family.

Your father received a nice promotion at the Bank and we were full of hope and joy. New Year's Eve we walked for hours around the City watching the crowds and lighted streets.

We bought a bunch of balloons for little Fred. At midnight, we had a drink to greet the New Year. Fred was up and he had the best time with his balloons.

We moved into a large apartment in an old house on the Bourg hill (Hunyadi János ut. 15) before our third Christmas and again spent the Eve with my parents and closest family. We had a tall tree and again many toys. Windup cars were Fred's favorite. The dinner was good. Even Nagypapa liked it, though he was critical of my culinary experience.

Papa had his first attack of bleeding ulcer in November and we spent a week before the holidays on Lake Balaton in a big hotel so that he should recover. Our Christmas was a quiet one. We both had the flu and high fever.

I was expecting Steve and did not feel like going out. One felt something in the air. "Political changes."

We had two little ones at this Christmas, Steven was a strong, chubby little boy and waddled around the tree and just stared at the lights and glittering ornaments. Nagypapa would not miss lighting sparkles … and Steve was looking amazingly at it. He was not scared like Fred was the first time and he was trying to catch the sparks…

APRIL 12, 1959, "SUCH TIES BIND EVEN BEYOND THE GRAVE"

The story of our father and Leopold Scheffler is of two "enemies" putting their lives on the line. As professional bankers, they had the courage and ethics to stand up for their convictions.

The German Commissioner from the Berlin Reichsbank and our father had worked together through the normal business transactions with Germany before the war. Their respect for each other and their relationship are evident in the letter from Leopold Scheffler wrote to our mother after our father died in 1957.

My Dear Mrs. Tarnay,

The good has already left us so quickly. I often think of him, especially when Hungary is the topic of conversation. He was so calm, matter-of-fact, and responsible. I officially always enjoyed having something to do with him. We never had any differences, we could express ourselves openly. Towards the end of the war we even lived together for a while. Such ties bind even beyond the grave.

April 12, 1959

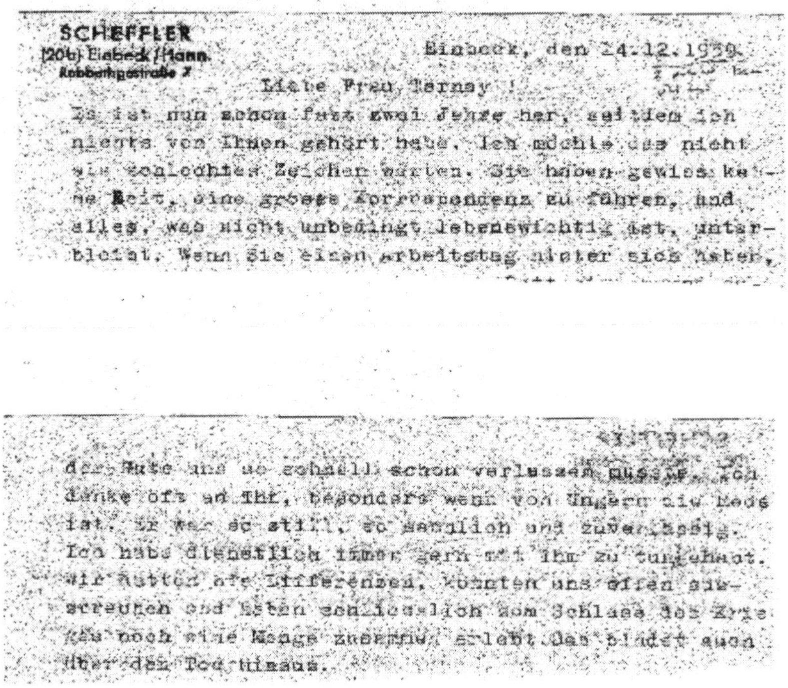

SCHEFFLER
(20b) Einbeck/Hann.

Einbeck, den 24.12.1959

Liebe Frau Tarnay!

Es ist nun schon fast zwei Jahre her, seitdem ich nichts von Ihnen gehört habe. Ich möchte das nicht als schlechtes Zeichen werten. Sie haben gewiss keine Zeit, eine grosse Korrespondenz zu führen, und alles, was nicht unbedingt lebenswichtig ist, unterbleibt. Wenn Sie einen Arbeitstag hinter sich haben,

der Gute uns so schnell schon verlassen musste. Ich denke oft an Ihn, besonders wenn von Ungarn die Rede ist. Er war so still, so sachlich und zuverlässig. Ich habe dienstlich immer gern mit ihm zu tun gehabt. Wir hatten nie Differenzen, konnten uns offen aussprechen und haben schliesslich zum Schluss des Krieges noch eine Menge zusammen erlebt. Das bindet auch über den Tod hinaus.

Figure 111: Letter from Leopold Scheffler written to our mother on April 12, 1959.

Figure 112: Steve Tarnay, Leopold Scheffler, our mother, and Mrs. Scheffler on the right in 1965, Germany. Our mother and Steve visited friends and relatives after WWII. During the visit, much time was spent talking about our families and the saving of the Hungarian Treasury.

Figure 113: Leopold Scheffler, his wife and our mother in 1965, Germany.

DECEMBER 10, 1961, "I'M NOT SCARED OF MOTHER!"

This is from Mrs. Vera Torzsay-Biber in 1961. She was very close to our mother during the time they were in Spital am Pyhrn. It shows the near family relationship of the MNB bank personnel.

—⁓—

Palo Alto, December 10, 1961

My Kati, my dear Kati,

Please do not be mad at me. Please forgive me for touching upon your healed, but still hurting wounds with my clumsy hands. But we knew nothing of your sadness. What I want to tell you, or at least what I am trying to tell you, maybe you will not believe this, is that we spoke of you often and I thought of you often through the long years.

Kati [*Torzsay's daughter*] said once, we were already here in America at the time, "Well, we're never again going to meet people like Kati in our lives," and we haven't. My Kati, I cried desperately after I hung up the phone, even though I don't usually cry anymore because I know that crying does not help. It does not make things easier.

Gyuri asked me why I did not speak with you for a longer time. He too is devastated by the news. I did not tell him that I didn't want to start crying over the phone.

I will always think of you as being put together of tiny steel springs. I know those little springs cannot be crushed, but I also know that there are many painful stages before becoming crushed.

And "must" is a strong word. Hapsi was a sweet little child. "István, you are scared of Mother, – I'm not scared of Mother." This has become a saying in our family whenever I become angry. Gyuri says he is not scared of Mother, or that he is scared of Mother, depending how he feels at the time.

When we decorate the Christmas tree, I am reminded of your tree ornaments that you hid so carefully from the Russians. And how right you were! I am sure you can still decorate a whole tree with them while the other things have become lost.

Of course, I cannot imagine what your sons are like; Frici, the dark eyed serious little boy, István, Mother's favorite, and chubby, roly-poly, convivial Hapsi. How much porridge he could eat! We are still the same old frivolous, eccentric family. Gyuri's hair has turned gray and he is quiet. My hair has not started to turn gray yet (I will be 60 years old in April), but I only dare mention this to you. Everybody here thinks I dye my hair. Well yes...things change.

Vivi has a cute little daughter named Veronika. She is 5 and a half years old already, but her parents can still not get over their surprise that they have such a pretty little daughter. We have not seen a lot of each other since we have been living 1500 miles from each other. Of course our phone bills are horrendous. In a frivolous moment, I promised Veronika that I would never die, but I have recently been having disturbing doubts that I shall not be able to keep my promise, although I am presently wonderfully healthy, but still...

My Kati, I am a very "clumsy" letter writer, but I do not worry even for a second that you will misunderstand me. I know you well, even though you don't know that and you don't even believe me. I couldn't even tell you who I like more: you, or serious little Zsuzsi Tarnay, who is only sometimes betrayed by her eyes?

You are not angry, are you?

Poem at the end of the letter.

> The weather is winter, the snow is falling,
> Joyfully glides the little sleigh,
> On it sit the spirited boys
> One of them drives the goat
>
> [*Missing lines*]
>
> The little sleigh has broken
> Indeed, many little sleighs have broken.

Hugs, Vera [*Mrs. Torzsay-Biber*]

JUNE 12, 1965, "THE NEXT SONG WILL BE A HUNGARIAN SONG."

It was almost ten years after our father's death. We were still living in our house on 11th Avenue in Los Angeles. We celebrated the wedding day of our brother Matt. Our mother describes her happiness. She was respected by other people for her strength and courage and ability to carry on after our father died. She rejoiced in her Hungarian roots and culture.

—∿—

My Dear Mother,

I cannot do anything else now after the wedding until I write you this letter. My heart is so full of happiness that I have to tell you how happy I am. And it is not just from me, but I heard from many friends how beautiful it was. It couldn't be anything else.

I know, they both are so charming and natural and they have true affection for each other. This and their happiness radiates and sticks to everybody.

Matt's mother-in-law really put together a beautiful and perfect wedding. Everybody had their own place at each table. Nobody had to go around and find a seat. There were 200 people at the dinner. It was a huge room with round tables and a long table at one side for the wedding party and where I sat alongside the bride's grandmother and where I could see everybody. In the middle of the room, there was a big area where they danced after the dinner.

Last night I cried myself to sleep with happiness and today I smiled all day with happiness.

It only sunk in when the young people started to get up and dance, my dear Mother, it was beautiful! Hapsi was so good and calm and Madeleine so charming and happy.

It was like a dream. The Mass started at 10 a.m. followed by the lunch at the restaurant. There they took pictures for an hour and after that the wedding family stood up one by one and received congratulations from everybody. At first everything went a little slow because everybody had to sign the guest book, but after that the procession started with the many handshakes. Hapsi was not bothered because my friends did not go in the line. They received a whole bunch of gifts and I think money too, because when I gave him a little money for gas for his trip he said he had plenty.

Madeleine wore a beautiful lace inserted dress, with a long veil, and the bridesmaids' dresses were beautiful. The four sisters were very sweet together and my three sons side by side. Peter Ronay was the fourth one.

I must say my dress, dear Mother, was very beautiful and the nicest of all the ones there. The coral jewel pin and the blue horsehair hat, and the peacock blue shoes were magnificent. Picu and Magdi were beside themselves about it and Kutko hardly recognized me.

I didn't have a lot to do with organizing this so very successful wedding. Hapsi did most of the family arrangement and I would have gladly helped out with affection and goodness with whatever needed to be done.

There was a very interesting scene. As you know Madeleine's father left the family, but his brother and sister were there. They talked to the mother-in-law and they were proud to know them and speak to them especially at times of special occasions and family get-togethers. An old acquaintance, that you also know from the letters I wrote you, István's friend's mother was sitting with the Flynn family. She came over to me and asked me to come over so the Flynn family could get to know me. They told how wonderful Hapsi was. These are very wealthy people, millionaires, and they were very nice to me, too. The sister's husband asked me to dance several times and after came over and sat near our table. I felt that I had to show that we are not like vagabonds and I was successful in doing this.

Figure 114: "Madeleine wore a beautiful lace inserted dress, with a long veil, and the bridesmaids' dresses were beautiful. My coral jewel pin and the blue horsehair hat, and the peacock blue shoes were magnificent."

Of course, my friend Rosemary Dieterli told everybody everything about us, since they helped us and took us under their wings after Papa's death and knew us very well. At the end, they said they would like to invite soon the young people to dinner. The

Uncle Flynn who works for a big building company would like Hapsi to come to work for him. This is just like a dream what is happening here. If someone is good, they are attached to them. And my Hapsi is very good. I don't know what the mother-in-law would say that I made friends with the family, but I did it for the young people so they can come closer together.

The morning was phenomenal. The four boys packed themselves into those stiff starched shirts and fumbled with all those buttons and straps that went along with tuxedo coat and they looked very distinguished. Little Frici with his army experience in shining shoes polished everybody's shoes to a mirror finish. They worked together and had a good time. Hapsi entertained with his good humor. I did put a word to them that they should be a little more serious and quiet during the ceremony.

Little Frici left early because he had to be at work at 4 a.m. and István is now sleeping. He was dead tired. You know he takes everything so seriously and helps everywhere. I think that he feels a little bad because he is the only one alone now. I understand that it is difficult, especially him who had such a close brotherly connection with them. And because of that I pray that God would help him also.

Sharon was sweet. She socialized with all of my friends.

Of course, she went along with me everywhere. I proudly introduced her and she was so nice and beautiful. She knows Frici so well and she smartly directs him and is modest. Today was also very nice. My friend Pista said it was elegant. He called me at home to tell me how beautiful the wedding was and up till now he was very critical about everything. For instance, he always said that I spoil the kids and he can't understand that it is just my affection for them. Now maybe he understands. At the wedding, I didn't speak with the Hungarians much except when I went around meeting everybody. I would rather talk with the family.

Now I write things as they come to mind, not in any order. The boys were in the processes of getting dressed, when Peter showed up. Hapsi said, "Finally he is here who is going to take my place today!" Peter got really frightened. He is a very big boy. He is two meters tall, like a bear, but like a little kid. My kids really like him.

The band was next to me and I asked them if they knew a Hungarian song. And they said over the microphone, "The next song will be a Hungarian song," after which everybody gave a huge clap. Madeleine's grandmother is the same age as you, amazingly dear old Lady. I liked her from the first moment we met. She said if I go see you, "Give my love to your mother." When they started the wedding dance, I cried and she quietly held my hand.

At the end, the usual habit is everybody goes around giving hugs to each other. All the old friends of My Frici came by and greeted me with tears in their eyes.

We waited till the bride and groom changed clothes for their honeymoon trip, meanwhile the kids decorated the car. They did all kinds of funny things. They wrote on the windows, they tied some cans on a string in the back of the car, and they followed them with their cars, honking their horns. Of course only their friends took part in the send off.

In a sure way, I mumbled to my friends what I remember my father told me, that I did not believe, that "You will also experience this in time." Later it came to my mind that I used exactly the same words as they did. I think you also know that Hapsi is much like Grandfather; his sense of style, his manners, and the way he dances, with old fashioned and sweeping gestures. This is why the dance was so nice and distinguished. Everybody was just staring at them. I will never forget that moment. Someone took movies and there were lots of pictures taken.

At the end I can sum it up. I feel so lucky that God gave me such abundant blessings. I do not know what I did to deserve this. Of course I did not see Hapsi very much. We danced for a couple of minutes. He said, "It's been a long time since I danced with you." When he was little, I brought him to dance school. All three of my sons are like their Dad. They do not show their emotions outwardly, but they can be very loving. The celebration and respect that was shown to me all came from them.

I was proud of the many friends of my Frici who came in his memory and who saw what became of the kids.

I am not ready yet, but the time will pass calmly. I will need to help Little Frici, but Sharon guides the family so well that they will also get ahead somehow.

I am putting a wedding napkin in this letter with all the kid's signatures and I will send the pictures when they are ready. My Dear Mother, everything was so much more beautiful and warm than how I have written you. The way it was cannot be expressed in words.

I'm cleaning the house now and pressing the agent to sell the house. I don't have time to think about the memories, there is much work ahead. I know you are waiting for my letter and I'm hurrying to send it in the mail.

With much much love and hug you with happiness.

Your Kati
June 12, 1965

A HUNGARIAN DANCE: A NEW SONG AND A "CSERKI" CSÁRDÁS DANCE

Our great uncle Alajos Tarnay wrote a popular romantic Csárdás song, "The Steam Train Goes Down Its Way" ("Megy a Gözös lefelé"). When Mother suggested a Hungarian song at Matt's wedding, it was a Csárdás song like our Uncle's. It is also a symbol of our continuing Hungarian heritage and customs in our family.

"A New Song", written by Steven Tarnay is meant to be a fast popular Hungarian tempo, called a Cserki. Our great uncle Lojzi composed the original words and music. The words have been changed to fit the story of our family. The "Cserki Csárdás" would be enjoyed by our new Hungarian dance generation.

—⚒—

The Steam Engine Folk Song
Original by Alajos Tarnay
Adapted by Steven Tarnay

[Csárdás Dance, Pattogósan (bouncing)]

The Steam Locomotive is Leaving

Steaming down the railroad tracks
Gold and treasures on its back
Never ever looking back
Leaving Hungary tears a rolling
Eyes of red and wet from crying
Eyes of red and wet from crying
We may never see our homeland. May God's love be with you always
We say goodbye, but not forever. Don't forget me if you love me

The Steam Locomotive is Coming Back

Steaming back on the railroad track
Smoke and soot coming out its stack
Looking forward never back
Coming home with tears a rolling
Eyes of red and wet from crying
Eyes of red and wet from crying
My dear Hungary here I am. Take me back within your arms
Love me again and forever. Once again we are together

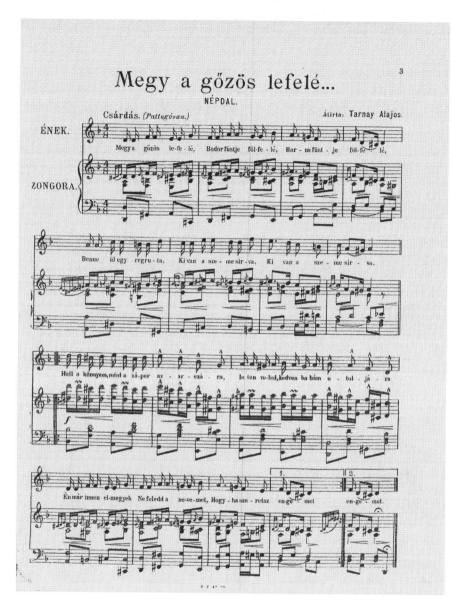

Figure 115: By Tarnay Alajos

REFLECTIONS BY STEVEN TARNAY

If our parents were alive today, they probably would say Hungary is a country straining, reaching out to find itself. With this story, we hope to inspire the youth of Hungary with the heroism of a small group of people who loved their beautiful country and her heritage.

This story brings out our culture in the many letters that tell of our parents' love for each other. The two driving forces, the love of Family and the love of Country always directed their path. The conflict between the two was there, but their love for each other never faltered. This enabled and drove our father to accomplish his heroic tasks. Our parents knew that they were in the middle of an important part of history in the making.

As Secretary to the President of the MNB, our mother held the highest position of a woman in the MNB. She was the woman that had the most influence in the successful operation of the saving of gold reserves and national valuables of Hungary. If our father could be considered the King of the story, our mother would surely be the Queen.

Today the gold may be in the Forint, but the shine and glitter are imbedded in the language and Christian Faith that created its culture and held the Kingdom of Hungary together for over a thousand years. The roots are still there and the shine can come back with time. This book is meant to give our new generation a glimpse of what it is to be Hungarian, so they can be at peace with themselves and their beautiful language.

When I wrote, "Do not forget me if you love me…My dear Hungary here I am. Take me back within your arms. Love me again and forever," I wrote it because the soul of Hungary is coming back. I knew this is what our parents would have wanted. Their story is told. May they now rest in peace.

IN RETROSPECT: WRITTEN BY KATHERINE TARNAY TO HER SONS, CIRCA 1965

We were hit by the war, actually by the occupation of our country by the German Army from March of 1942–1944. Thirty-four years have now since passed. Many events have been forgotten by me and are all unknown to you for you were just 2-4, too small to know the reasons for hardship, tension, the air raids endured by the family. You, My Sons, lived through it without knowing what was happening.

By recalling the times, reading old correspondence, visiting places, even though those all look different, they still remind me of the turbulent times, of people long gone which were part of our lives. Most of these events went by even for me, being busy day by day, but in retrospect the reality comes back after these many years. It may have been life, like it is for everybody, but with the difference that we were in the midst of history – war, turmoil, separation, all this in the true sense of the words.

Now I see what could have been done better, what all I and we all missed to understand due to unpreparedness, lack of information, subject to rumors. I wonder if those responsible had been really aware of what was happening. We were all in God's hands, which should give one courage, faith and hope in the present and future.

Whatever happens, we must say with St. Paul, "I fought the good fight." Were it wise or not, we do not know any more except that it has been our BEST.

—Kati Tarnay

DECEMBER 22, 2011, MASS IN MEMORY OF THE SIEGE OF BUDAPEST AND OUR FATHER

Budapest memorialized the Siege of Budapest and recognized the heroism of our father in a formal Mass in 2011. During the celebration, an Ave Maria prayer hymn was sung. The hymn was composed and verses written in 1920 by our uncle Alajos Tarnay. He was a famous composer and a friend and contemporary of Franz Liszt. The hymn was sung in the Latin at the Memorial Mass on December 22, 2011, at Matthias Church on Castle Hill.

As Father wrote to Mother so long ago during the Siege of Budapest, "They pray for us at every Mass. They ring the bells. They think of us."

Consummatum Est.

—*Steven Tarnay*

—///—

EMLÉK MISE

Budapest ostroma és Tarnay Elemér Frigyes emlékére

2011 December 22-én (csütörtökön) 18 órakor
a Mátyás Templomban

A misét celebrálja:
Süllei László plébános

Elhangzik:
Tarnay Alajos: Ave Maria

Közreműködik:
Tardy László karnagy
Tarkó Magda, ének
Schilling Eszter, hegedű

Tarnay Elmér Frigyes
(1906-1957)
A Magyar Nemzeti Bank egykori alelnöke
A második világháború végén az osrom idején
nagy segítséget nyújtott
Magyarország arany tartalékának,
a Szent István Koronának
és a nemzeti vagyonnak a megmentésében.
Ezt a verset feleségének írta a Várból 1944 December 22.-én.

Figure 116: Mass card

Memorial Mass

In Memory of the
Siege of Budapest and Frederick Elmer Tarnay

December 22, 2011 in Matthias Church, Thursday at 6 o'clock in the Evening
Mass Celebrant

Pastor Fr. László Süllei

Music
Ave Maria by Alajos Tarnay
Director László Tardy
Soprano Magda Tarkó
Violin Eszter Schilling

Frederick Elmer Tarnay [1906-1957]

A vice-president of the Hungarian National Bank. He was a great help in rescuing
the nation's gold reserves, the Crown of St. Stephen, and our nation's valuable assets.

*[The next line refers to the next page on the bulletin which is the note Father wrote to
Mother, "The Siege of Castle Hill"]*

This verse was written to his wife on Dec. 22, 1944 from Castle Hill.

—⚭—

Ave Maria
By Tarnay Alajos

Virgin Mary full of grace
In the twilight of the day, you light up the world!
It is a wonderful journey on a beautiful day when you are here
When you are with me, Mary, I am happy at night and cradled in peace.
I rest peacefully on your rose petals
And in the morning, Mary, Blessings like dew
Will come down from you!

—⚭—

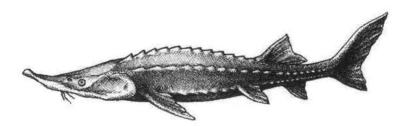

Figure 117: Danube Sturgeon

FREDERICK ELMER TARNAY AND KATHERINE TARNAY

APPENDIX

Acknowledgments

Lee Tarnay, my son, for his grandmother's (Katherine Tarnay) eulogy

Lorena Tarnay, my daughter, for inspiration and encouragement

Irén Tarnay and Joe Hari, my wife and stepson, for love and support

Erdélyi Lujza, transcription of Hungarian handwritten letters

Bényi Eszter, contribution of family source material

Feketené Balogh Judit, translation and advice

Puskás Attila, attorney, legal advice

Musci Réka, translation

Kiss Sandor, translation

Pomozi Arpádné, translation and support

Adam Schmidt, advice

Ladáyni Kati, history of the MNB

Agnes Engelmeyer, history

William Lower, advice and support

Irén Puski, advice

Toth Attila, translation

Bathó Edit, historical input

Rozalin Jánkovics, (in memoriam) for her support and history

Magyar Nemzeti Bank Archives

Liesa Scholze, German translation

Michael Ross, review

Daniel Hoffmann, German translation

Congresswoman Nancy Pelosi, for encouragement and support

Cythia Becht, Loyola Marymount University; for archives and historical support

Stephen Újlaki, LMU Dean of Film and Television, for review and advice

Dr. Vásárhelyi Judit, Széchenyi National Library Budapest

Mary M. Hedge, editing

Francie Hedge, Musical Illustrations

Krisztina Vaprezsan, translation

Dr. John Horváth, Parliamentarian, Budapest Heritage Foundations.

Chronological Sequence of Events

1932 — Our father, Frigyes Tarnay, (originally Puschmann Frigyes) starts work at the MNB.

1934 — Our mother, Katalin Tarnay starts work at the MNB.

February 13, 1938 — Our parents' wedding day.

1939 — Start of WWII. (September 1, Germany invades Poland)

1943 — Our father receives promotion to head the Foreign Exchange and Clearing Section of MNB.

March 19, 1944 — Leopold Scheffler is appointed German Commissioner to oversee the moving of the MNB Gold Reserves and personnel to Germany.

October 15, 1944 — Germany takes control of Hungary. Arrow Cross appoints Temesváry as head of MNB. Jánkovics Lászlo becomes Manager of MNB.

November 12, 1944 — Bank moves to Veszprém. They carry St. Stephen's Crown.

December 4, 1944 — The personnel in charge of protecting the Crown of St. Stephen is detached from the MNB at Veszprém

December 5, 1944 — Sunday, Memorandum from Jánkovics regarding Scheffler and our father. Our father and Scheffler leave Budapest.

December 7, 1944 — Scheffler and our father arrive in Veszprém.

December 8, 1944 — Friday, first train leaves Veszprém to Fertőboz.

December 15, 1944 — Friday, The Bank business section moves from Veszprém to Sopron with trucks.

December 25, 1944 — Christmas on the train in Fertőboz.

.January 15, 1945 — Signing of Agreement between MNB and Germans to keep control of gold by MNB.

.January 17, 1945 — First train leaves for Spital am Pyhrn from Fertőboz with bank notes and food.

.January 20, 1945 — Order by Scheffler for the train to leave Fertőboz.

.January 22, 1945 — Second train leaves for Spital from Fertőboz with gold.

March 30, 1945 — Good Friday, the last strip of Hungary is taken by the Red Army.

May 4, 1945 — Our father travels through German lines to contact Americans in Salzburg.

May 7, 1945 — The German SS makes last attempt to steal the gold in Spital am Pyhrn.

May 7, 1945 — Americans enter Spital am Pyhrn and save the gold.

May 8, 1945 — End of WWII.

June, 1945 — MNB personnel travel to Frankfurt to inventory the gold with the Americans.

November 1945 — Our father returns from Frankfurt.

July, 1946 — The gold is returned to Hungary.

Aug, 1946 — Our family leaves Spital am Pyhrn to Innsbruck, Austria.

November 13, 1948 — Family receives refugee American sponsorship letter from McLean in New York

July 15, 1949 — Our family leaves Innsbruck, Austria for the U.S.A.

August 12, 1949 — We arrive in Boston, U.S.A.

March 18, 1957 — Our father dies at age 51 after the 1956 Hungarian Revolution.

February 4, 1984 — German Commissioner Leopold Scheffler dies.

December 26, 2005 — Our mother dies at age 97.

Background – Family History

Our father's name was Frederick Puschmann II. He was born January 25, 1906, in Magyarovár. His parents were Frederick Puschmann I, who was Chief Veterinarian in Magyarovár and Aranka Steiner, house wife and also a Veterinarian. Puschmann Frigyes I parents were Ignatious Puschmann and Amalia Mészáros from the famous Mészáros family. A picture of the family's royal crest follows. Aranka Steiner's father, our great-grandfather had two brothers who were priests and the younger one Steiner Fülöp became a bishop. Our family name was changed from Puschmann to Tarnay for security reasons during the German occupation of Hungary in 1942.

Our mother's parents were Tarnay Kálmánn, Royal Hungarium Ministerium Councilor from Jászberény, and our grandmother Tótth from Révfülöp. She inherited the famous Balaton summer Tótth Villa mentioned in the letters in the story. Our grandfather's brother, Tarnay Alajos was a famous piano and song composer and teacher at the famous Academy of Music in Budapest for 25 years.

The Tarnay name originated in 1848 when it was taken up by Jászberény Stephen Taczmann and his wife Kristina Szalay family. The Taczmann family changed their name to Tarnay, a Hungarian name. The name originated from the river near Jászberény named Tarna. The majority of our parents' lives as young adults were during reign of Miklós Horthy.

Figure 118: Puschmann Coat of Arms
Mészáros family crest from our father's side. His great grandmother's
maiden name was Amelia Mészáros.

PUSCHMANN FAMILY TREE

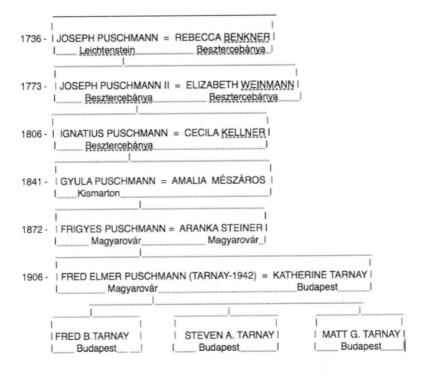

1736 - JOSEPH PUSCHMANN = REBECCA BENKNER
Leichtenstein   Besztercebánya

1773 - JOSEPH PUSCHMANN II = ELIZABETH WEINMANN
Besztercebánya   Besztercebánya

1806 - IGNATIUS PUSCHMANN = CECILA KELLNER
Besztercebánya

1841 - GYULA PUSCHMANN = AMALIA MÉSZÁROS
Kismarton

1872 - FRIGYES PUSCHMANN = ARANKA STEINER
Magyarovár   Magyarovár

1906 - FRED ELMER PUSCHMANN (TARNAY-1942) = KATHERINE TARNAY
Magyarovár   Budapest

FRED B. TARNAY
Budapest

STEVEN A. TARNAY
Budapest

MATT G. TARNAY
Budapest

Figure 119: Taczmann (Tarnay) coat of arms from our mother's side

TARNAY FAMILY TREE

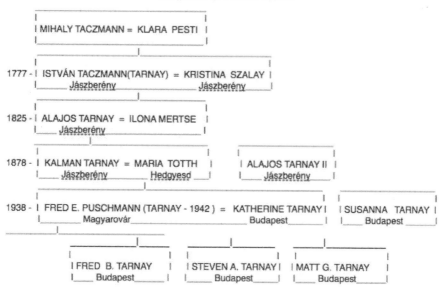

The Tarnay Family Tree

THE EARLY YEARS OF THE FAMILY IN HUNGARY

Figure 120: Fred Puschmann I and our grandmother Aranka (Steiner)
Puschmann in Mosonmagyaróvár, Hungary.

Figure 121: Our father on the right and his brother Ödi around 1914,
near Mosonmagyaróvár, Hungary

Figure 122: Our father's family listening to radio around 1920. Our father, his brother Ödi, our grandfather Frigyes Puschmann I , and our grandmother Aranka (Steiner) Puschmann. Mosonmagyaróvár, Hungary.

Figure 123: Our father hunting around 1925.

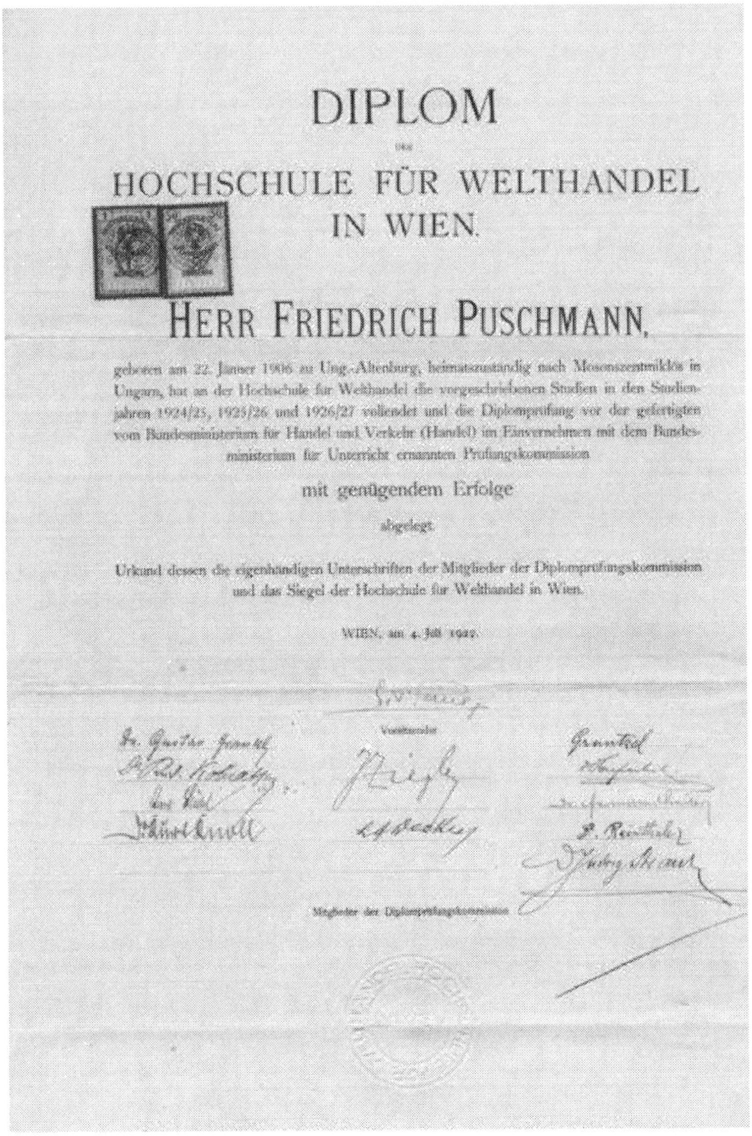

DIPLOM

der

HOCHSCHULE FÜR WELTHANDEL
IN WIEN.

HERR FRIEDRICH PUSCHMANN,

geboren am 22. Jänner 1906 zu Ung.-Altenburg, heimatszuständig nach Mosonszentmiklós in Ungarn, hat an der Hochschule für Welthandel die vorgeschriebenen Studien in den Studienjahren 1924/25, 1925/26 und 1926/27 vollendet und die Diplomprüfung vor der gefertigten vom Bundesministerium für Handel und Verkehr (Handel) im Einvernehmen mit dem Bundesministerium für Unterricht ernannten Prüfungskommission

mit genügendem Erfolge

abgelegt.

Urkund dessen die eigenhändigen Unterschriften der Mitglieder der Diplomprüfungskommission und das Siegel der Hochschule für Welthandel in Wien.

WIEN, am 4. Juli 1927.

Vorsitzender

Mitglieder der Diplomprüfungskommission

Figure 124: Frederick E. Tarnay Diploma.

Herr Friedrich Puschmann. Born 22 January 1906 in the Hungarian-Altenburg, under the local jurisdiction of Mosonszentmiklós in Hungary, studied at the University of World Trade, completed the required studies in the Academic Year 1924/25, 1925/26 and 1926/27 and successfully completed the final examination before the Ministry of Trade, Manufacturing and Transport (trade) in agreement with the Federal Ministry of Education's appointed examiners.

Figure 125: A Catholic Ball at the Famous Vigado in Budapest in 1936.
Our father is at the right end of the table in the foreground. Notice the
Császár army uniformed men towards the back.

Figure 126: The city of Jászberény Ministers meeting at the Tarnay Károly Villa kb.1860

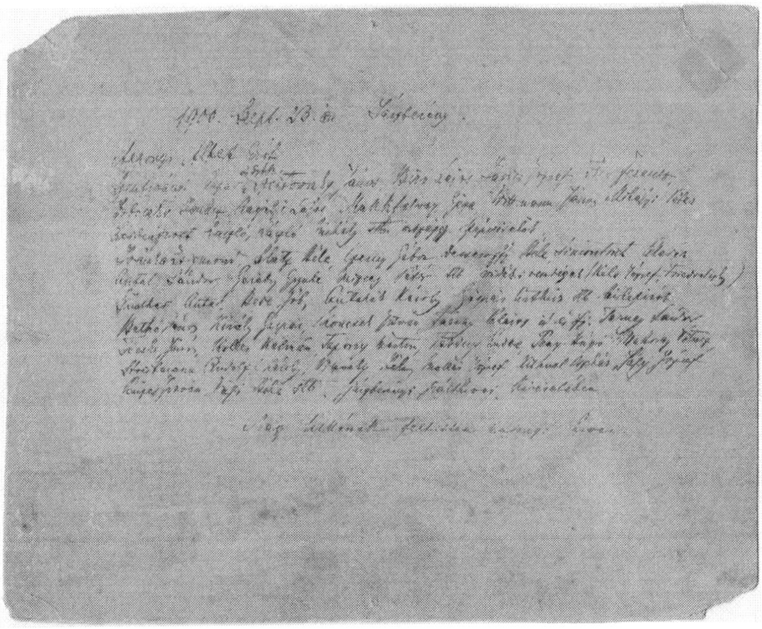

Figure 127: Back of picture with the names

Figure 128: Alajos Tarnay I (1825-1908), our great-great grandfather on
our mother's side

Figure 129: Around 1915, a family gathering at the Tarnay Villa and vineyard in Révfülöp

Figure 130: Family Gathering, Close up detail

Figure 131: A tennis tournament at Margaret Island in Budapest. Many MNB employee gatherings were held at the Island.

Figure 132: A MNB banquet at the Ritz Hotel at the Dunapoloda in Budapest. The Ritz was near the chain bridge and was bombed out in WWII. Our father is the first one on the right. The Dunapoloda was a popular place for the MNB personnel and their families.

Figure 133: Around 1940, our mother working at her desk as the
Secretary for the MNB President

PERMISSION TO MARRY

Since both our parents worked at MNB, they needed permission to marry. The following is a translation of the letter from the president of the Bank at the time.

—⚬—

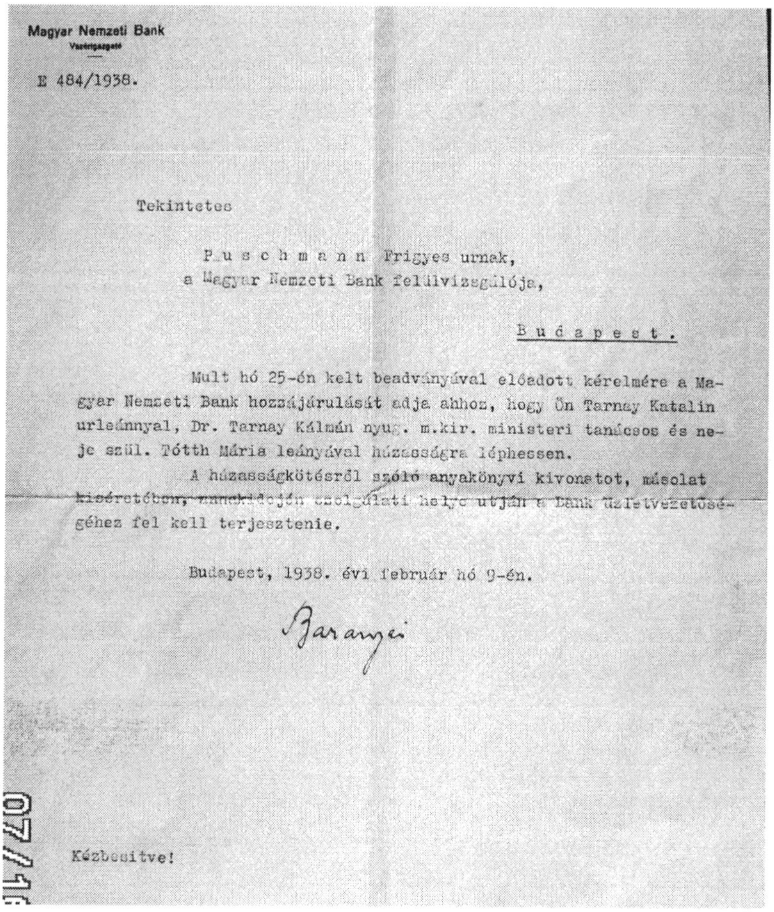

Magyar Nemzeti Bank

E 484/1938.

Tekintetes

P u s c h m a n n Frigyes urnak,
a Magyar Nemzeti Bank felülvizsgálója,

B u d a p e s t.

Mult hó 25-én kelt beadványával előadott kérelmére a Magyar Nemzeti Bank hozzájárulását adja ahhoz, hogy Ön Tarnay Katalin
urleánnyal, Dr. Tarnay Kálmán nyug. m.kir. ministeri tanácsos és ne-
je szül. Tótth Mária leányával házasságra léphessen.
A házasságkötésről szóló anyakönyvi kivonatot, másolat
kiséretében, annakidején szolgálati helye utján a Bank üzletvezetősé-
géhez fel kell terjesztenie.

Budapest, 1938. évi február hó 9-én.

Baranyai

Kézbesitve!

Figure 134: Permission letter from the MNB president

To the Honorable Frigyes Puschmann, Examiner of the Hungarian National Bank, Budapest,

With regard to the request handed over with the petition dated the 25th of the previous month, the Hungarian National Bank grants its consent for you to enter into matrimony with Miss Katalin Tarnay, daughter of Dr. Kálmán Tarnay, retired Royal Hungarian Ministerial Councilor, whose wife's maiden name was Maria Tótth.

The marriage certificate, along with a copy, shall be submitted to the Management of the Bank when appropriate.

Signed BARANYAI – President of MNB
Delivered!

Figure 135: February 13, 1938, our parents' wedding in the Árpád Alsóvízivárosi St. Elizabeth Parish, in Budapest. Founded in 1687.

Figure 136: Our parent exiting the church, the Árpád Alsóvízivárosi St. Elizabeth Parish, in Budapest. Founded in 1687.

AUNT ZSUZSI

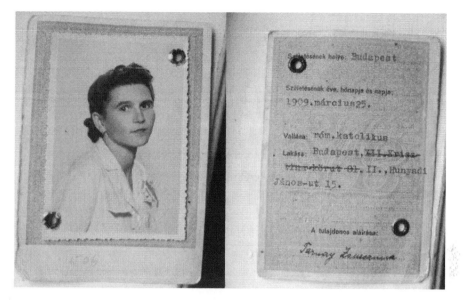

Figure 137: MNB Identification card of Tarnay Zsuzsanna, the MNB Librarian.

A great amount of credit for this book has to be given to our aunt, Tarnay Zsuzsanna for her librarian abilities in collecting and preserving so many of the documents, letters and photos that make this story possible.

Zsuzsanna Tarnay was our mother's sister. She was employed as the librarian for the MNB from May 16, 1939 to August 31, 1946. She was on the official list of employees in 1944. She returned to Budapest from Spital am Pyhrn, Austria, along with our grandparents.

She was not allowed to return to work for the MNB and was put under constant surveillance. The State also took away her home as well as our grandparents' home. She cared for our grandparents until they passed away.

—≈—

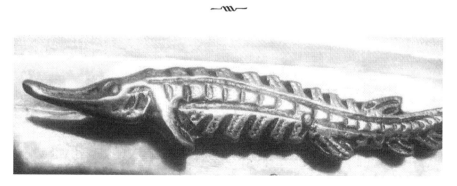

Figure 138: A Danube sturgeon pin of our Aunt Zsuzsa
(Photo by Steven Tarnay)

1944, MEMORIES OF RÉVFÜLÖP BY FRED B. TARNAY (SON)

Révfülöp is the most peaceful place I remember. When we left, I was six years old and I have always thought of it as the home where I grew up. The setting by Lake Balaton with the vineyard sloping down to the water, the peach, apricot and almond trees in fruit and the grapes ready for harvest, the house with the large glass enclosed veranda looking over the sun rising on the water still warms my heart; it is still home for me. It was our grandparents' place, 8 acres of land first settled by my grandmother's ancestors (Tótth) who built the house and planted the vineyard. Grandfather made changes and added to the maintenance building as well as planting the fruit orchards.

Because of the war and the danger in the cities, our parents took us out of Budapest to live there 60 miles west of the city. I had started school in Budapest, but things were so unsettled that I was enrolled in the grammar school in Révfülöp. Not sure what grade it was, but I remember making the number 4 hundreds of times it seemed on my slate pad.

Father took the train or drove to the city, but sometimes stayed in our Budapest flat during the work week and came out on the weekends....

We basked in the care and attention of our grandparents. Grandfather and I walked to town for haircuts and a lemon sherbet afterwards. We walked through the vineyard and he would talk of the grapes and how to check for ripeness.

We went through the trees bordering the property by the lake and he showed me how to make a whistle from a green filbert sapling, which I still remember how to do. You take a 2 inch cut, work the bark loose, and slide it partially off the wood. Make a flat cut for the airway, a notch for the whistle well, and then slide the bark back. Open the bark where the notch was.

I remember the pocketknife he used to also make grafts in the vines. Zsuzsi saved that knife for me and I still use it in the garden at times. I helped Grandmother in the kitchen to shell peas and pit the sour cherries picked from the big tree near the water well. Some work was always required in the vineyard, but the big event was the harvest in the late summer.

Grandfather had a small wooden bucket that strapped to your back made for me just like the workers full sized ones to pick the grapes. I would work alongside the men picking grapes and hauling the full bucket to the wine press in the cellar. We would get to taste the fragrant grape juice as it flowed out of the press. When the big wine barrels that stored the wine were empty, grandfather would get me to climb in the barrel and scrape the inside clean. There was a large opening in the top I could fit through.

We didn't have cows, but the neighbor had a herd and I would go get milk and cream every morning. Grandmother would set me up with a butter churn. I would make the butter, but didn't like it as it was boring.

The fall harvest was also time to prepare for winter. Grandmother would make plum butter in a huge outdoor pot on a fire. She would stir it slowly with a big wood ladle which Zsuzsi saved for us. (I have it) The jam was canned and part of it used to trade for other goods that were needed.

We had pigs, sheep, chickens, geese and goats. Pigs were slaughtered in the fall and the sheep in the spring just before Easter. We needed help with cleaning and cutting up the animals. Neighbors came to help and received part of the yield. Every part of the pig was used for something. Sausage was made using the cleaned gut.

Everything was made in large quantities both for sale and to last through the winter. The kitchen was full with the neighborhood women making bread and cherry strudel. A large table was set up in the middle of the kitchen and women on every side pulled the paper thin dough until it covered the table. The women talked a lot and it was loud, I remember. Then sugar, butter, sour cherries and spice was spread and rolled up into long strudel logs. Grandmother's kitchen smelled wonderful. It had a wood stove and oven.

A goose was chosen for the coming Christmas and stuffing it began. Grain was forced down its beak and worked down its neck until its gizzard was full. This was repeated until Christmas when it was roasted and served.

One day Father saw a weasel in the woodpile, got his rifle and shot it. Some fruit trees were full of birds, sometimes so thick you could hardly see the leaves. Father now loaded bird shot in the rifle and it rained birds. I got to use a gun for the first time. You didn't have to aim much, just point it at the tree. The ground was covered with birds which were buried there to feed the tree for next season.

The maintenance building held all the tools and things needed to work the vineyard and farm. Part of the building was Gonga's place. Gonga was her nickname; I never knew what her real name was. She was sort of taken in by my grandparents as a grown person after being orphaned. That's all we ever knew. She worked in the fields and helped my grandparents around the house with cleaning, sewing and cooking. Her place in the maintenance building had two small rooms, one a bedroom and a living room of sorts. It was spotless and painted white. Gonga would get rid of mice by making a paste of bread and ground glass and place it near the mouse holes. She helped care for us as children, she was a loving nanny. Gonga died soon after my grandmother passed away.

Our favorite pastime was going to the lake. We always loved the water and I think that was ingrained in us children. It was a short walk across the road that ran behind the property. Families had their own cabanas on the sandy shore. We swam and splashed and almost learned to swim. We chatted with neighbors and spent most of the day there on the water.

Friends had boats and took us sailing on the lake. The ferry that crossed the Balaton docked nearby and sometimes we took it just for the ride across the lake.

Father came home one weekend and brought me a red glider. We launched it from the veranda stairs and it flew over the vineyard, but eventually it crashed so badly it couldn't be fixed…

JANUARY 29, 1946, CORRECTING THE REPORT BY STEPHEN COTTELY, FORMER MNB MANAGER

Stephen Cottely was in Frankfort with our father inventorying the gold with the Americans during the summer and fall of 1945. Stephen Cottely wrote his recollections of the MNB journey from Hungary and how the gold was saved. Cottely directed this report to Torzsay-Biber, who was the acting manager of the MNB in Spital am Pyhrn.

Frigyes wrote the following correction document to Mr. Richard Quandt retired MNB President whom the Americans assigned as the administrator of the MNB and custodian of the MNB possessions. The Bank officially went back to Hungary, but the possessions were still not returned. This was approximately November, 1945 after MNB Bank manager Torzsay-Biber was jailed in Budapest.

My father was representing the Bank working with Scheffler. In this document he clarifies the position of Leopold Scheffler and his role with the Bank.

Scheffler clearly went against the wishes of the MNB Arrow Cross president Temesváry and the other German authorities who wanted to take the gold to Germany. Scheffler as the Commissioner in charge of the gold and personnel, allowed all the personnel to leave together with the train from Veszprém to Spital. It was Scheffler's negotiations with Austrian officials that resulted in obtaining Spital as a place for the gold and the personnel.

Frici describes the events that took place when the MNB switched the destination for the gold from Vorau to Spital am Pyhrn after leaving Veszprém. In a key correction, Frici mentioned that Scheffler acquired the help of German soldiers to load the train so it could leave on time from Veszprém. The German soldiers were paid by the MNB.

—⁓—

- 3 -

Ez a jutalmazás kétségessé teszi azt, mintha
ᐱként 100 pengőt és 1/2 kg zsirt utalt ki. ̶X̶x̶x̶x̶x̶x̶x̶x̶x̶x̶x̶x̶x̶x̶x̶x̶x̶x̶x̶x̶x̶-
̶x̶x̶x̶x̶x̶x̶x̶x̶x̶x̶x̶x̶x̶x̶x̶.̶ ᐱa német katonaság önkényesen és erőszakosan
avatkozott volna be a kiüritésbe.

12.old. Andre László kivel közölte, hogy a szerelvénynek
este 7 óráig el kell hagynia az állomást ?

̶x̶x̶x̶x̶x̶x̶x̶x̶x̶x̶x̶x̶x̶x̶x̶x̶x̶x̶x̶x̶x̶x̶x̶x̶x̶x̶x̶x̶x̶x̶x̶x̶x̶x̶x̶x̶x̶x̶x̶x̶x̶x̶x̶
̶x̶x̶x̶x̶x̶x̶x̶x̶x̶x̶x̶x̶x̶x̶x̶x̶x̶x̶x̶x̶x̶x̶x̶x̶x̶x̶x̶x̶x̶x̶x̶x̶x̶x̶x̶x̶x̶x̶x̶x̶x̶x̶x̶x̶x̶
̶x̶x̶x̶x̶x̶x̶x̶x̶x̶x̶x̶x̶x̶x̶x̶x̶x̶x̶x̶x̶x̶x̶x̶x̶x̶x̶x̶x̶x̶x̶x̶x̶x̶x̶x̶x̶x̶x̶x̶x̶x̶x̶
̶x̶x̶x̶x̶x̶x̶x̶x̶x̶x̶x̶x̶x̶x̶x̶x̶x̶x̶x̶x̶x̶x̶x̶x̶x̶x̶x̶x̶x̶x̶x̶x̶x̶x̶x̶x̶x̶x̶x̶x̶x̶x̶x̶x̶x̶

Hiányzik a felterjesztésben annak a megemlitése, hogy a
Külügyet az elnök utján feljegyzés formájában megkerestük az állam-
közi szerződés megkötésére. Ennek szövege melléklendő volna, mert
felterjesztés csupán állitja, hogy az elnök ezzel a kérdéssel nem
törödött, de ezt semmivel se bizonyitja. A Külügy - bár az elinté-
zés megsürgetésére a Bank az elnököt felkérte - erre a feljegyzésre
nem válaszolt és a Bank semmiféle elintézést nem kapott. Ezért a
Bank maga vette kezébe az ügyet és a pénzügyminisztert kérte fel,
hogy Boden utján a szerződést hozza létre.

Célszerünek t... anám Tornay igh. és Bethlen e. kirchdorfi
és a magam salzburgi utjával kapcsolatban megemliteni, hogy ebben
a vállalkozásban Tuboly e. és Sipos gépkocsivezető is résztvet-
tek, egyrészt azért, mert mint tanuk a vállalkozás megtörténtét
és lefolyását igazolhatják, másrészt, mert a vállalkozás kocká-
zatát ők is vállalták. A 27.oldalon a szöveg javitandó volna:
Tornay és Bethlen nem Linzbe, hanem **Kirchdorfba** utaztak. A következő
bekezdés negyedik szava "mindketten" helyett "mindhárman" szót
kell helyezni. ᐳami helyes is volt, mert tudomásom szerint az
amerikaiak hamarabb érték el, mint Linzet.

A felterjesztés nem mutat rá azokra az erőfeszitésekre,
amelyeket a Bank abban az irányban tett, hogy amikor Voreu nem
bizonyult megfelelőnek, a Bank olyan helyre kerüljön, ahol érté-
kek a személyzettel együtt maradhassanak. A legfelsőbb németható-
ságok már ugy döntöttek, hogy a Bank értékei és a személyzet külön-
külön helyeztessenek el, ezzel szemben sikerült a Banknak Schefflert
is olyan irányban befolyásolnia, hogy az ausztriai hatóságoknál
igyekezzék olyan telephely kiutalását elérni, amely a Bank érde-
keinek megfelel. Célszerü volna tehát Spitalnak, mint végleges te-
lephelynek a megszerzésére vonatkozó eseményeket és adatokat is leirni.

A leirás teljességéhez tartozna Sopron, a fiókok és a ▪

Figure 139: Section of Correction document report written by our father
concerning the Stephen Cottely Report.

JANUARY 29, 1946
CORRECTIONS TO THE "PRESENTATION" (REPORT BY STEPHEN COTTELY) AS AN AUDIT REPORT.

By Frederick E. Tarnay

I do not consider it appropriate at this time to verify the content of the report (by Stephen Cottely) that is being here corrected because this can only be established in direct discussion with the author(Stephen Cottely) in an effort to bring to light and establish the differences in the report. It is not known who is the source of information in Cottely's report; hence we make corrections only against any assumed mistakes and incorrect statements.

Apart from this, I do consider it necessary to record in writing the history of the fleeing the Bank, with special regard to the coercive circumstances of the relocation; to give an account of just the bare facts; free of any emotion and subjective influence; with the purpose of having it available at any time the need for it might arise. Moreover, I consider it absolutely necessary to hand over such document to Mr. Quandt, retired president, in his capacity as the officially appointed custodian of the Bank's possessions, informing him and perhaps others to see the story objectively.

Therefore, I make my observations from this viewpoint and emphasize that I comment only on those events that I am familiar with through my official assignment.

In general, while striving for an appearance of objectivity, the "Presentation" is nevertheless woven through with subjective and emotional moments. These might give the impression that the documented writing reflects the events with a certain slant. There is a strong impression of washing of the documentation of a series of small, insignificant events and incidents and drawing from them compelling conclusions with a strong exculpatory flavor.

Page 7. Mr. Scheffler's assignment doubtlessly included the relocation of not only the valuables, but of suitable personnel as well, hence his interests were not constrained to the valuables.

In the beginning, based on the Bank's data, he understood a head count of 250-300 and he took his steps and sent his reports to the competent German authorities, based on that. His objections to the latter increase in the head count was therefore not based on principle or practical reasons, since he was afraid such would make it more difficult to settle the Bank. Hence he would not object to claim that, along with the president, he would have used a head count as low as possible. Such a claim is contradicted by the fact that, upon the Bank's request – and against the president's (Temesváry) stand – he supported the substantial expansion and filled out the documents (Ausweis), even though he could obviously have summarily denied doing so.

I need to mention this because the German pressure was obvious toward relocating not only the valuables, but personnel in sufficient numbers as well. This, I believe, cannot be ignored. For example, the Slovak National Bank was relocated despite the fact that, as far as I know, they had hardly any gold. When in February of last year, I was in Pozsony on an official trip, Dr. Virsik, the President of the Sl. National Bank complained to me that the Germans had ordered their relocation and, although they had no substantial valuables, they would be compelled to follow the order.

Page 9. In place of the introduction of Chapter III, I recommend the text below. For the original text bases its conclusion on 1) Mr Scheffler's interest in the gold 2) on his almost regular visits at the Bank, and among other things, behavioral clues. In my opinion, there is no need for such assumptions and conclusion, as it was a public knowledge, further revealed by his announcement, that his assignments include the relocation of the Bank and of the gold.

In the course of his dealings with the German authorities in the matter of relocating the Bank, Scheffler always introduced himself as "der deutsche Betreuer der (the German handler of the Hungarian National Bank").

We are weakening the manifestation of the German duress when we draw conclusions regarding Mr. Scheffler's role based merely on such outward signs.

From the viewpoint of maintaining a Commission of our Government, there was no threatening the interest in our valuables which were displayed by the (German) military and civil authorities occupying Hungary.

After the events of March 19th, 1944, in order to organize the Hungarian-German economic ties and to oversee the Hungarian economy, the German government named Dr. Boden a Permanent Commissioner of Economy, next to the German Ambassador Plenipotentiary. Scheffler, the Director of the Reichsbank, belonged to the staff of this PCE, with the tasks of conducting German-Hungarian financial transactions, of keeping an eye over the operations of the Hungarian National Bank and later, of the execution of its relocation. In this capacity he constantly urged the relocation of the Bank's precious metals, because – contrary to the statements by all official German sources – he feared quick worsening of the situation at the front lines.

"When the Bank moved its operations to Veszprém, Scheffler's staff relocated (near Sopron): he himself moved to Veszprém on December 7, 1944. By then the city was already threatened. On the same day, there appeared (etcetera)..."

The white-collar bank employees were working hard in the loading, but became exhausted. Hence the Bank hired day laborers as well and requested help from the Hungarian military. When the pace of loading still fell short of the need, the idea surfaced whether to request help from the German Military. Scheffler did obtain their help. The management of the Bank ordered payment of 100 pengő plus half kilogram lard per German soldier per day. This compensation casts doubt on the German Military's part in the evacuation being arbitrary or violent intrusion.

Page 12. To whom did László Endre communicate that the train must leave the railroad station by 7 p.m.?

The Presentation fails to mention that, in order to enter into the inter-governmental contract, we sought the foreign Ministry via the President, in the form of a note. The text of this ought to be attached, because the Presentation merely claims that the President did not care about this matter, but shows no proof of it. Although the Bank requested that the President press for action, the Foreign Ministry did not answer this note and the Bank rectified no action whatsoever. For this reason the Bank took the matter in its own hands and called upon the Minister of Finance to establish the contract via Boden.

In connection with the trip of the deputy director Tornay and auditor[?] Bethlen to Kirchdorf and my trip to Salzburg, I would consider it proper to mention that Auditor[?] Tubloly and chauffeur Sipos also participated in this undertaking, in part because as witnesses they can attest to both the fact and the course of this undertaking, in part because they also submitted themselves to the risks thereof.

The text on page 27 ought to be corrected to read: Tornay and Bethlen traveled not to Lintz, but to Kirchdorf. This proved right because, to my knowledge, the Americans reached Kirchdorf sooner than they reached Linz. The next paragraph, the fourth word "both" should be replaced by the words "all three."

The Presentation does not point out the efforts the Bank exerted, after the location in Vorau proved inadequate, towards settling the Bank at a location where the valuables and the personnel could remain together.

The highest German authorities had already decided that the Bank's valuables and personnel would be located separately. Contrary to this, the Bank was able to influence Scheffler to try to approach the Austrian authorities for designating a place of settlement satisfying the Bank's interests. Hence it would be proper to document in writing the events and data related to acquiring Spital as the final place of settlement.

For completeness, it would behoove to include the history of the fleeing to Sopron to safeguard the bank branches and printing press from Veszprém.

Spital am Pyhrn, January 29, 1946.

"THE GOLD RUSH FROM HUNGARY"

It was 1956 when our father wrote this story. The timing could not have been more appropriate. Later that year on October 23rd came the Hungarian Revolution. The harsh years had gnawed away at his health and he felt an urgent need to write his story of the historic events that unfolded during the train journey.

Our father sent this story out in the hopes of having it published. He was unsuccessful. When the Hungarian Revolution erupted, he didn't have time to pursue the publishing as he was occupied in helping in the Revolution. The strain of the events took its toll on his health and he died soon after on March 18, 1957. He was able to help save the nation's gold, but not his country.

Figure 140: Map of the MNB train route (Scale 50 miles per inch, or 80 km per in., or 31 km per cm, (Sopron to Linz 112 miles). The route went approximately 350 miles from Budapest to Spital am Pyhrn, Austria. Veszprém to Fertőboz took 3 days. Traveling at night, we stopped and zigzagged to avoid a chance of robbery and the advancing Russians. Fertőboz to Spital am Pyhrn in Austria was a direct route of several days' duration. (Route drawn by Steven Tarnay; 1914 map, copyright unknown)

SUBMISSION: "THE GOLD RUSH FROM HUNGARY"

By Frederick E Tarnay, 1956

Cover Letter

Attached please find the manuscript of a true story titled "The Gold Rush from Hungary" written by myself. The story was inspired by the article, "The Secret Voyage of Britain's Treasure" published in the November 1955 issue of the *Reader's Digest*, and presents in a way a counterpart to that story relating how a similar gamble was undertaken on the side of the Axis powers during World War II. It is however rather a personal account of the whole transaction in which I played an active part.

I was born in Hungary in 1906. As a graduate of the College for World Trade in Vienna I entered the services of the National Bank of Hungary in 1932 and was working in the foreign exchange and foreign trade department of the Bank. When World War II entered its last phase in 1944, I was head of the Foreign Trade Section.

In October 1944 when the constitutional Government was overthrown by the Germans and replaced by a Nazi puppet Government, I offered my resignation to the new Board of Directors. This however was not accepted and I was warned by the new General Manager if I did not stay at my post and follow the new regime's policy I'd be put to death.

The story of my family's flight before the Russian invasion is told in my article. I did not want to stay in Hungary because: 1) I did not want to see my wife raped to death by Red soldiers and myself wind up somewhere in Siberia; 2) Everyone with a little common sense could figure out that under Soviet military occupation and under the terms of the shameful Paris Peace Treaty that sooner or later Hungary must go Communist… and I did not want to share the blessings of a communist state.

When the war was over we stayed in Austria as refugees for 4 years until the Displaced Persons Act opened the gates and we were admitted to this country in 1949. It was hard to start a new life in an entirely new world with three little kids, but if you work hard and have endurance you cannot fail in this wonderful country. Now we are citizens, we have a steady job, have our own home, a good car, in other words we are a happy American family.

Preface

"In the November 1955 issue of Reader Digest Leland Stowe tells us the story of "The Secret Voyage of Britain's Treasure" i.e. how the treasures of the Bank of England have been secretly moved across the submarine infested North Atlantic to Canada in World War II.

When I finished reading this story a crowd of memories started swarming in my mind, memories of a similar venture of a small nation in South East Europe which tried to save its treasures from being captured by Russians and "secured" by the Germans under the most turbulent and adventurous circumstances in the very middle of the fighting between the German and the Red Army. This country was Hungary.

The valuables involved were of course smaller than those of Britain's treasures, but for a small nation they meant just as much as the gigantic amounts for a world power. The total gold reserves of the National Bank of Hungary, as well as all deposits and securities safeguarded by the Bank, were moved from Hungary abroad to a little alpine village in Austria, accompanied by employees and their families. Besides the gold and the deposits, also the total stock of unissued banknote at a face value of 700,000,000 dollars was transferred to Austria.

The estimated total value of the removed assets amounted close to 1 billion dollars. The problem and the task was similar to that of the Bank of England, but the way and the circumstances under which it was carried out, were entirely different.

The primitiveness of the means of transportation and the way these Treasures were stored ridiculed the most elementary measures of security and precaution and would have given the cold chill not only to experts, but to people less familiar with the rules of safeguarding money and valuables, as well.

If we add to this that the whole transaction was carried out in the last phase of a lost war when order and law were in the state of disintegration, we have to admit, it was a miracle that everything was safely turned over to the U.S. Army.

To use the words of the U.S. Ambassador, J.F. Montgomery, Hungary was an "unwilling satellite" of the Axis Powers in World War II. As a small country, squeezed in between two big totalitarian adversaries, Germany and the Soviet Union, it had not too much chance to keep out of the war. For four years it managed to escape the German occupation, but in 1944 when Rumania was about to surrender to the Red Army, Hitler did not want to take the same chance with Hungary and overran the country on March 19th, 1944.

Technically Hungary was still an ally of the Axis, but de facto it was a prisoner of the Germans, a prisoner who was not enthusiastic at all to be liberated by the Red Army.

The ideal solution for Hungary would have been an invasion and liberation by the Western Powers from the Balkan Peninsula, yet the Yalta agreement killed this idea and along with it the hope of 100 million people (the Poles, Czechs, Slovaks , Hungarians, Rumanians, Bulgarian and Baltic Nations) to be really liberated, was gone.

The Gold Rush from Hungary
By Frigyes Tarnay (unpublished manuscript)

In October 1944, half of Hungary was invaded by the Red Army. The Regent of Hungary, Nicolas de Horthy, decided to quit the hopeless war for the country and conclude a military armistice with the Soviet Russia.

The Declaration of surrender was broadcast to the nation on October 15th, 1944. The Germans, of course did not agree with this move and their reaction was quick and radical. They arrested Regent Horthy, dismissed his cabinet and put a Nazi puppet government in power.

The new Government immediately started a large scale evacuation program and ruled to move everything valuable. In the first place of course the gold reserves and treasures of the country to Germany in order to save them from being captured by the Russians. Virtually there was no alternative because the treasures, being located in a territory occupied by the Germans, left no doubt that in case the Hungarian Government would refuse to evacuate the treasures, the Germans would rather take them by force to Germany than let them be seized by the Red Army.

For the protection of its treasures, the National Bank of Hungary started building underground shelters and vaults in 1938 since the tensions in international affairs left no doubt that sooner or later a war will come. In these massively built modern shelters, the Bank could continue its business operations without being interrupted by alarms and air raids. One of these huge shelters was built in Budapest on the Western side of the Danube in the so-called Tower Hill District, the oldest part of the city... Uri Street 72. Inside of this hill there are plenty of natural caves and caverns used as shelters and hideouts way back during the Turkish Wars 400 years ago. In World War II the various Government agencies located in the Tower District built their air raid shatters in these caverns. Some of them had been adjusted to public shelters and served as last refuge for the starving and horrible suffering population during the long lasting siege of the Tower by the Russians.

The second and even larger shelter was built in the city of Veszprém situated in the midwestern part of the country close to the Lake Balaton (Jokai Street, 31 Veszprém). It was equipped with modern printing machines and with all facilities to secure the function of the Bank during a war.

In November 1944 the situation became critical in Budapest, the capital of Hungary. The Red Army stood before the outskirts of the city and if you felt so inclined, you could take the street car to have a ride to the battle lines.

Budapest had seven huge, beautiful bridges across the Danube. All of them were undermined, ready to be blown up by the Germans in case they had to retreat to the West bank of the river. I felt not a bit at ease when every day I had to cross one of these bridges to get to my office and it was not more encouraging at all when one morning one of the mines went off by accident and in the heaviest traffic jammed street cars, horsed teams, automobiles and hundreds of passengers fell in the cold waves of the Danube.

In the beautiful and once so happy streets of Budapest, guns, tanks and all kinds of equipments were moving into position and at nights you could see the flashing of gunfire from the battle lines. And on top of this every day and night the efficient visits of the U.S. Air Force, the crazy barking of the antiaircraft guns and the thunder from the hits of the bomb loads.

Because of these almost permanent alarms and air raids, the Bank moved into the first underground shelter in the Tower Hill. But not for long. When Marshall Tolbukhin's army crossed the Danube in the South and the danger that Budapest might be encircled became imminent, the Bank decided to move to its second and last shelter in Veszprém.

Our gold reserves (32 tons) and all other assets were already stored there. We had to safeguard not only our own valuables, but also the masterpieces of the Museum of Arts, the treasures of the Historic Museum and even the most sacred relic of the nation, the thousand year old Holy Crown, an award of Pope Sylvester II to King St. Stephen for the conversion of the pagan Magyars to Christianity, was hidden there.

We left Budapest on December 5th, 1944 forming a small convoy of automobiles and tried to take the highway to Veszprém. We had no luck, it was already blocked and pounded by Russian gunfire and so we had to use the side and dirt roads filled with refugees and retreating German units. It was quite an experience and a hard test on the driver's skill. Imagine a traffic jam on a soft, muddy road churned up by tanks and heavy armored equipments, crowded with the largest variety of vehicles from wheelbarrows and oxen carts to Tiger tanks.

When we finally arrived in Veszprém we had only a couple of days to get settled in our new quarters and offices. The military situation became so alarming that the families of the employees living scattered in villages and resort places at the Lake Balaton were picked up by trucks and brought to the shelter in order to have them ready to be moved out with the Bank in case the Russians should break through to the city.

On December 9th, 1944, we received the bad news that the Red Army reached Lake Balaton and is no farther than 16 miles from the City. A wild panic broke loose. The gold and valuables were still sitting in the vault and no sufficient trucks or railroad cars were at our disposal for their transportation. We had to get railroad cars by all means if we wanted to leave the danger zone. Our efforts to obtain them from the State Railways and from the Hungarian Transportation Center were futile, for the whole railroad system was under the control of the German Army.

Fortunately, I must say, the bank had a German Commissioner delegated by the German Government to supervise the operations of the Bank since the country was occupied by the Germans. I informed him about the situation and within a few hours we could start loading 1 coach car and 7 freight cars.

That night the whole personnel of the Bank were feverishly working to load the cars and get them out of the city as quickly as possible. 32 tons of gold representing a value of 33 million dollars packed in wood boxes weighing 110 lbs each were placed on the floor of three plain 15 ton box cars. Their capacity marked as "for 40 men or 6 horses," but gold being known as heavy stuff there was still plenty of space left for 2 guards and their families to live on this precious carpet during two long winter months.

The women and children were squeezed in the coach car and finally at midnight the train carrying hundred millions of dollars and a desperate crowd of crying and worrying women and children left the city with the orders to pull as close as possible to the Western border, but not to cross it until further instructions.

A unit of the Royal Hungarian Gendarmes was attached to guard the valuables during this voyage of uncertain destination. The men had to stay and load the cars we expected to get from the Germans the following days. There was a great shortage in railroad cars and we had to take any type of freight cars, open or covered ones, available. For instance we had to put 100 tons of silver ingots safeguarded by us for the Royal Treasury, in seven open hoppers just like a dumped load of coal.

Fortunately the Russian offensive had been stopped and a German counteroffensive had thrown them back to a safe distance from Veszprém.

One day I even tried to make a business trip back to Budapest, but after 20 miles of driving 3 Russian fighter planes appeared above our car and started firing. In no time I took to the bushes on the roadside. One of the shells hit the ground close to me, but when they passed and kept on firing I saw that their target was a train standing at a small village station loaded with German tanks.

The planes made several circles over the train and kept it under permanent fire. They did it undisturbed because the Germans did not return the fire either from the ground or from the air. Nevertheless not one of the cars or tanks was hit, but a good lot of the houses in the village caught fire from the shells. They sure were poor flyers and gunners. This incident and the information I gathered from drivers coming from the direction of Budapest made me give up my plan and return to Veszprém.

By the German counteroffensive we gained time enough to load everything we wished to take along. Successively we had about 80 cars loaded and assembled into a train at a small station named Fertőboz near the city of Sopron and the Lake Fertő on the Western border.

About 500 people, among them my family lived in this train during the two cold winter months.

An almost insoluble problem was how to heat these cars. The coach had steam radiators, but there was no locomotive to supply the steam. And the freight cars were not equipped with heaters of course. We needed stoves desperately, but it was impossible to get them. The stores were closed and practically empty anyway. What saved us in this case, believe it or not, was the so much scolded red tape.

When one day we went to the railroad station to load the cars assigned to us, to our great surprised we found one of them filled with stoves. Just the kind of camp stoves we could use for our railroad cars. Nevertheless, we honestly reported this fact to the railroad official and asked for replacement. He however, ignored our apparently bothering and under the prevailing circumstances, I admit, ridiculous complaint and declared that according to his records that car is empty thus it must be empty and he is not going to give us another car. Seeing that he stubbornly stuck to his infallible records, we did not insist further, closed the door of the car and sent it as it was after our families to Fertőboz. The problem of the fuel to heat the stoves with was solved too.

Along the tracks of the station where our train was standing was a little forest of young trees, too big a temptation for men with freezing families to leave them unharmed and let them grow bigger. Two months later, the train left the station and the owner's only worry was how to replant his forest.

The greatest problem however was to find a safe place for these immense valuables loaded on plain freight cars and exposed to the daily air raids of the U.S. Air Force. You have to realize that main targets of the air raids were the strategically important railroad tracks, bridges and highways in order to cut off the supply lines of the Germans. Thus a railroad station was the worst place we could keep our treasures and families. Every time an air raid came the women and children had to leave the train and hide in the ditches and bushes as far as they had time to run.

Another reason to leave the station as soon as possible was that the Station had only one restroom and one well for 500 people and the sanitary conditions became unbearable.

We knew that not before long we had to move somewhere in Germany for there was no doubt that pretty soon Hungary will be occupied by the Red Army.

We were determined to stick stubbornly to the idea that the valuables and personnel with their families are inseparable and composed an indivisible body in which the employees and their families formed a protective wall around the gold and the treasures.

Therefore our first objective was to find and get an appropriate location where the treasures and the staff with their families as a community can be resettled and sheltered. Then before we could leave the country we had to arrive at an agreement with the German government bearing the guarantee that we may move and stay together with our treasures We may guard them ourselves even on German territory and independence and integrity will be secured during our stay in Germany.

The attempts of a special delegate of the Bank and our efforts through the diplomatic channels to obtain an adequate location from the German government having failed, I was instructed to get in touch with the German commissioner and solve the problem as quick as possible.

An urgent solution was imperative, for in case of a rapid Russian advance the Germans would have evacuated our treasures even by force to Germany and would not have cared what happened with the personnel. I was present when a telephone call came from Berlin for the German Commissioner suggesting that the gold be put into vaults of the Reichsbank in Vienna, the silver be shipped to Magdeburg and the treasures of the Museums to Berlin. And as to the personnel … well, they can take refuge in the Province Upper Austria (at that time called Upper Danube) like other Hungarian refugees. This would have meant the complete loss of control over our assets and had to be prevented by all possible means.

Fortunately the German commissioner shared our idea of indivisibility and ignored these instructions.

When he finished his talk with Berlin and saw how upset I was about those "suggestions" from Berlin, he told me not to worry and reassured me that "we'll find something for our treasures, but we have to go ahead immediately." And so we did.

Our idea was to pick one of the old cloisters in Upper Austria at that time confiscated from the religious orders. We gathered information about old monasteries, studied the maps and then went to the Gauleiter (governor) of the Province Upper Danube with our request and suggestions.

We did not anticipate having an easy job, because the Governor's Province was already flooded with refugees and our application for sheltering our valuables and our personnel was just another headache for him. Yet to our surprise he was very cooperative and although he could not assign to us the place we chose, he assured us that we are going to have even better shelter in an abandoned cloister in the village named Spital am Pyhrn.

He called the bürgermeister, mayor of the village right away. When he could not get him he interrogated the switchboard girl of the local post office about the conditions in the cloister and left a message for the bürgermeister that the gold of Hungary will be sheltered in his village and he will receive more instructions next day. "You folks are going to be famous," he finished his talk to the switchboard girl in his broad Upper Austrian accent.

So finally we knew where we were going to be settled and by having a definite destination point our hottest problem seemed to be solved for a while at least. We would have preferred a location farther West, but Upper Austria was assigned to Hungarian refugees and it would have taken longer to get something in another Province. The Governor authorized us to get in touch with the bürgermeister and work out the details of our resettlement in the village.

As soon as the agreement with the German Government was signed and our new quarters in the village were prepared, the green light was turned on for our train" to leave the little village station in Hungary and cross the border to Austria.

One half of the train with banknotes and food left on January 17th, 1945. The second half carrying the gold and the other treasures as well as the personnel and their families left Hungary a week later. On their way to Spital am Pyhrn they lost a "gold" car at a ranging station. Otherwise they arrived safely. There was "some" excitement about the loss of that car, but it was quickly recovered and joined the train a couple of days later in Spital am Pyhrn.

The village of Spital am Pyhrn is situated in the southern part of Upper Austria at the foot of the Alpine Pass of Pyhrn alongside a road of strategic and commercial importance dating back to the Roman times. In the early Middle Age this road and the Pyhrn Pass were used by the crusaders and the pilgrims on their way to the Holy

Land. They took shelter in a hospital at the site of the present village. Hence the name Spital which means hospital in German. (There are two more towns in Austria carrying the name Spital and this was the source of a very shocking misunderstanding on one occasion about which I'll tell later).

In the 12th century a church was erected here which of course underwent several renovations and alterations during the centuries. In its present beautiful baroque style was rebuilt in the 18th century.

The basement of the church forms a large crypt where the priests and dignitaries of the village were buried. Now it is not used anymore. Almost all tombs and vaults for the coffins are empty and the skulls and the bones of the buried are removed and piled up in a separate consecrated room of the crypt.

It was closed in by a thick wall of banknote crates, a poor substitute for the steel walls of an armored vault. The other valuables were put into the premises of the cloister, a huge old building with plenty of rooms and storage spaces. These rooms and the crypt however were by far not the ideal storage spaces for our treasures and assets and under ordinary circumstances any expert would have been horrified at a suggestion to put these tremendous valuables behind a plain rusted iron door with a simple padlock like that of the crypt.

No armored steel vaults… no automatic alarm equipments… no combination locks… unless you call a combination of regular door locks with padlocks a combination lock. By entrusting the keys of this very primitive form of combination locks to two officials in charge, we had the dubious satisfaction of having complied with the safeguarding rules of the bank, or at least we did our best to do so.

The crypt was almost permanently flooded with ground water, which soaked a great part of our banknotes, but of course did not do any harm to the gold. Although we tried to make these storage rooms as safe as we could, much could not be done in this respect and we mostly had to depend on the alertness and trustworthiness of a gendarme unit of 34 men armed with only plain repeating army rifles. Not a single machine pistol was in the whole unit that guarded the treasures day and night.

The office rooms of the Bank were in the cloister, the quarters of the employees with families in hotels, inns and private houses of the village. The single men and women had two separated dormitories in the cloister, the families got one room each in which they had to cook, live and sleep. Yet it was a relief after the much more rugged camping life in the railroad cars.

The men had to fell trees and cut the wood rationed by the German authorities. In addition to the official rations, we were allowed to go to the forests and pick fallen dead wood. As the time passed, food became scarcer. As long as we had some reserves from Hungary the situation was not so bad, but when they were gone it was hard.

When the war was over the misery became even worse and you could really say the rations were not enough to live on, but too much to let you die. Only the American food supplies saved us from starving to death.

And it would be unfair not to dedicate some words of commemoration to the "unknown" Hungarian horses. These poor animals pulled out thousands of wagons loaded to the utmost with refugees and their belongings from Hungary. Then when the war was over they were ridden by American GI's for pleasure and then because there was no fodder to feed them and no food to feed the people, they made their last contribution: they were slaughtered and their meat was distributed among the starving refugees and the Austrian population.

I was ordered to stay in Hungary with our branch office in the city of Sopron on the Western border. I stayed there until the Russians took that city, too. Frankly I do not know why, because I spent most of my time either in the basement of our office building or when the air raid alarm warned us in time I drove to the surrounding forests where we felt much safer than in the basement of our one story office building. If these smaller buildings got a direct hit the cellars and basements usually turned into your grave.

Besides that, I had to take turns in digging fox holes and tank traps in the snow covered frozen ground around the city.

After the fall of Budapest in February, 1945, the Russians launched a new and successful offensive moving closer and closer to the Western border of the country.

Good Friday (March 30th 1945) found the last strip of Hungary taken by the Red Army.

Consummatum Est....

The Russian attack on the City of Sopron came as a surprise and the evacuation of our branch office was a panicky 50-mile run up to the Austrian village Reichenau in the high Eastern Alps, where we thought we could take a breath and then move farther to our headquarters. Very soon we realized that we had not run far enough. The Russians kept on coming with unexpected speed and since the truck sent to our rescue from our headquarters was seized by the German Army we had to abandon a broken truck loaded with Hungarian currency as well as our business records and all our personal belongings. The personnel and families fled walking and hitch hiking to Spital a/p carrying 200,000 dollars worth of foreign currency stock stuffed in their pockets.

When the war was over, I went back to Reichenau, at that time under Russian occupation, to investigate what happened with our valuables and belongings. I learned that everything, the load of currency on the broken truck included, was looted during two weeks of fierce fighting between the Germans and the Russians.

Our truckload of money was gone of course. The crates had been broken up and millions of dollars in pengő notes were dispersed among soldiers and civilians as well.

Bundles of notes were scattered in the streets and nobody wanted to miss the chance to become rich once in his life. You cannot blame them. In that no man's land the arms had the word, law and justice were silenced.

The only things left were our apparently unattractive business records and books. When the battle was over they were collected with other rubbish, incinerated and reduced to ashes.

When the Russians took the village they ordered the population to turn in all our notes. Then the Russian soldiers used the money to buy wine and liquor in Hungary. The money was not officially in circulation, but who would have questioned the validity of the money offered by a Russian soldier? The fact that he paid for something was a miracle anyway.

An innkeeper and his wife gave me this account about the fate of our abandoned belongings. I scared them to death when in the evening I knocked on their door and asked for room and some food. This was a very unusual thing that time because all restaurants and hotels were closed and nobody dared to walk in the streets after the sun went down.

The town was filled with Russian soldiers who had lots of fun by hunting for souvenirs, preferably for watches and fountain pens, but the top of their pleasure was the riding and of course wrecking of bikes if they could get hold of one.

My innkeeper complained bitterly that one night a bunch of Russian soldiers knocked on his door and after lecturing him about the "Kulturera" (culture) in Russia, took everything they found and liked in his home. The innkeeper took a 50 pengő note out of his wallet and solemnly handed it over to me as a souvenir and as the only copy "saved" from our lost stock on the broken truck.

The Russian invasion of Austria was stopped by the Germans for a couple of weeks in the Eastern Alps. This was the last effective resistance of the German Army and when it was ground up the danger grew from day to day that the Russians will catch us before the Americans would reach our village.

Some attempts were made to move the treasures westward to a safer location, but the Governor who was plenipotentiary Commander in Chief on our territory suppressed the slightest initiative to pull out of his Province. "Abhauen gibt's net" (no desertion) was his brief and resolute answer to our suggestions.

In the second half of April, the situation became desperate. It was evident that the final collapse and the end of the Third German Reich established by Hitler for at least 1000 coming years, is only a question of a few days.

The road winding from the Pyhrn Pass through Spital a/p became very busy. Retreating German units and refugees were moving down the village and pulling westward. Long columns of convicts in their striped clothes and Jews from concentration and forced labor camps were driven on the road.

I'll never forget the look of a Jewish man in a column which stopped right in front of our window. He lifted his eyes toward me and pointed to his mouth indicating that he is hungry. I picked up some bread and hurried from the second floor down to the street, but the column was already moving again and my man was gone. I only saw the end of the column, the guards urging the sick and the weak ones supported or pushed on wheelbarrows by their campmates.

This commotion on the roads was a sign that the Russians are rapidly moving ahead and the situation was getting chaotic. In the vicinity everybody knew of the gold being hidden in the crypt of the Church. We feared an assault of the mob, of irregular troops or gangs of escaped prisoners who would take advantage of the last tumultuous days of the war and plunder the cloister and the crypt.

The other hazard was the Russians taking the village ahead of the Americans and everything becoming a prey of the Red Army. So the crucial question was who will reach the village and the gold first, the Russians or the Americans? We had to act.

A group of the staff decided to contact the American Army as soon as possible. We sent two couriers to Kirchdorf, a town only 25 miles north of Spital a/p with the instructions to stay there until the town is taken by the Americans and then hand over a letter notifying the U.S. Forces of our location and asking for urgent protection for our treasures.

I volunteered to go to Salzburg and try to contact the American Forces there. This meant that somehow I have to get through the German lines. I needed papers from a German authority to pass the check-points of the German lines with a car. I disclosed our plan to the German Commissioner and asked him to get the necessary papers for one of my colleagues, the Chauffeur and myself.

Although to a German this sounded like instigation to conspiracy (treason) I personally knew him well enough to be sure that he'd not denounce us and would not refuse this last request. I was right! He willingly agreed and next day I had the passes.

The purpose of the rite (negotiations with the German Legation) given in the passes was of course a phony one, but the papers worked all right. Almost in every town our car was stopped by German military police for checking our papers.

It was not a comfortable feeling to know that in case they would search my body and find the letter to the U.S. Forces, they would have shot us on the spot for high treason.

But we were lucky and reached safely the outskirts of the city of Salzburg. Here we found the road blocked by German Police. They told me the city surrendered to the Americans and the occupation of the town was already going on. This was good news for me. All I have to do, I thought, is to stay here and wait until the first American tank shows up. I sent back the car with my colleague and then with a heavy rucksack on my back, I stayed close to the road and kept on watching.

Finally after two hours of waiting an American tank rolled up and stopped in front of me. The crew was very friendly and the first thing they did when the heard me speaking a little English, was to give me a package of American cigarettes (Chesterfields) something I had not seen for a very long time. They made jokes and looked very happy.

This was the most for me. I had not seen happy faces since I did not know when. With us everybody was worried and bored, everybody looked tired and worn out. These guys looked well fed, in high spirits, relaxed and always ready to make jokes.

Upon advice of the tank crew I went into the city to find the U.S. Military Government. Although a curfew for civilians was announced by the military loudspeaker car, I went around in the downtown section of the city, but could not find any military authority established yet and had to return to my room in the outskirts.

Next morning German snipers fired at the crew of the tank and wounded a soldier. This incident could not stop me however from walking downtown again and looking for the Military Government.

I finally found it in the town house and succeeded in handing over my letter to an American officer. He read it and was immediately willing to go and have a look at our treasures, but when I told him that the village is 70 miles away and still occupied by the Germans he looked disappointed and disinterested. He put the letter in his pocket and turned to another applicant. This attitude was not too encouraging and I decided to find somebody who shows more interest in my letter.

I went to the American Counter Intelligence Corps and presented the copy of the letter to a young second lieutenant of the U.S. Army. When he was through with reading he declared he is not in charge of this kind of cases, yet since I happened to come to him with this important looking letter he feels responsible and is going to take care of it.

Answering his questions I told him the approximate value of our treasures and gave him the exact location of the village. He made some notes, copied the letter on his typewriter and rushed out of the office uttering a "Come back tomorrow" to me. Next day he informed me that the letter and his report have been wired to the G-2 3rd Div. of the U.S. Army and upon my request he confirmed this on the letter.

I felt great relief when I left the office room. My mission was carried out and no more could be done on my part. Now everything was up to the American Army.

Yet I could not relax until I learned that Spital a/p was really taken by the Americans. I wanted to return immediately, but civilians were not allowed to leave the city and no means of communication were available for the public. Everything was still in the state of war although the war was technically over.

Two weeks later the Bank sent a car for me with a special pass of the U.S. Army. It was good to see my family and my friends again. There I heard what happened during my absence and how dangerous the situation was in the last days before the Americans occupied the village.

The day after I left for Salzburg a German military commission of 3 German officers entered the Bank and wished to talk to the management. The head of the delegation identified himself as the delegate of the 6th German Army and pointed out that his mission is to secure the treasures of the Bank before the American Army would occupy the village. To our objections he answered that the treasures must be saved as long as there is the slightest chance to do so. However we did not yield and the commission said that they will report to their commander and left the Bank.

Next day the Governor of the province called us by phone and asked what were our intentions. The General Manager told him we want to stay where we are and to turn over everything to the Americans. He asked the General Manager to see him in the neighboring village. There he informed him that he agrees with our intentions, but is afraid that the Bank will be plundered by irregular German military gangs and wants the Bank guarded by a strong German unit commanded by a reliable officer. The commander will be instructed to surrender to the Americans and to nobody else. And indeed within a few hours a German unit of 25 soldiers and 5 officers, each one of them armed with machine pistols joined our gendarmes and took their positions around the Church and the cloister. The commander presented the written order of the Governor which was in accordance with the promises made by him, so we had no doubt that the intentions of the Governor were all right.

Next day, it was May 7th 1945, was a hot day. The situation was chaotic; nobody knew what's going on and what's going to happen in the next few hours. Words came that a resistance was prepared by the Germans in our narrow valley and they are going to blast roads and bridges. As the topographic conditions were suitable for a defensive operation, we feared the German will delay the occupation of the village by the Americans and in the last minute we will lose our treasures.

The delegates of the 6th German Army returned and informed us that the commander insisted that the gold be moved to a secure place at once and for this purpose there were 6 railroad cars at our disposal. We informed them about the orders of the Governor and called the commander of the German guard. He showed the written order of the Governor and told a captain of the commission that he wants to talk to him confidentially.

When they left, the head of the delegation began to persuade the general manager that the gold had to be taken away. He reassured him that he arranged everything: The gold would be moved to a place where nobody would find it. He would care for it and that only the General Manager and he would know the location of the cache.

This was a pretty obscure proposition which of course could not be but refused by the General Manager. The situation was saved by the returning Commander of the

Guard who declared that according to the orders of the Governor the treasures had to stay where they were. Then the delegates left in a hurry.

We suspected they went to the Governor to make him change his orders. The General Manager tried to call the Governor, but could not get him. Therefore he wrote a protesting report to him and it was just finished when the screaming of sirens came from the street and the first American tanks were rolling through the village.

We were saved. The American Army won the race with a slight margin against the Russians who took the Pyhrn Pass, only 3 miles ride from the village.

The Americans disarmed the German unit. They left the rifles of the Hungarian Gendarmes and agreed that the Bank be guarded by them as before. For a couple of weeks they gave reinforcement to the Hungarian unit, but later the Bank was guarded by the Royal Hungarian Gendarmes during 4 years following the end of the war.

So it happened that while the Kingdom was abolished long ago in Hungary, a small unit of the "Royal" Hungarian Gendarmes still existed and guarded Hungarian properties in the mountains of a foreign country.

The discovery of our treasures was quite a sensation and the 'Stars and Stripes" reported it under the headline "Hungary's Gold Cache found in Alpine Village by 80th Division."

Right after the village was taken by the Americans even General Patton, Commander of the 3rd Army inspected our place and the treasures.

Then the Bank was ordered to turn over the gold to the U.S. Army. It was moved from the crypt of the Church and loaded on 3 American Army trucks. Accompanied by 2 tanks the precious load was taken to Frankfort a/M and placed into the vaults of the Reichsbank, at that time the headquarters of the Finance Branch of the American Forces. So after 5 months of being moved from one odd place to another the gold finally landed from the vaults of the crypt to the definitely safer vaults of the Bank.

Four officials (among them myself) were working in the U.S. Headquarters in Frankfort a/M furnishing all information wanted by the U.S. authorities. Frankfort a/M is about 600 miles from Spital a/P and at that time no communication, not even mail services was established between Germany and Austria. So, for a couple of months we did not know anything about our families.

The boundaries of the occupation zones were not final yet and rumors went around that some parts of the American Zone will be turned over to the Russians. We wanted to be sure that nothing like this will happen with our families in Spital a/P and inquired in the competent department of the U.S. Headquarters (I wish we did not). An American major gave us the answer which was one of the hardest blows in my life: The village Spital a/P will be turned over to the Russians within two weeks.

We do not remember how we got out of that office, but I know we all must have looked pale and pitifully helpless. Fortunately this state of despair lasted only a couple of days and turned into rejoicing when an American Lt. Colonel informed us that Spital a/P is going to be connected to the British Zone.

This was not true either, but we could take it. The truth was that Spital a/P remained all the time in the American Zone, only these two American officers happened not to know it because from the three Spitals existing in Austria one of them picked Spital am Semmering in the Russian Zone, the other one looked at Spital a/Drau in the British Zone on the map and both of them missed our Spital a/Pyhrn in their own zone.

If these two gentlemen ever happen to read these lines I herewith wish to assure them that we were fully aware of their good intentions and knew that they only wanted to help us with their information.

In Frankfort a/m the gold was meticulously checked by American experts by weight, numbers and pieces against our books and also the origin of every gram was painstakingly investigated.

It was a great satisfaction for us to learn that not one gram of gold was missing when this big gamble was over.

The deposits and other assets of the Bank including the banknotes and the treasures of the museums stayed in Spital a/P safeguarded by the Bank's employees and the gendarmes under the supervision of the U.S. Military Government. Except some foreign owned assets and the banknotes, subsequently everything was returned to Hungary. Since a new currency, the Forint 2 was issued in Hungary in 1946, the pengő notes stored in Spital a/P became worthless and there was no use returning them to Hungary. With a face value of about 700 million dollars they were sold to an Austrian paper mill for 400 dollars.

— And the gold? Well, in accordance with the stipulations of the Peace Treaty of Paris it was turned over by the U.S. Government to the Hungarian Government and shipped back to Soviet dominated Hungary.

I frankly admit this was not the end I was dreaming of when the story started. But I have the satisfaction that in a team of fine cooperating colleagues, I did my best and had my good share in turning over these treasures of my former country into the safe and trusted hands of the U.S.A., hoping that once they will be returned to a real free Hungary. Now, I only have the comfort that I had no part whatsoever in returning them behind the Iron Curtain.

Eulogies to Katherine (Katalin) Tarnay from Those Who Loved Her

Eulogy
By Lee Tarnay, her grandson

Katherine Tarnay was many things in her 97 years of life, but to my sister Lorena and me, she was Grandma-our only Grandma – and for a time, the closest thing to a mother we had. At her age, most people think about a quiet retirement. Indeed she might have returned to her beloved fatherland (Hungary) to be with her sister.

Events/God intervened however and our journey with Grandma started in earnest somewhere around 1984 when her son Steve (our father) divorced. Grandma at that time was in her seventies, experiencing poor health, and was increasingly unable to keep a place up by herself. But when she saw that she was needed, she came north to help her son raise us for more than 8 years. As with her own children, Grandma was always there when we needed her and by helping us I think she regained much of her health and renewed propose in life.

Our relationship with Grandma was on the surface was turbulent during the time (my adolescence) with many a "borzasztó" accompanied comments about our attire and or behavior. Underneath it all though, we knew that this tension only meant that she cared deeply. Eventually, we could not help but yield to her sense of grace, desire for us to better ourselves, and her faith in God, in herself, and ultimately, in us.

My last memory of her was from this past July, when we drove all night from Yosemite to see her after Dad (Steve) called saying that she was fading fast. I'll never forget the look on her face as we walked into the room: Her body jerked as if she had just entered it suddenly from behind the veil of those cloudy, wide eyes. Now though, her face shone, every wrinkle seemed to be screaming with the love and good will that she could no longer express with words. That severe pursed expression she had so often worn was gone.

As I sat there gazing back at her, trying to make small talk and convince her to stick around a little longer to meet more great-grandkids, my words only seemed to be getting in the way. Finally, I just stopped trying and just gazed back at her. She gazed right back at me, her eyes shining, "I love you, too," in the dim hospital light, and shrugged almost playfully, but with some chagrin mixed in. What more is there to say at the end? The only thing I could think of was, "Thank you Grandma. "

Although she didn't die that evening after we said goodbye, I got that twinge in my stomach that told me I wouldn't see her alive again. She lived on, probably by will alone, until the day after Christmas early in the morning. I fancy myself a scientist, but I like to think that huge squall of wind lightning and thunder that woke us around that time was one last affectionate yet powerful "borzasztó" commemorating her passing.

—◊—

MOTHER'S EULOGY - JANUARY, 5, 2005

By Matthew Tarnay, her son
Holy Cross Cemetery, Culver City, Ca.

It is only in retrospect and with years of reflection that we can understand and appreciate what our Mother has done for us. The memories of my Mother are strongest from the time our Father died up to the time I left home. With the passing of our father, Mother was suddenly faced with raising three teenagers who were looking to her for support and direction.

Mother worked and saved diligently to be financially sound and free of debt —this is what gave her a sense of independence and pride—she did not want to be vulnerable or dependent on anyone.

While she saved, she did not give up her sense of style. She always looked put-together, wearing just the right scarf, jacket, skirt and even kitchen apron.

In Mother's effort to save, all three of us experienced the grocery shopping trips every two weeks to the Grand Central Market in downtown in Los Angeles. As to which of us went with Mother depended upon who was old enough and available to drive at the time. Mother was adamant about shopping at the Grand Central Market to get everything fresh and at a good price. The local grocery store was too expensive. Also, I think the Grand Central reminded Mother of Hungary, where shopping and negotiating at different food stalls was the way of life. Our role was to follow Mother around to all the food stalls and carry the heavy bags of groceries. She had her favorite dry goods, vegetable and meat stalls. Mother was an expert food shopper. She knew exactly what she wanted and how to barter with the butchers to get the best cut of meat. This was our Friday routine; not one that any of us enjoyed, but one that all three of us seem to remember.

Another way Mother saved is with lunch bags. She would fix our lunches every day, using recycled the grocery bags. These bags, of course, were well worn and wrinkled, but according to Mother, just fine for holding lunch sandwiches. When you go to Loyola High School, which is a very preppy school, it is bad enough to have to bring your lunch; and if you do, the condition of your lunch bag is scrutinized as much as the clothes you are wearing. I think Fred might have been lucky enough to escape the brown bag torture. The social pressure, mostly self-inflicted, was so acute that I bought new lunch bags and, without Mother's knowledge, changed the bags when I got to school.

The Saturday afternoons spent in the kitchen watching my Mother cook were the best. It was here that we talked and I felt comfort. I was fascinated by Mother's ability to create great Hungarian dishes with such simple tools and basic ingredients; the weinerschnitzel, plum dumplings and dobos torte were just a few of our favorites. I recall especially the skill that she had carving a large leg of veal into beautiful clean filets for making weinerschnitzel. Even today, Fred, Steven, and I talk about Mother's great cooking. One of us has Mother's carefully hand written recipe book and hopefully, when time and energy allows, we will have it translated and published for the family.

Mother's strong faith and devotion to the Catholic Church was instrumental in our receiving a good education. Mother put a high value on education; she had graduated from University in Hungary, spoke four languages, was well read, and loved classical music. She made a great effort that Fred, Steve, and I attend Loyola High School because she believed that the Jesuits were great educators. I know that she worked very hard to convince the Jesuits they were lucky to have the three of us attend Loyola on a financial scholarship.

It was important to Mother that she could live on her own terms and be financially secure. She continued to live frugally, investing carefully, and at the end, her estate was in good shape. I am sure it gave her a sense of pride and honor that she was able to raise us and not be a financial burden to her children.

Throughout her life in America, Mother's thoughts and memories were about Hungary. Had it not been for wanting to be close to her children and grandchildren, she would have returned to Hungary in a heartbeat. I remember the many letters that went back and forth to Grandmother and Aunt Zsuzsa, at a time when it took 3 to 4 weeks for letters to arrive. These letters were her lifeline to the country that she loved and the life she left behind.

Finally, Mother can now join our Father to stroll together across the Chain Bridge and walk the beautiful boulevards of Budapest.

May she live in our memories in peace and joy
By Matthew Tarnay (Son)

—⟋⟍—

www.drlaura.com/b/Important-Lessons-Learned-from-My-Mother/497104411729081609.html
[Dr. Laura Email of the Day]

Important Lessons Learned from My Mother by Fred Tarnay
05/10/2013

We escaped from Hungary in late 1945 with the Communist army just a few miles from our door. A makeshift train had been quickly assembled by a band of patriots including my father. We and other families loaded whatever we owned into boxes and set off towards the border.

We didn't know if we would make it safely, as the Communist army was still at our heels. There was also little food and we often left the train to go into farmers' fields to gather whatever we could to survive. We came under attack from fighter planes and had to run and hide in the forest. As we lay in the woods my mother covered us with her body as we heard bullets whiz by and hit the branches above us. What I remember most was my mother always doing what had to be done, putting her fears and feelings aside as the survival of her family came first.

After spending several years in Europe, we realized there was no hope for freedom and no going back to our beloved ancestral homeland. My father had been in government and was an outspoken critic of both the Nazis and the Communists. We would have simply been executed as many were that stayed or went back. So we left everything behind, home, relatives, and belongings, everything that was dear to us because freedom was more precious than that, and came to America as displaced persons. We applied for American citizenship and became citizens five years later.

Those first years in America were difficult. We had no work history here and had to start again in mid-life. It took its toll on my parents. My father died suddenly and left my mother to care for three teenage boys. She again put her fears and feelings aside and put the survival of her family first. She worked harder than ever and saved every penny she earned. Jobs were difficult to get and keep; she spoke broken English and had an accent that was not appreciated. She went on day by day until we were all out of high school and in college. My mother taught us to become independent because she saw she could not give us what other parents could and we would have to earn that for ourselves. Because of her love and dedication, we survived. She passed away at 97 and left a legacy of love of family, of hard work, of character, as well as an estate put together by a poor woman one penny at a time.

But she left me the greatest gift of all. I married a woman like that.
Fred Tarnay

(From my uncle Fred about my grandma and grandpa and all they did to make our amazing lives here in America possible. The quiet heroism and hard work never stopped for Grandma: 40 years later, she would step up to help raise me and my sister and her example made a huge difference in our lives. She was never peaches and crème... more like peaches and cottage cheese (a combo she and I often enjoyed for breakfast... I still do... and think of her...)

Leland Tarnay, grandson

—⁂—

EULOGY TO KATHARINE TARNAY

By Fred B. Tarnay, her son

Her trust in God was the rock that anchored her. She was a devout common sense (orthodox) Catholic, and lived her faith daily. No matter how poor we were or where we were, she found a way to make sure we received our first communion and confirmation, not an easy task in wartime. She kept God and the church present in our family and showed us that prayer was to be relied upon. Some earliest memories from Hungary were being at Sunday Mass in Matthias Church, sitting next to our parents, our father reading from his missal.

During the flight from the homeland, our parents worked with the Vatican and Catholic Relief Services to request and distribute food and clothing to all those in need. She managed the inventory stored in a rented room in Innsbruck, he managed the distribution. We often had religion at our table for dinner in those days. The conversation was always who was in need of real help, not only material goods, but where do we go from here. Do we wait to return to the homeland or look to settle in another country? The Vatican war relief services had contacts throughout the world and it was this way they were able to provide many families with the ray of hope to resettle. And they did. Argentina, Brazil Venezuela, New Zealand, South Africa, America, Canada, Britain, Italy. We developed a wonderful stamp collection as we kept in touch with our friends in exile.

During the times when our father was very ill, she would kneel for long periods at his bedside and pray so fervently that her clenched hands trembled. When he was in for a major operation, she spent the entire waiting hours praying in the hospital chapel.

She chose a Catholic education for her sons. We were taught by the Salesians in grammar school and the Jesuits in high school. When our father passed away and she could no longer afford it, the school waived the tuition. After we were done, she repaid the school with the only thing she had of value, a 16th century New Testament that had been in the family for generations. It first went on display at the priory in Palo Alto and then at Loyola Marymount University.

"Look to the rock from which you have been cut and to the quarry from which you have been hewn," says Isaiah.

She is the rock from which we were cut.

HER FAMILY

She loved her homeland and she loved her family. Not many personal things can be saved in fleeing a country during wartime, but she made sure that what she treasured most remained intact for us to inherit. These were her/our family records. Birth and death certificates, school records, pictures and personal letters were saved, stashed away in boxes for her to reminisce and our generation to discover. She remembered our pre-war family days in a letter to her granddaughter.

"In 1938 the battles were far from us and we were a happy family. But 3 years later we found ourselves in the center of all the fighting."

We were a happy, relaxed family. Our Christmas tree in Budapest was lit with real candles, for a magical minute only. We shared the moment with uncles, aunts and grandparents. Our Christmas tradition after that was that on Christmas Eve, we stayed in our room until we heard the strains of 'Silent Night'. Having had very little, we were always grateful for receiving anything at all. The period of peace in Budapest soon turned to concern for our safety, then into full preparations to flee the country for our lives.

What followed was the saga of the train escape later documented by our father. Memories of her from that experience include fleeing into the nearby forest as the train was being strafed by Russian aircraft. She covered her young children with her body as the bullets flew above and tree branches fell around us. To feed us when we ran out of food, she went into the fields for green apples and somehow cooked our meals from those.

She was a master chef; she made everything from scratch. She learned from her mother, cooking over a wood stove. She was also a master seamstress. Our clothing during the war years was made from old drapes *a la* Sound of Music. We were clothing carbon copies, the three of us. The Trapp family learned everything from her.

But the most significant part of her family life was her love for her husband, our father. They had something very special between them. It surfaced rarely, whenever they had a moment to relax together. After he passed away in our youth, you could tell she missed him terribly-daily – for almost 50 years… Together at last.

HER FATHERLAND

If there was one theme that ran through her life, it was her love of the Fatherland. She was a true Hungarian, a patriot, child of the Carpathians, daughter of Attila and Arpad. She considered herself in exile here, and had she been alone she would have returned to her homeland given different circumstances. English was her fourth language; to her it came in last after Hungarian, French and German. Both she and our father deplored all socialism not only for its inherent evil, but especially when it gained the power to control her beloved country and resulted in misery, devastation, and the death of untold millions. The poet describes it well:

Her Fatherland

If there was one theme that ran through her life, it was her love of the Fatherland. She was a true Hungarian, a patriot, child of the Carpathians, daughter of Attila and Arpad. She considered herself in exile here and had she been alone, she would have retuned to her homeland given different circumstances. English was her fourth language, to her it came in last after Hungarian, French and German. Both she and our father deplored all socialism not only for it's inherent evil but especially when it gained the power to control her beloved country and resulted in misery, devastation, and the death of untold millions.

The poet describes it well:

"I ask not for my homeland.
Forth in the world I'll stray.
I know too well the bitter truth
That I must go away.
My smith! My court smith! Come and turn
My brown steed's shoes for me,
Changing the front shoes for the back,
That he seek not the homeward track,
And I, in truth, shall not come back
To lovely Hungary!

"Hungarians and Szeklers,
Folk of my countries twain,
Heroic souls that love me,
God bless you once again!
Patak, may God be with you!
The Russian rules you know,
God save you, Munkacs, ne'er I'll see
Thy fort I love so tenderly
In this sweet land, my Hungary,
For ever more, I vow!

"But Hungary still loves me,
And Transylvania, too,
Pities and grieves for me till death;
Even their children's faithful breath
Will wish for me anew!
When I have long departed,
You'll sigh me back once more;
When I have long been dead, I trust,
You'll mourn me, and bring home my dust.
And gather up my crumbling bones
To bear them to this shore!

"But where the ocean bellows,
And where the far winds blow,
And where the stars go falling,
In death and exile - this Magyar now must go."

From 'The Poetry of Hungary – In Quest of the Miracle Stag'
Adaptation from the Kuruc Poems — 19th Century Ballads of national resistance and protest against invading forces. Many of the Kuruc poems have become folk songs still sung in Hungary and Hungarians in exile, in disapproval and demonstration against foreign influence, occupation and oppression, most recently the socialists/communists.

F. Tarnay 01-04-06

Figure 141: Adapted by Fred B. Tarnay from: Makkai, Adam, ed. Trans. Watson Kirkonnel. "The Exile of Rakocz." In Quest of the Miracle Stag the Poetry of Hungary an Anthology of Hungarian Poetry from the 13th Century to the Present in English Translation. Vol 1. Trans. Watson Kirkonnel. Hungary: Turtia Publishers, 1996. N. pag. Print.

Index